Stephen R. Beggs, America Project Making of

Pages from the Early History of the West and Northwest

Stephen R. Beggs, America Project Making of

Pages from the Early History of the West and Northwest

ISBN/EAN: 9783744712521

Printed in Europe, USA, Canada, Australia, Japan

Cover: Foto ©ninafisch / pixelio.de

More available books at **www.hansebooks.com**

PAGES

FROM THE

EARLY HISTORY

OF THE

WEST AND NORTH-WEST:

EMBRACING

REMINISCENCES AND INCIDENTS OF SETTLEMENT AND
GROWTH, AND SKETCHES OF THE MATERIAL
AND RELIGIOUS PROGRESS

OF THE

STATES OF OHIO, INDIANA, ILLINOIS, AND MISSOURI,

WITH

ESPECIAL REFERENCE TO THE HISTORY OF METHODISM.

BY

REV. S. R. BEGGS.

CINCINNATI:
PRINTED AT THE METHODIST BOOK CONCERN.

R. P. THOMPSON, PRINTER.
1868.

Entered, according to Act of Congress, in the year 1868, by

S. R. BEGGS,

In the Clerk's Office of the District Court of the United States for the Southern District of Ohio.

CONTENTS.

CHAPTER I.
Autobiographical—Ancestry—Life in Southern Indiana—Conversion 9

CHAPTER II.
Early Methodism in Indiana—Notable Preachers—Conferences—Districts and Circuits 17

CHAPTER III.
Compilations from Smith's "Indiana Miscellany" 31

CHAPTER IV.
The Same continued—The Pious Wife and Impenitent Husband—Remarkable Conversion 44

CHAPTER V.
Received into Missouri Conference—Remarkable Experiences in the Primitive Itinerancy 51

CHAPTER VI.
Introduction to the Illinois Work—Minutes of the First Conference 59

CHAPTER VII.
Pioneer Experiences—Home Again—Pleasant Conference Occasions 67

CHAPTER VIII.
Quakers and Infidels at a Methodist Meeting—A Primitive Baptism 75

CONTENTS.

CHAPTER IX.

Marriage—Rough Experiences of a Young Bride—Painful and Perilous Journeyings........ 81

CHAPTER X.

Mission Work in Chicago, 1831-32—Terrors of an Indian Raid—A Home-Made Fort........ 94

CHAPTER XI.

Privations in Chicago—Division of Illinois Conference—Incidents of Labor........ 103

CHAPTER XII.

A Clear Conversion—Statistics of Desplaines Mission—Rock River Conference formed........ 114

CHAPTER XIII.

History of Peoria—A Curious Church-Building Enterprise... 122

CHAPTER XIV.

Sketch of Rev. Jesse Walker—Interesting Narrative from his own Manuscript........ 131

CHAPTER XV.

Statistics of Early Methodism in the Fox River Region—Aurora and Ottowa........ 143

CHAPTER XVI.

Early Methodism in Middle Illinois—Sangamon County—First Settlement of Peoria........ 151

CHAPTER XVII.

Miscellaneous Statistics—The Plainfield Work—How Roberts became Bishop........ 161

CHAPTER XVIII.

Biographical Episode—The Author's Work and Experiences on the Christian Commission, in 1864........ 169

CONTENTS.

CHAPTER XIX.
Chicago Methodism—Great Religious Struggle and Victory.... 175

CHAPTER XX.
The First Chicago Churches—Canal-Street, Clark-Street, and Indiana-Street... 182

CHAPTER XXI.
The Chicago Indian Massacre of 1812—Mrs. Kinzie's Narrative 191

CHAPTER XXII.
Mrs. Kinzie's Narrative continued................................. 200

CHAPTER XXIII.
The Author's Observations on the Indian Character—Causes of the Sauk War... 213

CHAPTER XXIV.
Indian Anecdotes—How Jesse Walker dealt with them........... 221

CHAPTER XXV.
Chicago—Origin of Name—Incidents of Early Settlement—First Methodist Preaching................................. 227

CHAPTER XXVI.
Our Publishing Interests—The Methodist Book Concerns in New York and Cincinnati................................. 236

CHAPTER XXVII.
First Baptist Church in Plainfield—Methodism in Plainfield.. 241

CHAPTER XXVIII.
A Sketch of Methodism in Lockport................................ 249

CHAPTER XXIX.
History of the Illinois and Michigan Canal—A Great Undertaking under Great Difficulties................................ 260

CONTENTS.

CHAPTER XXX.

A Sketch of the Conversion and Ministry of Rev. John Hill—Extraordinary Effects of his Preaching........................ 268

CHAPTER XXXI.

Anecdotes of Bishops Roberts and Soule—Singular Incident—Sketches of Western Methodism.................................. 274

CHAPTER XXXII.

Western Methodism—James B. Finley—Nolley—Bangs—M'Kendree... 293

CHAPTER XXXIII.

Administration of Discipline—Rev. John Sinclair................ 301

CHAPTER XXXIV.

First Session of Rock River Conference........................... 311

CHAPTER XXXV.

The Prairie State—Its Beauty, Resources, Population, and Destiny 317

CHAPTER XXXVI.

St. Louis in the Olden Time—Its First Newspaper—Progress of Methodism in Illinois.. 321

INTRODUCTION.

BY T. M. EDDY, D. D.

Years ago, when the writer first came to the North-West, among his earliest and most hearty greetings was one from Stephen R. Beggs. We found so pleasant a spirit, so happy a disposition, so cheerful a retrospect that we sought further acquaintance. His experience ran back into pioneer days, swept along the rough places, and wound among the bridle-paths of frontier settlements. So interesting were his reminiscences that, at our request, he wrote a portion of them, which appeared in successive numbers of the North-Western Christian Advocate. Artless, natural, just, they attracted favorable attention, and called out an expression favorable to publication in a more extended and permanent form.

The thought of *a book* came to him as an amazement. He, Stephen R. Beggs, become the author of a duodecimo volume! He had never thought of entering into history, much less writing it. When he made his way from one appointment to another by blazed trees, and stood up on a puncheon floor and preached in the dim glare of one or two tallow candles, kept alight by the snuffing of backwoods fingers, he would have laughed outright at the prediction that he should ever make a book to be read by the light streaming into richly carpeted parlors from patent gas-burners.

Yet why not? These early Methodist pioneers have led an eventful life, and its record is almost as marvelous as any thing in the annals of chivalry, and possesses the glitter of romance They have a knowledge of persons, places, and events essential to a perfect history of our Church in the West, and, unless written, it dies with them. Written, and not printed, it will be of no service to the future historian. A few years ago autobiographic literature was overdone, and yet the poorest, stalest, and least enduring had its value, and from such ephemeral annals will history be enriched.

The author was at the laying of foundations in the North-West, both political and ecclesiastical. He was in Chicago ere it *was* Chicago. He rocked the cradle of young Methodism here, but, musical as he is, would never sing to it a lullaby. He has told the story as he knew it, and as other careful observers have recited it. He was here among the Indian troubles when Black Hawk was devastating the country, and that, too, is told. He has labored in Ohio, Indiana, Illinois, and Missouri when there was more hard work than pecuniary compensation.

With his own experience he has connected anecdotes, sketches, stray waifs of biography, and incidents in danger of being lost.

He sends it forth, especially commending it to his old friends, the associates, lay and cleric, of earlier days. There are many yet living, for of tough stock and hardy fiber were those pioneer folks. They will read, and "remember the days of former times." We commend it to younger readers. It is well to see, amid our present, what was the character of our near past. Those days can never come again; changes of population and society make them impossible. The scream of the locomotive has scared the saddle-bags out of sight, and almost out of existence. New duties, new conflicts, new responsibilities are upon us. But let us keep in sympathy with the heroic aggressions, the chivalrous spirit, the daring and doing which made "the paths straight" for our present. For this there is nothing like the facts as they were, and some of them the author has told.

OFFICE NORTH-WESTERN CHRISTIAN ADVOCATE,
Chicago, April 25, 1868.

PAGES

FROM THE

Early History of the West and North-West.

CHAPTER I.

My great-grandfathers were born, the one, James Beggs, in Ireland; the other, Charles Barns, in America, of English extraction. One of my great-grandmothers was born in Ireland, the other in England; the maiden name of one being Hardy, of the other, M'Dow. My grandfather, Thomas Beggs, was a native of New Jersey, where he married Sarah Barnes, and afterward emigrated to Virginia. He lived in Rockingham county, till the breaking out of the Revolutionary War. He joined the patriot army, and became an officer in the commissary department, and died of camp fever in 1779 or 1780. He had four sons and one daughter. His three oldest sons had large families—that of John consisting of one son, James, and eight daughters. James had four sons—Charles, John, Stephen, and Thomas. John married Hannah Barnes; James married Mary Custer; and Charles married Dorothy Trumbow.

All settled at an early day in Clark county, Indiana. John Beggs was Judge of the Court; James was State Senator for nine years, joining the Methodist Episcopal Church in 1791; Charles was a member of the Legislature for several years, and served as Captain of a light-horse company in the Indian War, participating in the battle of Tippecanoe. He moved to Illinois in 1829. He still lives, at the advanced age of ninety-two; and during the Rebellion was as bitter against the "Tories," as he termed the rebels, as his family had been in '76. My father and mother, James Beggs and Mary Custer, were members of the Methodist Church from 1791 to the day of their death, a period of three-fourths of a century; and if I am an ultra Methodist, I came honestly by it.

I was born in Rockingham county, Virginia, March 30, 1801. When I was four years old, my father moved West, stopping about two years in Kentucky; and then settling in Clark county, Indiana, on the Ohio River, about seventeen miles above the falls at Louisville, where my father passed the rest of his life. My father had scarcely cleared off a small piece of ground—he had bought a heavily timbered farm of one hundred and sixty acres—and erected a log cabin, when the whole family, father, mother, and five children, myself excepted, were taken sick with chills and fever. In the absence of a physician, a brother Methodist administered the novel remedy, calomel; and we all soon became convalescent.

Father, however, attempted work too soon, and one damp day took a cold, which resulted in an attack of rheumatism that kept him laid up for nine years, unable to do a day's work. This was a sore affliction to us all, especially to mother, upon whom it imposed heavy responsibilities. These misfortunes induced father to exchange his large farm for a smaller one, with some improvements. My elder brothers held the plow, and I drove or rode the team; and we thus managed to raise grain enough for the supply of the family and the stock through the first Winter. Subsequently, father was elected to the Legislature, finally serving as a Senator more than ten years, greatly to the comfort of his family. He was a great stickler for grammar, receiving the name of "Mr. Syntax," by which he was known for years.

Among other deprivations consequent on the newness of the country, was that of shoes. I was seven years old before I ever rejoiced in the possession of a pair. Little did my parents or I myself see, in this pioneer life of the boy, God's hardening process, preparatory for the hardships of the uncultivated fields of his vineyard.

During our youth we enjoyed all the manly outdoor sports, such as hunting, wrestling, jumping, ball-playing, etc.; but swearing, lying, and dancing were eschewed and detested. As for dancing, I felt something as Daniel Webster expressed it, who said he never had sense enough to learn. It really seemed such hard work, that I had a fellow-feeling with the heathen, who, seeing how hard people exerted themselves in that "amusement," wondered why they did not make their servants dance as well as do the rest of their drudgery.

My father, though not a very large man, was very athletic. I had the reputation of being the strongest man in Clark county. John Strange, one day, saw me walking at a short distance; and stopping in amazement at my apparent strength, said that if I could only get my feet properly set, I could rock the earth. I was just six feet in hight, and weighed from one hundred and eighty-five to one hundred and ninety-nine pounds. I have passed a generally healthy life; and now, 1868, my health is good, my lungs sound, and I am free from dyspepsia, or other chronic ailment.

What little schooling we got was in the Winter, in a school-house, which it may be worth while to describe: built of round logs; the window, a rude opening filled with white paper, greased with lard to admit the light; the benches made of "slabs" split from logs, and so high that the smaller children's feet could not touch the ground, that being all the floor we had; one entire end of the structure being used for a fireplace, the chimney built of split sticks, plastered over with mortar. With the improvement of the country, our advantages became greater. The old Dillworth spelling-book used to cost one dollar, equal to four dollars of our money.

From early youth I had a desire to become a preacher. This I manifested in conducting meetings in innocent play among the children, or alone in the deep forest, going through with the regular order of exercises. I learned to think that if a man could read, and write, and sing, and pray, he had about all the qualifications needed for the itinerant work. When I was about twelve years of age, the Indian troubles began in Scott and Clark counties. My fears I can vividly recall. I expected the savages would kill me; felt that I was not prepared to die, and would have made any sacrifice, could I have felt that I was not an accountable being.

When the news came of the "Pigeon-Roost massacre," nearly all the settlers north of us fled across the Ohio, leaving their effects behind. Returning, they built a fortification around my father's house, which was of stone. Here they remained for days, in constant expectation of the Indians. Several block-houses were built to the north of us, the occupants of which would flee to our fort on every fresh alarm. The "Pigeon-Roost massacre," of which I spoke, occurred at a settlement of that name, formed in 1809, and which, confined to a square mile of land, was five or six miles distant from neighboring settlements.

On the afternoon of the third of September, 1812, Jeremiah Payne and a man by the name of Kauffmann, were surprised and killed by a party of Indians while at work in the woods, about two miles from the settlement. The Indians then—Shawnees, ten or twelve in number—attacked the settlement about sunset, and murdered one man, five women, and sixteen children. The bodies of some of the victims were burned in the cabins where they were slaughtered. Mrs. John Biggs alone escaped with her three small children, reaching a settlement six miles distant near daylight.

A number of the militia of Clark county proceeded to the scene of the massacre, where they found only the mangled and half-consumed bodies of the dead, and the ruins of the houses; and the remains were all buried in one grave.

From a child I enjoyed the advantages of religious education, and was taught at school, as well as at home, to read the Bible. I formed the habit of prayer very young, and continued it regularly till my conversion in the nineteenth year of my age. At that time I visited a camp meeting at Jacobs' camp-grounds, seven miles above Louisville, which began October 6th. On Sabbath afternoon, after a powerful sermon by Rev. James Ward, of the Kentucky Conference, I took my place at the altar, among seekers of religion. The deliverance, on which I had fixed my determination, did not come till sunset. I can never forget those first bright joys of pardoned sin, nor cease recalling, when I think of that blessed hour, the shouts of joy that arose like the "sounds of many waters," "Glory to God in the highest!" multiplied, as they were, by scores, till two hundred were converted. Among these seven of us were licensed to preach, the most of whom entered the itinerant work.

Soon after my probation expired I was appointed assistant class-leader. It was a heavy cross to address in reproof and exhortation, as well as comfort, the old alike with the young; yet I found, as I have ever found, His grace sufficient for me. I was soon afterward licensed to exhort, by Rev. Samuel Glaze. Blessed in these labors,. I was speedily licensed to preach. I had long felt this necessity laid upon me, though I shrank from the great duty; but the resolution once formed, and the step taken, I felt wonderfully blest. This occurred at the local conference at a quarterly camp meeting near Salem, Indiana.

I resolved that after two years' schooling, I would offer myself to the Annual Conference as a probationer. Rev. James Armstrong, who succeeded Rev. C. Ruter—under whose untiring labors six hundred had been added to the Church on the circuit—insisted that I should at once receive a recommendation to the next Annual Conference, which was to be held at St. Louis that Fall. He held that I could better receive my education and graduate in the "Brush College," as most of our preachers had done. After much anxious and prayerful reflection, I finally said: "Here am I." My recommendation was presented, and I was received; and glad am I to this day that I began when I did and as I did.

This one lesson I learned: to look to the Lord, whence cometh our help. I know that I have thus formed a habit of trust stronger than I should have done, had I waited to receive a liberal education. Yet I realize what a blessing and what a power a sanctified education is.

The great revival above mentioned was attended with many extraordinary physical manifestations, in which both the converted and the unconverted were alike exercised. Some laughed so excessively and so long that it seemed as though they would literally "die laughing." Bending backward as far as they could, they would laugh at the top of their voice, then bending forward almost to the ground, they would continue till they well-nigh lost breath, then straightening up and catching breath, they would renew their convulsive laughter, repeating the same phenomena for an hour or more, till completely exhausted they would fall down in a swoon. The "jerks" were also very common in the prayer meetings, particularly among the women. Sometimes three or four were affected at once, being thrown flat on the floor, and when forced to their feet by a couple of strong men, "jerked" irresistibly back and forth. Often have I seen a frail woman surpass the utmost strength of two strong men.

Elder Hamilton was preaching on one occasion when several became affected in this way. It prevented his going on with his discourse, as he thought it all assumed, or at least a thing which could be controlled. That very night, however, after retiring, he was himself seized with the "jerks." On finding them to be a reality, he fervently prayed the good Lord to deliver him from what he considered an affliction, promising that if similar occurrences took place again at his meetings, he would make the best of it. They were so prevalent in places, in these early days, that Peter Cartwright said that he had heard of the dogs and hogs having them; a fact to which brother John Stewart bears the testimony of personal observation.

Brother Cartwright tells of one man whose neck was actually broken while thus exercised. The falling "exercise" was also very common; those affected by it lying apparently lifeless for hours. The subjects returned to consciousness with a bound, and generally with a shout of "*Glory to God!*" President Edwards, for his personal satisfaction, examined carefully into these phenomena, and gave it as his deliberate conviction, that these "foxfire" and "wildfire" conversions, as they were termed, were often among the most powerful and lasting that he had ever witnessed.

CHAPTER II.

As early as 1802 Methodists ventured within the present limits of Indiana, among its few scattered settlers. The first was Nathan Robertson, who moved from Kentucky to Charlestown, Clark county, in 1779. Three years later a small class was organized near Charlestown. This class built the first chapel in the State, on David Roland's land. This was afterward burned down, and another erected a mile farther north, called Gassaway, or Salem meeting-house. It was made of hewed logs, and still stands in a good state of preservation, though not used for worship. In the old church-yard in which it stands, lie the remains of my revered father and mother, of two brothers and a sister, all members of the Methodist Church. Within the walls of this church I was faithfully warned to flee from the wrath to come, and pointed to the Lamb of God, who taketh away the sins of the world, by some of the best men the Church has ever produced. The class was very strong in faith and in numbers, embracing a hundred members at the close of Calvin Ruter's Conference year, 1820.

Wm. Cravens made a practice of meeting the class at his appointments, where he would examine each member, asking them if they drank strong drink.

All who confessed to doing so and who would not promise total abstinence, he would direct to sit on a separate bench. At the close of the class meeting he would have a prayer meeting in their behalf. If no reformation followed these efforts, he had them tried promptly and turned out of the Church. He was a very large man and of great strength. His sermons were original and powerful. His eccentricity was proverbial. In one of his sermons before election he said he would as soon vote for a horse-thief as a dram-drinker or whisky distiller.

On one occasion, in calling for mourners, he set out three benches, one for seekers of religion, one for backsliders, and the other for hypocrites, and they all had occupants. On the hypocrite bench was a man who had two wives. Cravens was soon by his side, and said: "I understand that you have two wives; are you determined now to forsake this woman and go and live with your lawful wife?" The man replied "no." "Be off, then," said Cravens; "you can't get religion here!" He could strike as hard in a few words as any man I ever heard.

Once he was preaching at a camp meeting. Among the preachers on the platform were a slave-owner and a lawyer. Speaking of the qualifications of the ministry, he said he "would as soon hear a negro play a banjo, or a raccoon squeal, as to hear a negro-holder or a petty lawyer preach;" then turning abruptly to the two men he exclaimed,

"How dare you lay your bloody hands on this Sacred Book!" He termed all instruments of music introduced into churches wooden gods. Rev. Mr. Fillmore once preached where brother Abbot led the singing in a choir in which they had instrumental music. After the service he asked brother Abbot how he liked the music, whose only reply was, "Your wooden brother did very well to-day." A bass-viol being once introduced into a choir when Cartwright preached, he announced the hymn with the invitation, "We will fiddle to the Lord, my brethren." Brother A. E. Phelps told me the following story of the manner in which Rev. J. Gruber once disposed of a choir difficulty: there being a division in the choir, he wished to have the whole matter turned over to him. When the choir began to sing he began to roar on a shell which he had procured. This, of course, put a stop to the singing. On the choir starting again at his request, he began to blow again, exclaiming, "I can't sing, but I am a roarer on this shell!"

To Joseph Williams belongs the honor of being the first itinerant preacher appointed to a circuit in Indiana. In 1809 the Indiana district was formed, embracing the entire area of the territories of Indiana, Illinois, and Missouri. Samuel Parker was the first presiding elder. In this year Silver Creek circuit was formed. It embraced all the settlements in the southern part of Indiana, reaching up the Ohio River to Whitewater circuit. Josiah Crawford had charge of it; returning a membership of one hundred and eighty-eight. In 1810 Silver Creek was a part of Green River district, Wm. Burke presiding elder, and Sela Paine preacher in charge. This district embraced, besides Silver Creek, the following circuits: Green River, Barren, Wayne, Cumberland, Danville, Salt River, and Shelby. The Indiana district was composed of Illinois, Missouri, Maramack, Coldwater, Cape Girardeau, and Vincennes circuits, Samuel Parker presiding elder. At the close of this year, 1810, Silver Creek returned four hundred and forty-eight members. In 1811 Wm. Burke was presiding elder on Green River district, and Isaac Lindsey had charge of Silver Creek circuit. The number of members returned was 397. The total number returned from Indiana was 1,160. In 1812 two additional circuits were formed in Indiana, Lawrenceburg and Patoka. Silver Creek was this year connected, under the charge of Wm. M'Mahon, with Salt River district, James Ward presiding elder.

In 1815 the Western Conference was divided into the Ohio and Tennessee Conferences. The Indiana circuits were assigned to two different Conferences; Whitewater and Lawrenceburg in the Miami district, and Silver Creek in Salt River district, being within the bounds of the Ohio Conference. The total membership in the State was 2,176—all gathered in within five years. In 1814 Charles Harrison was appointed to Silver Creek, Jesse Walker presiding elder. The number of members reported in Indiana was 1,759. In 1815, 1,504 were returned, the decrease being due to the War. Shadrach Ruark was preacher in charge on Silver Creek circuit, Charles Holliday presiding elder. In 1816 Joseph Kinkaid went to Silver Creek. This year Blue River was detached from Silver Creek circuit, under the charge of John Shrader. It extended down the Ohio and out to the head waters of the Patoka. There were now six circuits in Indiana, with a membership of 1,877. In 1817 Joseph Pownal was sent to Silver Creek, and John Cord to Blue River, Samuel H. Thompson presiding elder.

This year there were six circuits in Indiana, with a membership of 1,907. In 1818 John Cord was sent to Silver Creek. A new circuit, Little Pigeon, was established; seven in all, with nine preachers and 3,044 members. I have been thus particular about the introduction of Methodism into Indiana, of the districts of that Conference, and especially of Silver Creek circuit, because it was there that I passed so much of my early life and entered upon the work of the ministry. Brother Wm. C. Smith thinks that the first Indiana meeting-house was erected in 1808.

It was in this year that the first circuit—Whitewater—was formed. I think the claim to precedence lies between the Meek's Church, as it was termed, and the Robertson meeting-house, three miles north of Charlestown, Clark county. There was also one built at an early day near my father's. The date

I can not give. It was the first that I recollect attending. Thomas Allen and James Garner were the preachers. I told a playmate that I liked the former the best, because he did not swear so much as old brother Garner. That building was subsequently burned, and afterward the old Salem meeting-house was erected one mile further north.

Since the first rude log cabin meeting-house was erected in Indiana, the work of church-building has gone on, till the number reaches about 1,300; many of them magnificent buildings, costing from thirty to seventy thousand dollars. What has God wrought through this "pioneer" Methodist Episcopal Church! Wm. C. Smith thinks the first camp meeting in Indiana was held in Wayne county. I think that about the same time we held one on the Robinson camp-ground, Clark county.

Brother Smith, in his sketch of Miami district, says that T. Nelson and S. H. Thompson, who preached on Whitewater circuit in 1810, then went to Kentucky—Nollechuckie circuit—and neither of them ever returned to Indiana to labor. S. H. Thompson was on the Illinois district in 1817, and I recollect distinctly his sermon at our quarterly meeting at old Salem meeting-house, Clark county. His powerful sermon and his fresh, manly look, all left an ineffaceable impression on my mind. I thought him one of the handsomest men I had ever seen. He was so good a hand at soliciting aid for our Church charities, that he bore the name of "beggar-general." His strong appeals were almost resistless. On one occasion he closed his appeal by telling the people to come forward and lay their offerings on the table. Among those who responded was a gentleman who put his hand deep into his pocket and took out a handful of silver to get some change. Thompson saw him, and, as if supposing that he intended to lay all upon the table, exclaimed at the top of his voice, "Thank God for one liberal soul!" By this time all eyes were fixed on the "liberal" gentleman, who could not help laying down the entire handful. But Thompson illustrated his precept in this respect by example. He generally headed the contribution; and so generous was he in his offerings, that he not infrequently had to borrow money to get home with. Indeed, he was hardly an exception. The liberality of the Methodist preachers was remarkable; giving beyond their means, they yet realized that it was more blessed to give than to receive.

In this connection, I may appropriately introduce some account of the early history of Methodism in Northern Indiana, with sketches of a few of the prominent preachers. Among the many whom I heard preach, were brothers A. Joslin, James Conwell, A. Wood, James Havens, John Morrow, J. Strange, A. Wiley, J. L. Thompson, Calvin Ruter, James Armstrong, George Hester, and Richard Hargrave. Wiley was a superb preacher; beginning slowly, and deliberately, and cautiously, but surely making his way to the hearts of his congregation, till his deep feelings seemed to take charge of his tongue, and his whole soul would be poured out with his words. His appeals, always affecting, were sometimes overwhelming.

James Havens, as the Hon. O. H. Smith describes him, may be justly termed the Napoleon of Methodism in Eastern Indiana. He was hard to handle, physically, as well as intellectually; his strength of muscle being equal to his mental powers. At one of the Connersville circuit camp meetings, I once saw him, just as Strange was beginning his Sabbath morning sermon, take hold of a ruffian who was making a disturbance at the altar. He threw him literally "heels over head," giving him a tremendous fall, then holding him so fast as almost to strangle him; having fairly subdued him, he took the humbled rowdy to head-quarters for trial. Strange preached a most powerful sermon, resulting in the conversion of many souls. O. H. Smith regards Strange as one of the most effective preachers he ever heard. He does not hesitate to say that Indiana owes him a special debt of gratitude for his efforts through a long, laborious life, to form her new society on the enduring basis of morality and education.

A. Wood, D. D., and myself, were both young men when we became acquainted. He bid fair, at an early age, to become a useful man. He had a sound mind, a most felicitous elocution, and a zeal without bound. He preached always with all his power, frequently becoming so exhausted as to fall helpless into the arms of those near him. He still enjoys the best of health in his green old age.

The following sketches from his pen will give value to this book, written in reply to a request to furnish some recollections of the early Methodist societies in Laporte county, Indiana. He prefaces his personal sketches with some valuable statistics of the early Conferences:

"Previous to the year A. D. 1832, all the settlements of Northern Indiana were visited by missionaries from Michigan, which was then in what was called the 'North Ohio Conference.'

"Erastus Felton, in 1830, and L. B. Gurley, in 1831, preached in Laporte county. But in 1832 there was made an 'Indiana Conference,' and James Armstrong was appointed missionary. He moved to the county and settled on a farm near Door Village. James Armstrong was the evangelist of our Church in this county, influencing many Church members to move to it from older parts of the State; and remaining in the county as an enterprising missionary till his death, which occurred on the 12th of September, 1834.

"N. B. Griffith came to the county about the same time, but he settled in St. Joseph, where he also died in 1834. The first societies in both these counties were organized by these men. It may be in place for me to give some pen-portraits of them.

"Armstrong was of medium hight, and weight. His chin, lips, and nose sharp, eyes small, eyebrows heavy, forehead square and high, and hair thick set and dark. He was always neatly dressed in plain black. He had a good voice, with a free use of plain, English words of Saxon origin; nothing of the Irish brogue, but much of the fire, which, as he felt himself, he failed not to impart to others who gave him audience, till the bond became so strong between the speaker and hearer, that both were carried along with the force and beauty of the subject before them. He was what we called a 'topic preacher;' and before a promiscuous congregation, his memory, his imagination, and tact enabled him to conduct a controversy with great ingenuity for success to any cause he espoused. As a man and a minister he attached personal friends, who liberally sustained his enterprises and boldly defended his measures.

"Having been presiding elder over all the State of Indiana, from the Ohio to the lakes, he was a herald of the Gospel whom God owned and blessed, and his untiring industry and influence, devoted as they were entirely to the organizing of the Church in the then new settlements, place him on the page of our history as the leading evangelist.

"In the order of time, the societies were formed: first, at Door Village; second, at Springfield; third, at Robinson's; fourth, at Laporte; fifth, in Michigan City. At all these there were societies, and stated worship, before the year 1837.

"The first meeting-house was at Door Village; the second at Laporte; the third, Union Chapel; the fourth at Michigan City; and from these there have branched off all the societies in the county.

"N. B. Griffith had a ready mind, well adapted to organize religious societies in a new country. He was remarkably quick and correct in his knowledge of human nature—a discerner of human character on first acquaintance. Earnestly devoted to the one work of bringing men to Christ, his congregations were large and his labors successful. He died August 22, 1834.

"It is difficult to give a true history of our Church as bounded by *county lines*, for these were not the lines of circuits or societies in the first mission. In 1833 there was a missionary district, in which there was a Laporte mission. Elder Armstrong had charge of both district and mission. The former inclosed Ft. Wayne, Elkhart, St. Joseph, and Kalamazoo, as well as Laporte. On this district were four young unmarried men; namely, R. S. Robinson, B. Phelps, J. T. Robe, and G. W. Beswick. As the elder lived in Laporte county, this was the head of the district. These gave to the people not only the wisdom of the presiding elder, but the variety of these young men.

"The returns of 1833 give to Laporte 140 members; but this included Terre Coupee society, most of whom lived beyond the county line. The first camp meeting was on J. A. Osborne's lands, near

Door Village. At this meeting $300 was subscribed to build the first Door Village church; here, for some years, was the strongest society in the county. It had laymen and local preachers, whose *general* knowledge gave them influence, and whose devotion to the Church made them a power for usefulness.

"F. Standiford was one of those who came to this county. He was brought up in Maryland in the midst of old Methodists, and graduated to the order of elder as a 'local' preacher. He moved to Laporte from Putnam county, Indiana, having lived first in Kentucky after leaving Maryland. He was a representative 'local' preacher, assisting the itinerating preachers by his experience in knowledge of 'Scripture holiness.' There was, in the days of large circuits traveled by young men, a necessity for something more fixed than the occasional visits of the itinerating evangelist; and a society was favored when it had an ordained local preacher. This was the condition of the Door Village society. There were also tried *laymen* in that band of men, who, though they had come, some from Ohio, others from Virginia, and others from New York State, yet met with one accord in one place, and were blessed of God. Many of these have finished their careers, and rest from their labors. F. Standiford, A. Stearns, and J. Sale, have passed on, before those who yet remain to see the fruits of planting the Church in this beautiful prairie.

"Of traveling preachers, who did betimes something

to build these societies, and who have passed away, I now call up E. Smith, A. Johnson, G. W. Baker, J. Garner, W. F. Wheeler, G. M. Beswick, J. Jenkins, and W. Poney. All these had at some time contributed to the ministerial work of a quarterly meeting at Door Village. The first and strongest off-shoot from this old stock was Union Chapel, on the south end of Door Prairie, composed largely of a colony from Clark county, Indiana, relations of 'Robertsons' and 'Garners,' who formed the first Methodist class in Indiana Territory in 1802. The leading laymen and local preachers were *sui generis* Methodist, of old Maryland and Ohio stock—oral—hospitable—earnest—loyal."

CHAPTER III.

For the subject-matter of this and the following chapter, I am indebted to brother W. C. Smith's "Indiana Miscellany;" from different portions of which they are compiled.

It has generally been thought that Methodism was introduced into Indiana, in what is known as Clark's Grant, which included a portion of what is now Clark and Floyd counties. In later years it has been stated that a class of Methodists was formed in Clark's Grant, as early as 1802; but upon what evidence or authority we do not know. We do know that Rev. Hugh Cull, a local preacher, settled in the Whitewater country as early as 1805, having visited the country the year previous. The first circuit in Indiana was called Whitewater, and belonged to the Ohio district, in the old Western Conference. It embraced all the country from the Ohio River along the eastern line of the territory, as far north as there were any white settlements, which was in the region where Richmond now stands, and west to the land belonging to the Indians. This circuit was probably formed in 1807. It appears upon the Minutes of the Western Conference, in the year 1808, with Joseph Williams as preacher in charge, and John Sale presiding elder of the district. The settlements visited by Mr. Williams were remote from each other; the traveling was laborious and hazardous; the roads along which he passed were Indian traces and newly blazed ways; the streams were unbridged; the country was full of ravenous beasts and the much-dreaded Indians. The emigrants, to whom he ministered, could afford him but few accommodations. He labored faithfully, hunting up the Methodists who had pitched their tents in the wilderness, and at the end of the year returned 165 white members and one colored. According to the most reliable data, these were all the Methodists who had to this date been organized and numbered in Indiana. In 1808 Indiana contained but one circuit, with 166 members of the Methodist Episcopal Church. Now, 1866, there are four Annual Conferences, with a membership of about 100,000 in the State. How great the change in fifty-eight years! Mr. Williams has the honor of being the first itinerant Methodist preacher appointed to a circuit in Indiana. We would, if we had the particulars of his life and death, give them to the public to perpetuate his memory. In 1809 he was sent to Scioto circuit, in the State of Ohio, and in 1810 he located. In 1809 Indiana district was formed, and Samuel Parker was appointed presiding elder. It was composed of the following circuits: Illinois, Missouri, Maramack, Coldwater, Whitewater, and Silver Creek. Though but two circuits of this district were in Indiana, we give its entire bounds, that the young men, who are now traveling circuits and districts in the State, may see the extent of the fields of labor our fathers had to cultivate. This district covered all the territories of Indiana, Illinois, and Missouri. It required, surely, a man of strong nerves and stout heart to travel such a district at such a time. In traveling this district Mr. Parker had to go from the eastern boundary of Indiana across Illinois, and then across the Mississippi River into Missouri. In some places many miles of unbroken wilderness intervened between the settlements he had to visit. This year Silver Creek circuit was formed, and embraced all the settlements in the southern portion of the territory, and up the Ohio River to Whitewater circuit. Hector Sanford and Moses Crume were appointed to Whitewater, and Josiah Crawford to Silver Creek. The most northern appointment on the Whitewater circuit was the cabin of George Smith, which was about two miles from where the city of Richmond is now situated. At the close of this year the preachers returned 352 members for Whitewater circuit, and 188 for Silver Creek, making an increase of 374. In 1810 Whitewater was placed in the Miami district, with John Sale presiding elder, and Thomas Nelson and Samuel H. Thompson circuit preachers. This district was composed of the following circuits: Cincinnati, Mad River, Scioto, Deer Creek, Hockhocking, White Oak, and Whitewater. Silver Creek was in the Green River district, William Burke presiding elder, and Sela Paine circuit preacher. This district was composed of the following circuits: Green River, Barren, Wayne, Cumberland, Danville, Salt River, Shelby, and Silver Creek. Indiana district was composed of Illinois, Missouri, Maramack, Coldwater, Cape Girardeau, and Vincennes circuits. Samuel Parker was returned to the district, and Wm. Winans was appointed to Vincennes. Nelson and Thompson, who traveled the Whitewater circuit this year, both rose to considerable distinction, particularly Mr. Thompson. The next year Nelson was sent to Rapids circuit in Mississippi. Mr. Thompson was sent to Nollechuckie, in the State of Tennessee. Neither of these men ever returned to Indiana to labor.

Sela Paine, who traveled the Silver Creek circuit this year, was sent the next to Natchez circuit, Mississippi.

Vincennes circuit appears on the Minutes of the Conference this year for the first time, making three fields of labor in Indiana. What the dimensions of this circuit were we have no means of knowing. Vincennes was an old French post, under the influence of the Roman Catholics, a hard place in which to plant Methodism. Mr. Winans, who had been sent to Vincennes this year, had been admitted on trial in the Western Conference the year before. He was a young man of promising talents, and made a good impression on those who heard him preach. It was difficult for him to get the people of

Vincennes to come to preaching, so wicked and so much were they under the influence of the Romish priests.

The following incident is said to have occurred this year: General William H. Harrison was Governor of the territory of Indiana, and resided at Vincennes. Young Mr. Winans had an appointment to preach one night, in a small room in town. General Harrison and one other person composed the congregation assembled to hear the young preacher. There was but one candle to give light, and nothing to place *that* upon. The General held the candle for the young preacher to see to read his hymn and text. Mr. Winans preached faithfully to those two hearers. After this he had no trouble in getting a congregation to preach to. At the close of this year the preachers returned 484 members from Whitewater circuit, 235 from Silver Creek, and forty-three from Vincennes, making a total of 765, an increase of 418; showing that Methodism began to take a deep hold upon the pioneers in Indiana. In 1811 Whitewater circuit was continued in connection with the Miami district, Solomon Langdon presiding elder, and Moses Crume in charge of the circuit. The people hailed Mr. Crume's return to them with great delight. He had traveled the circuit as junior preacher two years before. He made his impress upon the people so deeply this year, that he was ever afterward a great favorite among them. Isaac Lindsey was sent to Silver Creek circuit this year. It remained in connection with the Green River district, with William Burke as presiding elder.

Vincennes appears on the Minutes this year as "St. Vincennes," in connection with the Cumberland district; Learner Blackman presiding elder, and Thomas Stilwell circuit preacher. Mr. Blackman was a man eminent for his talents, piety, and usefulness. During the course of his life he traveled over a very extensive territory of country, ranging from Pittsburg to New Orleans, and was highly esteemed by all who knew him. This year the preachers reported 368 members from Whitewater circuit, 397 from Silver Creek, and 325 from Vincennes, making a total of 1,160, or an increase of 395. In 1812 two additional circuits were formed in Indiana; Lawrenceburg and Patoka. Whitewater and Lawrenceburg were connected with the Miami district, Solomon Langdon presiding elder. Silver Creek was connected with Salt River district, James Ward presiding elder; while Vincennes and Patoka were connected with Wabash district, James Axley presiding elder. Walter Griffith was sent to Lawrenceburg, Robert W. Finley to Whitewater, William M'Mahon to Silver Creek, James Turner to Vincennes, and Benjamin Edge to Patoka. These men were all faithful and useful.

Walter Griffith, who traveled the Lawrenceburg circuit this year, was afterward made presiding elder, and filled that important office with great acceptability and usefulness. Robert W. Finley had been a Presbyterian minister for several years, and was the father of Rev. James B. Finley, who rose to such distinction in Ohio. At the close of the year there were returned from the five circuits in Indiana a total membership of 1,121, which seems to present a decrease in the number of Church members; but from some cause, there were no returns from Lawrenceburg and Patoka circuits. This accounts for the apparent decrease in the number of members.

In 1813 the old Western Conference was divided or discontinued, and the Ohio and Tennessee Conferences were formed out of it. The circuits in Indiana were placed in these two Conferences, Lawrenceburg and Whitewater were placed in the Miami district, and Silver Creek in the Salt River district, all within the boundary lines of Ohio Conference. Patoka disappears this year. William Dixon was sent to Lawrenceburg, John Strange went to Whitewater, and Thomas Nelson to Silver Creek.

At the close of this year the number of Church members reported were as follows: Lawrenceburg, 489; Whitewater, 847; Silver Creek, 555; Vincennes, 175; Patoka, 110. Total membership, 2,176.

In five years, two thousand, one hundred and seventy-six members had been gathered into the Methodist Episcopal Church in Indiana, and this though the country was new, and though but a small portion of the territory was inhabited by white people.

This large increase shows that the men who had been sent into the wild wilderness to cultivate Immanuel's land, had done their work faithfully, and God had crowned their labors with success.

In 1814 Moses Crume was sent to Lawrenceburg circuit, David Sharp to Whitewater, Charles Harrison to Silver Creek, and Zachariah Witten to Vincennes. Patoka does not appear on the list of appointments this year. Charles Holliday was appointed presiding elder of Salt River district, and Silver Creek being in his district gave him connections with the work in Indiana; and Jesse Walker, being presiding elder of Illinois district, and Vincennes being in that district, he was brought in connection with the work in Indiana.

The number of members reported at the close of this year was 1,759, showing a decrease, which was caused by the derangement of the work produced by the war in which the country was then engaged. In 1815 John Strange was sent to Lawrenceburg, William Hunt to Whitewater, Shadrach Ruark to Silver Creek, John Scripps to Patoka, and John Shrader to Vincennes, with the same presiding elders that traveled the districts the year before. The number of circuits was not increased, but their boundaries were greatly enlarged.

The terror among the settlers, caused by the war, and the constant danger from the Indians that infested the country by thousands, had caused many of the inhabitants to return to the old States for safety. Among them were many Methodists, causing a great decrease this year. There were reported to Conference a total of 1,504.

In 1816 David Sharp was sent to Lawrenceburg, Daniel Fraley to Whitewater, Joseph Kinkade to Silver Creek, John Shrader to Blue River, Thomas A. King to Patoka, and Thomas Davis to Vincennes. Blue River circuit had been formed out of a part of Silver Creek. It extended down the Ohio River and out to the head-waters of Patoka. We now have six circuits formed in Indiana. The war being over and the country becoming more quiet, the inhabitants who had fled for fear of the Indians began to return, with many new emigrants. The preachers were enabled to report this year a total of 1,877 members, an increase of 373 over the past year.

In 1817 Russel Bigelow was sent to Lawrenceburg, Benjamin Lawrence to Whitewater, Daniel M'Henry and Thomas Davis to Patoka, James M'Cord and Charles Slocomb to Vincennes, John Cord to Blue River, Joseph Pownal to Silver Creek.

Missouri Conference having been formed, all of Illinois and all of Indiana, except Lawrenceburg and Whitewater circuits, were placed in that Conference. The other circuits were in the Illinois district, with Samuel H. Thompson for presiding elder. Moses Crume was placed over the Miami district, in the Ohio Conference; which brought him back to Lawrenceburg and Whitewater circuits, where he met a hearty welcome from the people. The preachers on the six circuits, in Indiana, reported at the close of the year a total membership of 1,907, being a small increase over the past year. In 1818 Samuel West and Allen Wiley were sent to Lawrenceburg, William Hunt to Whitewater, Charles Slocomb to Patoka, Thomas Davis to Little Pigeon, John Shrader and John M'Cord to Vincennes, Othniel Taebert to Blue River, and John Cord to Silver Creek. Little Pigeon was a new circuit just formed, and embraced the country south-west of Blue River circuit. We have now seven circuits, traveled by nine preachers. The preachers reported to Conference at the close of this year a total of 3,044 members, an increase of 1,037.

In the year 1819 the work in Indiana was so arranged as to place the circuits in two Annual Conferences, namely, the Ohio and Missouri, and to form three districts; namely, the Lebanon and Miami, in the Ohio Conference, and the Illinois in the Missouri Conference. There were three new circuits formed, which appear upon the Minutes this year for the first time; namely, Madison, Indian Creek, and Harrison. The circuits were placed in districts as follows: Whitewater in Lebanon district, with Moses Crume presiding elder; Lawrenceburg and Madison in Miami district, with John Sale presiding elder; and Silver Creek, Indian Creek, Blue River, Harrison, Vincennes, Patoka, and Pigeon, in Illinois district, with Jesse Hale presiding elder.

Allen Wiley and Zachariah Connell were sent to Whitewater circuit, Benjamin Lawrence to Lawrenceburg, John T. Kent to Madison, David Sharp to Silver Creek, William Mavity to Indian Creek, John Pownal to Blue River, William Medford to Harrison, John Cord to Vincennes, John Wallace and Daniel M'Henry to Patoka and Pigeon. This was a year of considerable prosperity. The whole number of members in Indiana was 3,470, giving an increase for the year of 426.

In 1820 the districts and circuits were again changed, and supplied as follows: Miami district, Ohio Conference, Walter Griffith presiding elder; Whitewater circuit, Arthur W. Elliott, Samuel Brown; Lawrenceburg, Benjamin Lawrence, Henry S. Farnandis; Madison, Henry Baker, William H. Raper; Indiana district, Missouri Conference, Samuel Hamilton presiding elder; Silver Creek circuit, Calvin Ruter, Job M. Baker; Indian Creek, John Shrader, John Everhart; Blue River, John Stewart, Joseph Pownal; Patoka, John Wallace; Vincennes, Daniel M'Henry. Pigeon and Harrison do not appear on the Minutes this year.

This year Calvin Ruter commenced his labors in Indiana. He had been admitted into the Ohio Conference two years before, and was now transferred to the Missouri Conference. The whole number of members returned this year was 4,399, giving an increase of 929. In 1821 Charlestown, Bloomington, Ohio, Mount Sterling, and Corydon appear on the Minutes as heads of circuits. The presiding elders continued upon the districts as they were the past year. This year James Jones was sent to Whitewater, John P. Durbin and James Collard to Lawrenceburg, Allen Wiley and William P. Quinn to Madison, Calvin Ruter and William Cravens to Charlestown, John Scripps and Samuel Glaize to Blue River, Daniel Chamberlin to Bloomington, Job M. Baker to Vincennes, Elias Stone to Patoka, John Wallace to Ohio, George K. Hester to Mount Sterling, and John Shrader to Corydon. The aggregate membership for this year was 7,314. Methodism was now advancing rapidly in the State.

In 1822 Allen Wiley and James T. Wells were sent to Whitewater, Henry Baker to Lawrenceburg, James Jones and James Murray to Madison, with Alexander Cummins for presiding elder. James Armstrong was sent to Charlestown, George K. Hester to Flat Rock, John Wallace and Joseph Kinkade to Blue River, John Cord to Bloomington, David Chamberlin to Honey Creek, John Stewart to Vincennes, James L. Thompson to Patoka, Ebenezer Webster to Mount Sterling, Job M. Baker to Corydon, and William Cravens to Indianapolis, with Samuel Hamilton for presiding elder. Indianapolis now appears on the Minutes as the head of a circuit, for the first time. In 1866 there were five Methodist preachers and one missionary stationed at Indianapolis, and the charges in the city belong to four Annual Conferences. The borders of Methodism had rapidly enlarged. The men, into whose hands the work had been committed, were fully devoted to their calling. In 1823 the number of circuits had increased to fifteen. Two new ones had been formed in Connersville and Eel River. Cummins and Hamilton were continued as presiding elders. The appointments of the preachers were as follows: Whitewater, Russel Bigelow and George Gatch; Lawrenceburg, W. H. Raper; Madison, J. Stewart and Nehemiah B. Griffith; Connersville, James Murray and James C. Taylor; Charlestown, James Armstrong; Flat Rock, Dennis Wiley; Blue River, W. M. Reynolds and George K. Hester; Bloomington, John Cord; Honey Creek, Hackaliah Vredenburg; Vincennes, John Ingersoll and Job M. Baker; Patoka, Ebenezer F. Webster; Mount Sterling, Stephen R. Beggs; Corydon, James L. Thompson; Indianapolis, James Scott; Eel River, William Cravens. The whole membership this year was 7,733, giving an increase of nineteen.

CHAPTER IV.

The Divine Being will always take care of those who trust in him, and unreservedly devote all their time and strength to his service. He will support, sustain, comfort, and deliver them in time of trouble.

In the year 1828, when Stephen R. Beggs traveled the Wayne circuit, Mrs. H., who then resided in Richmond, was deeply convicted of sin; she was awakened under a sermon preached by Mr. Beggs, from Psalm 1, 14, 15: "Offer unto God thanksgiving; and pay thy vows unto the Most High; and call upon me in the day of trouble: I will deliver thee, and thou shalt glorify me." She had a long and hard struggle, but after weeks of deep penitence, found redemption in the blood of the Lamb; her burden of guilt was taken away, and her "mourning was turned into joy." So intense was her agony of mind before she found peace in believing, that she was almost incapable of attending to her domestic duties; so great was her joy when she felt all her sins were forgiven, that she shouted aloud the praises of God, saying: "Now, Lord, from this time forth, in weal or in woe, in sickness or in health, in tribulation, in distress, poverty, persecution, living or dying; I am thine—thine forever!" She connected herself with the Methodist Episcopal

Church, casting in her lot with the little persecuted band in Richmond. Her husband was a very wicked man, violently opposed to her piety, particularly to her being among the Methodists, who, on account of their religion, were not in the sweetest odor in the nostrils of most citizens in town. He not only refused to render her any assistance, but by every means in his power strove to block up the way, prevent her from attending Church, and break her off from her piety, abusing the Methodists with oaths and curses, threatening her with violence if she did not desist from her religious course. He often crossed her in domestic concerns, trying in every possible way to get her angry, thinking, if he could only aggravate her to madness, the victory would be won and his triumph complete; but in this he failed, while Mrs. H. was kind and affectionate, giving every necessary attention to the wants of her family, enduring the abuses heaped upon herself and the Methodists by her husband, never uttering an unkind word, or allowing a murmur to escape her lips. She did not allow his opposition or threats to deter her from the discharge of her religious duties, but was faithful in all things, always at class and prayer meetings, and always in attendance upon the preached Word. Her steadfastness continued as time rolled on, though the oppositions she met from her husband increased. A two days' meeting was appointed in the country a few miles from town. When the time drew near her husband forbade her going;

she flew to the Lord, who was her "stronghold in the day of trouble." Receiving, as she believed, an answer that it was right for her to go, she made every arrangement she could for the comfort of her husband during her absence. When the time arrived she took her two children, and, being aided by some kind friends, made her way on Saturday to the place of meeting, intending to return on Sunday evening. As the meeting progressed she was greatly blessed. While she spoke in the love-feast on Sunday morning, the Holy Ghost came down; every heart was thrilled, every eye melted to tears. It rained throughout the day on Sunday, which raised Whitewater beyond fording, and Mrs. H. could not return. There being several persons at the house where she was, they held a prayer meeting. During the exercises, Mrs. H. was called upon to pray. She poured out her burdened soul to God; never did woman plead for a husband with greater earnestness.

During all this time her husband was at home, raging like a madman. When Sunday night came and his wife did not return, he became furious. About midnight, concluding his wife had given herself to the Methodists, caring nothing for him, he resolved to burn up his house and all it contained, and "run away by the light." He went to work and packed up his clothes. When all was ready and he was about to kindle the fire to consume his house, it occurred to him that it would be *too* cruel to burn the house and all its contents, and leave his wife and children with nothing to help themselves. After a moment's pause, he concluded to leave the house and goods for her; but "he would go, and she should nevermore see his face." He took his pack and started, directing his steps toward Eaton, Ohio. When he had walked about four miles, suddenly the thought entered his mind, "This is just what my wife and the Methodists desire—to get rid of me." With an oath he determined they should not be gratified. "He would go back and devil them as long as he lived." Retracing his steps, when he reached town the day was dawning. He went to his house—which he had left after midnight, intending never to return—and put away his clothes. His passion had been wrought up to such a pitch that he felt he *must* have revenge some way. To this end he went to a liquor-saloon and took a potion, to nerve him more fully for his purpose. He then went out on the streets, intending to whip the first man that gave him a harsh word or an unpleasant look. To his utter discomfiture, every one he met was in a most pleasant humor; none gave him an unkind word. At this he was so much chagrined, he determined to commit suicide; but soon the thought occurred: "This is what my wife and the Methodists desire— any thing to get rid of me." Toward noon of this day, his wife returned home. As soon as she arrived he commenced cursing the Methodists, hoping thereby to provoke her to reply. He was again doomed to disappointment. In this he did not succeed, though he kept it up till a late hour in the night. Finding this effort to provoke his wife into a dispute failed, he now tried another scheme; that was to make her believe he would kill himself, hoping she would yield, rather than "he should do that dreadful deed;" at least, that "she would try to dissuade him from his purpose." Mrs. H. did not make any reply, but with her heart uplifted to God in earnest prayer, felt that he would overrule all for good. In a few weeks after this, the first two-day meeting held in Richmond was to come off. When Mrs. H.'s husband heard that the meeting was appointed, he gave her most positive orders not to bring any Methodists about the house at that time. She gave no promise, but as the time drew near made what preparations she could to accommodate a few friends.

When the meeting came on she invited two mothers in Israel home with her on Saturday. Her husband, finding they were in his house, would not go home till a late hour at night. On Sunday morning he ventured to the breakfast-table. While at the table the ladies invited him to go to the love-feast that morning. Instantly he said to himself, "That's my chance. The Methodists have door-keepers when they hold love-feasts, and they talk to those who are not members of the Church before they let them in. I will go to the door, but I will not go in. When I get there and they begin to talk to me, I will give the Methodists—preachers and people—a round cursing in the hearing of them all, and then turn away; that will be some gratification to me." When the hour for love-feast arrived, he accompanied his wife and the two ladies to the school-house where the meeting was held. As they drew near the door—there being quite a crowd there—he concluded to fall back a little, till all had passed in, "lest the door-keeper might not speak to him, and then he would lose the opportunity of doing up the job of *cursing* he had prepared himself for." When they had all passed in he stepped upon the door-step. The door-keeper swung the door wide open. He stepped in and halted. The door-keeper, putting his arm around, drew him a little forward and closed the door without saying a word. Mr. H. turned pale, and, trembling from head to foot, sat down.

The love-feast was a time of power. He never had been in one before—had not intended to be in this, "but was caught in a trap." He felt that his distress of mind was intolerable; that if the torments of the damned in hell were any greater than he had been enduring for months, he could not bear the thought. In that love-feast he resolved if there was any such religion as the Methodists and his wife professed, he would have it or die seeking. From this time he sought the pardon of his numerous sins. The struggle continued for weeks. So great was his distress of mind, that much of the time he could neither eat nor sleep. Now did Mrs. H. most devoutly pray that God would have mercy on her husband. He was clearly and powerfully converted at a camp meeting, joined the Church, and became as zealous in the cause of the Redeemer as he had been in that of Satan, and as ardently attached to the Church as he had been bitterly opposed to it. How wondrous the mercy of God! During all the time he was so fearfully opposing his wife the carnal mind I was fearful of being cast out. He was often heard to say, "The steadfastness of my wife, with God's blessing, saved me."

Had Mrs. H. yielded in the slightest degree, or faltered in her religious course, the probabilities are her husband never would have been converted, and she would have retrograded in her piety. The text from which the sermon was preached, that was the instrument in her awakening, made a lasting impression on her mind: "Offer unto God thanksgiving; and pay thy vows unto the Most High; and call upon me in the day of trouble; I will deliver thee: and thou shalt glorify me." To this she clung till she realized the fulfillment of the blessed promise.

CHAPTER V.

I was received into the Missouri Conference, October, 1822, and was appointed in charge of the Mt. Sterling circuit, Indiana, Samuel Hamilton presiding elder. This was a four weeks' circuit, lying mostly on the Ohio River, and extending north nearly to Pealey. It was a sore trial to my friends as well as me. They wept as I wept; and for the first few miles I indulged myself in a good "fit of crying." I constantly thought of what father said; that in a few years I would break down, and die poor and helpless, as he had almost nothing to give me. I was to have only $100 a year if I got all my "quarterage;" and very many, I knew, labored the whole year and did not get one-fourth their dues. But all such thoughts I had to banish, and rely on the simple promise of God, "Lo, I am with you always!" I thank him that to-day I can look back upon the realization of more than my expectations, both as regards things spiritual and things temporal.

Upon reaching my circuit, which was fifty miles from home, I had a harder task yet—that was, to let the people know what I had come for. I was a mere boy. Many of them had no suspicion that I was their preacher, and my numerous questions did not give them the hint; so I had to make a clean breast of it at last. I soon realized my inexperience—alone, on an old circuit, with no Hedding or Baker to instruct me in my duties in enforcing discipline. In no subsequent year did I have more Church trials to conduct, and more perplexing business to transact. But the more crushing the responsibilities, the more and more earnestly did I pray. I was fortunate, however, in at last having the advice of a few old preachers who lived on the circuit, and got through the year without any charge or suspicion of maladministration; at which I thanked God and took courage.

After a few rounds on my circuit the good work began. In spite of a three weeks' attack of pleurisy, I maintained the interest unremitted. Two camp meetings were held. At the first Elder Hamilton presided, preaching frequently with great demonstration of the Spirit and of power, especially in the conversion of souls. This led the way to a second, which was held among the hills of Patoka. Brother Hamilton was not present, but the local preachers—one a colored man—rendered most effective assistance. I had heard the doctrine of sanctification preached—the first time by William Cravens—and now, believing it as Scripture doctrine, and because thousands had lived in its enjoyments, I preached it to others and besought it for myself. Before the meeting closed, I, along with many who heard me, was blest with a deep experience of its truth. God's will became my will, and I learned to live in him continually. All my soul was love, and for weeks I could continually sing,

> "There's not a cloud that doth arise
> To hide my Savior from my eyes."

My long rides this year, continually breasting the storms of a very cold Winter, together with exposure in open houses, brought on a violent attack of pleurisy. In May or June I was obliged to travel on foot, my horse having become lame.

One morning I left brother Joseph Springer's for Rome, fifteen miles distant, where I was to preach at 11 o'clock. I journeyed—carrying saddle-bags and great-coat—over the most hilly portion of Indiana. Calling at a house to inquire the way, the owner was kind enough to assist me for some distance across a stream, and as we journeyed I introduced the subject of religion, and learned his religious history, which was substantially as follows: He thought religion necessary, and believed he would have experienced it had brother Hamilton remained in charge of the district; "For," said he, "I was at a certain camp meeting where he preached, and during the sermon I was affected with chills, alternating with contractions of the skin on my head. The preacher's voice was soon lost in a general shout, scores of penitent sinners exclaiming as one man, 'What must I do to be saved?' Then Hamilton paused for a quarter of an hour, as he said, to 'let the Lord preach;' then he began again, and in his mild, pathetic manner told of the goodness of God, and of the sinner's portion if he did not repent; and," said the friend, "he hurt me a devilish sight worse than when he preached loud." But, deprived of his favorite preacher, he was still in his sins, in which state I was obliged to leave him, after thanking him for his kindness, and exhorting him to go directly to God for the blessing.

Having filled my appointment at Rome, and being unable to get a horse, I concluded to try a raft on the Ohio River. I soon had one afloat, reaching my appointment, twelve miles down, in good time. I reached the next appointment—Troy—eighteen miles further down, in the same manner, by an extra use of the paddle; likewise, the next, six miles further down. Having no horse yet, I failed to reach the next appointment, sixteen miles distant, through a low, wet country; so I took my way across to a two days' meeting, to be held at brother Moore's the next Saturday and Sabbath. Here I expected to meet some local brethren; but none came, and the work all came on me—four sermons, besides several exhortations, the results of which were very encouraging.

On Monday morning, though ill prepared, I set out through a wilderness to my next appointment, the house of brother Combes, twenty miles away. After a vain attempt to get some rest at noon, among the busy subjects of the musketo kingdom, I resumed my burden, and my march through briers and obstacles numberless, and in due time reached my appointment. How glad the people were in those days to see their preacher! The Gospel feast was a feast indeed, generally a whole month between meals! This year may be summed up as a total of long, hard rides and great labor, both of preaching and settling Church difficulties. But it was a year of great spiritual comfort; not only for what I gained in it, but what I did, with God's blessing, for others. The membership on my charge had increased from 346 to 436. My horse never quite recovered, and I had to exchange for another.

It may be worth while to remark that I was no exception to the general rule in regard to Methodist preachers and their horses. I never lost a horse till I had traveled twelve years. My cash receipts for the year were $40. In addition to the camp meetings already spoken of, I visited another on the Blue River circuit—preachers in attendance, James Garner, senior, George Hester, and Wm. M'Reynolds. My efforts here were attended with such success that one brother came to me, and said that if I would go around the camp-ground and exhort, the people would all be converted.

I returned to my circuit inspired with new zeal for my work, not only for the rest of the year, but for the next year's labors. Returning home at the end of the year, I spent a few days there, little thinking, and caring less, where my next work would lie, and what it would be.

The Conference was a large one, inclosing Arkansas, Missouri, Illinois, and a large portion of Indiana; on which I might be sent 800 miles from home, the only mode of reaching my destination being on horseback. The Conference met at St. Louis, October, 1823. I was not present; but learned in a few weeks that I was appointed to Lemoin circuit—David Sharp presiding elder—in what was called the Boone's Lick country; the distance was 500 miles. Speedily getting my little effects together, I set out, leaving a circle of weeping friends and neighbors, to a land and among a people that I knew not. I crossed the Wabash at Vincennes, and soon struck the Grand Prairie, not knowing where I should find resting places, and Winter close at hand.

I was not a little comforted to meet brother Samuel H. Thompson—presiding elder, Illinois district—late one evening, on his way to a quarterly meeting. He insisted on my stopping over night with him. After some religious conversation, in which he gave me very good advice, he led the family prayers, in which he remembered not only me but my horse—suggesting what Mr. Wesley said, that when he prayed for his horse, he never lost any. He then gave me a "way-bill" to my circuit, being acquainted with the whole 500 miles I had to travel, which embraced the inhabited portions of Indiana, Illinois, and Missouri. I had not traveled far the next day before I encountered a snow-storm, which continued till late in the evening.

I at length reached old brother Padfield's, where I was received with open arms, and received much assistance in preparing for my journey. I preached before I left—my first sermon I preached in Illinois, some forty-four years ago. I crossed the Mississippi at St. Louis, spending the Sabbath with Rev. John Scripps, for whom I preached in the evening. I did not enjoy much liberty in this my first experience in the "pulpit," which was constructed in the old style, about six feet high and four feet square. I, however, did my best, no uncommon thing, perhaps; for if a preacher has not religion enough he has pride enough to do that.

Next morning I left, crossing the river at St. Charles. I every-where found kind, liberal friends. Passing through brother Redmond's work—Boone's Lick circuit—I spent Saturday and Sabbath at his quarterly meeting. Being entirely out of money, I had the good fortune to borrow twenty-five cents to help me across the Missouri River to my circuit. My horse being much worn down, I borrowed one that was both young and wild, to bear me on my first tour of my work. About thirty miles from the place I left in the morning, in the midst of a large houseless prairie, my horse took fright, and jumping from under me, left me and my saddle-bags by the wayside. In his haste homeward, he soon left the saddle also. I shouldered both and traveled back laboriously to the first house, where I left them and went on after the horse. Night soon overtook me. I missed my way and wandered I knew not whither, till, at length, I found myself on the banks of the Missouri. There was no house within two miles. It was very dark and the cold was becoming intense. At length, after prolonged hallooing, I persuaded the people to come over for me. I spent the night at the house of a deist. It took all the little money I had to pay my bill and ferriage back in the morning. I presently found my horse, which had been stopped by a friend, and mounting "bareback," returned to where I had left my saddle and luggage, and went on visiting my appointments, which were from eight to fifteen miles apart. I enjoyed good health, and was generally able to meet my appointments this year.

CHAPTER VI.

It was some time in July that I went up to assist brother Harris of the Fishing River circuit. It was the first camp meeting held on brother Baxter's camp-ground, near Liberty, about one hundred miles up the Missouri. Brother Harris and myself were the only Methodist preachers present; and we both preached and exhorted each in turn. The meeting grew in interest till Monday. I tried to preach on that day, and brother Harris was to preach a funeral sermon. When I closed, he commenced giving out the hymn,

> "And am I born to die,
> To lay this body down?"

When he came to the second verse,

> "Soon as from earth I go,
> What will become of me?"

the power of the Almighty came down in such a wonderful manner as is seldom witnessed. Brother Harris fell back in the pulpit, overcome by the influence of the Holy Spirit, and called upon me to invite the people forward for prayers. During my sermon I had noticed that one powerfully built man in the congregation was so filled with the power of God, that it was with difficulty he restrained his feelings; now was the time for him to give vent to his feelings, and his shouts of "Glory to God in the highest!" were such that the whole congregation seemed thrilled with the "power of God." It was as if a current of electricity ran through the assembly, setting on fire with the love of Jesus each soul in Divine presence.

It was a memorable time. The whole camp-ground was convulsed, and the invitation was no sooner extended than the mourners came pouring forward in a body for prayers, till the altar was filled with weeping penitents. It was as if the shouts of his "sacramental hosts were heard afar off." The meeting continued that afternoon and all night. Late in the night I went to brother Baxter's house to get some rest; but the work was so urgent—sinners weeping all over the camp-ground—that I was sent for to come back and continue my exertions; and there we wrestled, the Christian and the sinner, in one common interest, like Jacob of old, "till the break of day." On Tuesday morning scarcely a soul remained unconverted, or not seeking pardon.

The next Friday my camp meeting commenced, and bid fair for a great good; till a preacher of another denomination, who craved our success, requested the privilege of preaching. He was at first denied, but he urged his request till I gave him liberty to speak on Sabbath evening. His words fell with such a dead weight on the congregation, and at the close of his sermon so little interest was felt, that we were obliged to close the meeting without the usual invitations. But on the following morning we laid hold of the work again. My faith was strong that we should succeed, and victory turn on Israel's side. A profane man, witnessing the spirit of the meeting, remarked with an oath that "Beggs was like to take the ground." Our meeting proved a blessing to the class and neighborhood.

I finished my work here on this circuit by holding a camp meeting. On my way to Conference I attended a camp meeting, held by E. T. Webster, on the St. Louis circuit. We had good preaching and a successful meeting. Leaving the camp-ground we staid over night with brother M'Alister, and the next night arrived at St. Louis. Here for the first time I saw Bishop Soule.

Our Conference in 1824 was held at Padfield's, some twenty miles east of St. Louis. We had with us three Bishops—M'Kendree, Roberts, and Soule. It was the first Conference I ever attended, and it was a very profitable time to me. By the act of the General Conference, held the previous May, the Illinois work was set off from the Missouri Conference, which however met, agreeably to adjournment, at the same place. As the session possesses a historical interest, I shall give in this chapter an account of its proceedings. After the introductory exercises, conducted by Bishop M'Kendree, who presided, the roll was called, and about a dozen brethren responded to their names.

Jesse Hale and William W. Redman were appointed Stewards, and J. Dew, James Armstrong, and John Scripps were appointed a Committee to prepare memoirs of the deceased brethren. A resolution was introduced by the latter Committee, requesting Bishop Soule to preach on the camp-ground, at 11, A. M., October 24th, a funeral sermon, in memory of our much-revered father in Christ, William Beauchamp. Bishop Roberts then formally introduced Bishop Soule to the Conference, the members of which rose to receive him. The Committee also requested Bishop Roberts to preach the funeral of brother Samuel Glaze in the afternoon of the same day. The Committee to examine candidates for admission into full membership consisted of brothers Thompson, Walker, Scripps, Armstrong, and Cord. The Bishop then informed the Conference that Peter Cartwright and Andrew Monroe, elders of the Kentucky Conference, had, by transfer, become members of this Conference; also, by transfer, Uriel Haw and Edwin Ray, deacons in the same Conference; also, brother R. J. Dungan, a member on trial. The President announced that the Conference could draw on the Book Fund for $150, and on the Chartered Fund for $80.

The Conference then took up the question, "Who remained on trial last year?" The following were examined and continued: Orsenath Fisher, Andrew Lopp, Edward Smith, James E. Johnson, William Shores, William Moore, John Miller, Benjamin S.

Ashby, Joseph Edmondson, Rucker Tanner. The characters of the deacons were then considered, and the following were examined and passed: David Chamberlin, Dennis Willey, Ebenezer T. Webster, James Bankson, John Glanville, John Blasdell. The morning session was concluded by prayer by J. Hale. At 2, P. M., the Conference was opened by Bishop Soule, who presided. The character of deacons was taken up, and William W. Redman, H. Vredenburg, George K. Hester, and William M'Reynolds were examined, approved, and elected. The following brethren were then, on recommendation, admitted: George Randle, Samuel Low, Daniel Anderson, James Garner, Jacob Varner, John Fish, Shadrach Casteel, Cassell Harrison, Green Orr, Gilbert Clark. The stewards then called on the preachers for their claims and receipts, and Conference then adjourned, after prayer by brother Walker.

At 9, A. M., Monday the 25th, brother Roberts opened by prayer, Bishop Soule in the chair. The following brethren answered to their names: J. Walker, Jesse Hale, S. H. Thompson, Thomas Wright, J. Scripps, J. Patterson. John Scripps was elected Secretary, on the nomination of brother Armstrong. Bishop M'Kendree then announced God's afflictive dispensation in the removal, by death, of our highly esteemed brethren in Christ, William Beauchamp and Samuel Glaze, accompanying the announcement with deeply interesting and affecting remarks. During his remarks the Divine presence was sensibly felt.

After the singing of a suitable hymn, Bishops Soule and Roberts severally prayed. Proceeding to business, Bishop Roberts in the chair, S. H. Thompson and John Dew were appointed a Committee to superintend Divine service. J. Scripps, Thomas Davis, John Harris, J. Cord, T. Medford, Thomas Rice, James Armstrong, J. L. Thompson, Jesse Green, A. Munroe, William W. Redman, H. Vredenburg, Davis Willey, E. T. Webster, James Bankson, J. Glanville, J. Blasdell, William M'Reynolds, U. Haw, E. Ray, Samuel Hull, character passed and elected deacons; S. R. Beggs, F. B. Leach, Cornelius Ruddle, T. Randle, William H. Smith, Isaac N. Piggott, examined and approved; Deacon George Horn—transferred from the Tennessee Conference—examined and approved. Bishop M'Kendree then addressed the Conference on Missions.

The afternoon session was opened with prayer by Jesse Hale, Bishop Roberts in the chair. The following brethren were examined and approved as elders: Walker, Thompson, Hall, Scripps, Wright, Patterson, Harris, Davis, Cord, Stephenson, Sharp, Dew, Green, Cravens, (superannuated,) Medford, (located,) Armstrong, Thompson, Ruter, Hamilton, Delap, and Glaze, (deceased.) Richard Hargrave, who had traveled under the elder—Beauchamp, deceased—was, on recommendation, admitted. J. Scripps was superannuated. A resolution was passed requesting Bishop Roberts to furnish his funeral discourse—of Beauchamp—for publication. Jesse Walker, missionary of the Missouri Conference, reported in regard to his work among the Indians. On motion of brother Dew, brother Walker's mission was continued under the patronage of the Illinois Conference.

At the afternoon session, Charlestown was fixed upon as the place of the next meeting of the Conference, August 25th. The Missouri Conference was appointed to meet August 4th. On Tuesday morning the Conference adjourned.

The ninth session of the Illinois Conference was held September 5, 1832, Bishop Soule presiding. It had twenty-five members, of whom six are still living: Peter Cartwright, A. L. Risley, John Vancleve, S. R. Beggs, Robert Delap, J. S. Barger. I extract a curious item from the minutes of the tenth Illinois Conference, held at Union Grove, September 28, 1833, Peter Cartwright in the chair. After prayer by Samuel Mitchell, the following resolution was introduced by brothers S. H. Thompson and Stith M. Otwell: "That we, the members of the Illinois Conference, do agree to wear hereafter plain, straight-breasted coats." The yeas and nays were called, with the following result: Yeas—Taylor, M'Kean, Massey, Hadley, Fox, Mavity, Barger, Robertson, Vancleve, Thompson, Randle, James Walker, Deneen, Otwell, Beggs, Mitchell, Benson, Peter, Hale, Royal, (21). Nays—French, Phelps, Cartwright, Roylston, Sinclair, Trotter, Crawford, Fisher, Jesse Walker, Starr, Dew, (11).

The ministers of that day held to plainness of

dress, both for male and female, the straight coat and plain bonnet being insisted on by many. After a considerable debate, we agreed, before taking the above vote, to have brother Samuel Mitchell deliver an address on the plain, straight-breasted coat—old Methodist style.

One of the voters for the straight coat was appointed agent of M'Kendree College. In visiting some of the eastern and southern cities he for some reason changed the cut of his coat, and returned to Conference the next Fall in a frock-coat. The brothers were quite astonished, and must know the reason, as he had been among the most strenuous in contending for the straight coat. He took the opportunity, a great many questions being asked, to explain to the Conference in a body. He said, addressing Bishop Roberts, who presided: "As a number of the brethren have asked me my reasons for changing the cut of my coat, I wish to state that I have been reading Mr. Wesley on dress; and he does not fix upon any fashion or cut of coat, only let it be comfortable and plain. This frock-coat which I wear comes as near fulfilling that recommendation as any thing I can fix upon." The Bishop replied in his pleasant vein, telling the brother that he reminded him of a man who was made a Calvinist by reading Mr. Fletcher's writings. The anecdote was so applicable, that the brother wished no further time for explanation, and retired amid a roar of laughter.

CHAPTER VII.

THE Missouri Conference being divided, as stated in the last chapter, I was still continued in the Missouri division, and was appointed to Fishing River circuit. There were eighteen preachers then stationed in the Missouri Conference. Jesse Hale was my presiding elder. Members returned, 143.

It was a great trial for me to be absent another year from parents and friends. To visit them would necessitate a ride of six hundred miles, and I should then be three hundred miles from my circuit. Winter was close at hand. I made it a subject of prayer, and, after many tears and struggles, resolved to give up all for the Master's sake. In company with brother Benjamin Ashby, I set my face westward. We journeyed on together very pleasantly, sometimes preaching in the evening when an opportunity offered.

One evening, having found a resting-place rather earlier than usual, we sent out runners to call the people together for evening service. We soon had a house full, and it was decided that brother Ashby should preach and I exhort, as was the custom in those days. Being exceedingly weary, and having a comfortable seat, I soon fell asleep. Brother Ashby's voice failed him in the midst of his discourse and he called upon me. Some one who sat near had been kind enough to awaken me, and after rubbing my eyes I took his place, supposing he had finished his sermon. I told them I supposed they had heard enough from the preacher if they would improve it; yet, if they would bear with me, I would exhort for a short time. Very soon there seemed to be a deep interest felt, and loud responses of "Amen" were heard, and from the "amens" the responses arose to a shout. Many were greatly blessed, and it was an occasion of benefit to all.

After brother Ashby left me I was almost alone till I reached my circuit. I had scarcely commenced my labor, when a deep snow fell. My appointments were far apart; the country new; the roads often blind, or, worse, none at all, so that it was very hard getting back and forth from the stations. My circuit extended about seventy miles along the Missouri River, embracing some of the settlements west of the State line. I crossed the river twice in every journey, and once on a bridge of boards thrown across two canoes.

My quarterage this year was twenty-three dollars. My clothing that I had brought from home was by this time so nearly worn out that it was necessary to replace it with new. Some of the sisters spun wool, and made me a coat of blue and white cotton, a pair of white cotton pants, and one of mixed. One of the brothers gave me his old hat, which I got pressed, and then I was fitted out for Conference. It was held on the fourth of August, 1825, at Bailey's meeting-house, Sabine Creek, Missouri. The weather was very warm and the roads dusty, and, by the time I had reached my journey's end, my new coat had changed from its original color to a dusty brown. There were, however, kind hands and willing hearts who soon set me to rights. Under the combined influence of soap and water my coat came out as good as new, and, thanks to the "Marthas" of modern times, "who care for many things," I appeared in the Conference room next morning, looking quite respectable.

During the Conference, Bishop Roberts requested all the preachers who wished any private conversation with him to stay behind; I was among several who had requests to make, and when my time came to speak, I asked for a transfer to the Illinois Conference. My request was granted, and I started on a journey to Charlestown, Indiana, where the Conference met this year. On my way, I fell in with Samuel H. Thompson and Jesse Walker, at a camp meeting near Padfield's, and a most glorious time we had there. On our way, near Mount Carmel, Illinois, we attended another camp meeting, and the gracious outpouring of the Spirit converted many souls, and quickened the believers. The meeting closed, and we journeyed on, reaching Conference the first day after its session. I was then within five miles of my father's house. My parents and family were all at the Conference, but attending Divine service at Church. On hearing of my arrival, after two years of absence, they all left the meeting, and ran to greet the long-absent son. It was like the meeting of Joseph and his brethren. Weary and worn by sickness, with my travel-stained garments, they hardly recognized me.

After resting a few days, and receiving from my father a better suit of clothes, I started for my new circuit at Rushville, John Strange presiding elder. It lay mostly on Blue River, and east to Greensburg. This was a four weeks' circuit; appointments scattered over a large and thinly settled country, with mud and high water, at some seasons of the year almost impassable. The principal villages were Rushville, Greensburg, New Castle, West Liberty—now Knightstown—and Shelbyville. At the three last-named places, we had a good work, especially at West Liberty. Twenty or thirty of the leading inhabitants were converted and joined the Church. We held a camp meeting under the charge of the presiding elder, near West Liberty. Brother Strange preached at the opening of the meeting, and, in one of his prophetic and electrifying strains, told us that God would convert many souls then within hearing of his voice. Saturday, in the afternoon, he arose to advertise the order of exercises; and, seemingly without intention, began to exhort. One thought led to another, and in a very few minutes the whole encampment was trembling and crying. Several souls were happily converted to God; and from this to the close of the meeting we had a succession of conversions, some of which were most powerful and clear; many of the believers were quickened with such blessings of full salvation that its fruits may be seen at the present day. My last quarterly meeting was also a camp meeting, and we had a season long to be remembered.

I seldom left a circuit where the people seemed more unwilling to give me up. This year I attended four camp meetings—two on my own—one in Connersville circuit, and the other one mile east of Indianapolis. This was on my way to Conference. John Strange, James Havens, and others, with myself, were the preachers. O what a blessing we received! The meeting, closed on Monday, with many converts.

On our way to Bloomington, where Conference was to sit that year, as Strange and myself were riding along together, a stranger rode up by my side, and in conversation with us soon found out that we were preachers. Our plain coats, saddle-bags, and other equipage might have told him that. He turned to me and said, "Your name is Strange?" "No!" said I, turning to my companion, "that is the Rev. Mr. Strange." He seemed a little confused at his mistake, and had no more to say to me, but addressed his conversation to brother Strange.

This year our members numbered two hundred and eight. Bishops Roberts and Soule were with us, and our Conference was exceedingly pleasant and profitable to me. John Strange was a man of surpassing personal beauty, eloquence, and piety. Once, at the close of the sermon, he administered the sacrament. After a most impressive introduction, he was greatly annoyed by some boys throwing nutshells over the floor. Starting suddenly, as if awakening from a reverie, he said, "Did I say Christ was the Son of God? He is, to the humble, penitent believer; but to you"—pointing with his long finger toward the young men—"to you, sinner, arouse him, and he is the Lion of the tribe of Judah; and, by the slightest exertion of his power, could dash you deeper in damnation than a sunbeam can fly in a million of ages!" The effect was awful; the transition from the gentle and pathetic to the terrible was so unexpected that one of the young men afterward said that he felt his hair raise on end at the imagination of himself going with the velocity of thought toward the doleful regions. The leader of the disturbers is still living, and is a worthy member of the Church in Lafayette.

This ended the year 1826. At the Conference I received my appointment to Vincennes circuit, Charles Holliday presiding elder. I had a laborious year. The circuit lay one hundred miles along the Wabash River. Samuel Cooper was my assistant, supplied by the presiding elder. Our stations consisted of all the principal towns from Vincennes up to Cole Creek.

This year I attended four camp meetings. One of them was my own, and a precious time we had. On Sabbath afternoon Joseph Oglesby preached a most powerful sermon from the words, "The Master is come, and calleth for thee." No words of mine could do the sermon justice. It seemed as if every sentence uttered was a direct inspiration from on high. It was the eloquence of the Holy Ghost, and it came with power. I felt that I could not preach for a week afterward.

This year we had efficient help from the local preachers, J. M. Baker, Samuel Hull, and Hugh Ross, all good preachers; the two former having served in the ranks of the itinerancy. We had several revivals this year, some unpleasant occurrences also. At a watch-night meeting, held at Carlyle, some graceless scamps shaved the tail of brother Cooper's horse, and, to add to our mortification, followed us with derisive shouts, as we were passing out of town. This year I came nearer getting my quarterage than any previous one. It amounted to near ninety dollars. The membership numbered 442. I found brother Holliday, my presiding elder, a great help in establishing me in the work of holiness of heart. What a man of God was he! A Methodist preacher in very truth. I am afraid I should have gone astray had he not held me to the virtue of wearing plain apparel.

Our Conference was held this year, 1827, at Mt. Carmel, Illinois. I was one among the forty preachers who left Vincennes to attend Conference. Bishop Roberts presided, and we had a pleasant and profitable session. John Strange preached one of the most powerful sermons here that I ever heard from him or fr·m any one. Several older preachers remarked that he excelled even himself, and it was said by those capable of judging, that he was more eloquent than Henry Bascom. His text was, "Behold, I send you forth as sheep among wolves." To those of us who had taken our lives in our hands, and gone forth as pioneers in the wilderness to preach the Word of God, the text came home to our very hearts, and, more especially, when it was so ably dwelt upon by one who had shared our perils. The leading preachers at that time were Strange, Calvin Ruter, A. Wiley, Jas. Armstrong, Peter Cartwright, S. H. Thompson, A. Wood, Richard Hargrave, C. Holliday, S. C. Cooper, and Jesse Walker.

CHAPTER VIII.

THE next year, 1828, I was sent to Wayne circuit, on which Richmond and Centerville were the principal towns. My circuit bordered on the Ohio State line. William Evans was my colleague, and John Strange my presiding elder. This was a four weeks' circuit, and in it I preached nearly every day, and often twice a day. I found here some as devout Christians as I ever met, and often took encouragement by their holy walk and godly conversation. It was here, also, that I fell into doubts, and for six months there hung a deep gloom over my mind. I think that if ever I labored to save souls it was during this great darkness and fearful struggle with the archenemy. This struggle continued till I visited my parents, in Clark county, Indiana. Here, one evening while retiring for secret prayer in the old familiar place where I had wrestled many hours in prayer to God, I passed through another great struggle, and the day dawned, the clouds broke away, my sky became clear. For six months my peace was like a river, and I still lived an expectant of a better world.

This year I held a protracted meeting in Richmond, assisted by some of the local preachers. We were very successful. Some of the Quakers joined us, and the children of infidel parents were soundly converted to God. Here I administered the rite of baptism in Whitewater—the first time, at that point, that the waters of the forest stream had ever served that holy purpose.

Brother William C. Smith gives a full account of this meeting, which he introduces with a reference to the prosperity that attended my labors on the circuit at large. Now that a two days' meeting was announced for Richmond, he says, the attention of the people generally turned in that direction. A Methodist meeting was something new to most of the citizens, and created no little excitement, partly because they were curious to know what it would be like, and partly because these "hireling preachers" were about to disturb the quiet of the place. Some were anxious to keep the people from attending, and others to see the great sight. The meeting was held in the brick school-house on the public square.

When the time appointed arrived the Methodists came in from different parts of the circuit. Mr. Beggs and two or three other local preachers were in attendance. At their first coming together there was a very good congregation, and an excellent sermon was preached—one that stirred the hearts of the people to their very depths, and kindled anew the holy fire. At the close of the sermon the tide of feeling was running so high that the songs and shouts of the congregation were heard at quite a distance. This increased the excitement in the town, and at night the school-house was crowded. The Holy Ghost attended the Word that was preached, and also the exhortations that followed. An invitation was extended, and five or six presented themselves as seekers of salvation. This was a strange sight to many in the house. The pious gathered around the penitents, singing and praying till a late hour.

On Sunday morning a love-feast was held, and it was a time of great power and of religious enjoyment. At its close there was an invitation given to those that wished to unite with the Church. Several came forward. Among the number were three sisters, the Misses K., belonging to one of the first families in the town. Their father was rather inclined to infidelity. He had taken great pains to educate and prepare his daughters to move in the first circles in society, not dreaming that they would ever become Methodists. When the young ladies came forward some evil-designing person on the outside, who saw through the window what was going on within, hastened to Mr. K. and told him that the Methodists had got his daughters befooled, and that they were acting disreputably, lying prostrate upon the floor, etc. This statement, of course, exasperated Mr. K. very highly, and he immediately made his way to the school-house where the love-feast was, and demanded admittance. The door-keepers, not knowing who he was, refused to let him enter. He forced open the door, and went in trembling with rage. Going to where his daughters sat weeping, he took them by the hand and led them away. As they were going out the prayer, in subdued tones, Lord, have mercy on their souls, was heard in several places in the congregation. When they reached home with their father, and explained to him that all that they had done was to unite with the Church, he, upon learning the deception which had been practiced upon him, at once led them back to the schoolhouse, and to the seat whence he had taken them. He then went to Rev. Mr. Beggs, and requested him to make an explanation of his course and offer an apology for him that morning to the public. He remained to hear the sermon, and at its close asked the preacher home to dine with him. He expressed an entire willingness, since it was the wish of his daughters, that they should become members of the Methodist Episcopal Church. They did so, and have long been pious and influential members. Thus Satan was thwarted in his design, and preaching continued for some time, resulting in much good.

At the close of these meetings there were several applicants for the rite of baptism; some wished for pouring, others for sprinkling, and one wished to be immersed. As we went down to the stream for the purpose of baptism, it was just at the close of a quarterly meeting held by the Quakers. Some of them were on their way home, and had to cross the stream just below the place which I had chosen for the rite. They stopped in the stream to witness the sight, it being the first that had ever taken place in that region. Some of the young Quaker boys ran, whooped, and hallooed as if they were going to a fair. So great was the curiosity of the people, that they had collected by hundreds at the water's edge, and stood from fifteen to twenty deep along shore. One man took up a large boy and waded several feet into the water, that he might have a better view. As I was leading the sister out, I found that this man had roiled the water, and I asked him to change his position; he did so by going farther into the stream. After the immersion, the sister came out, shouting and praising the Lord.

As an instance of the rudeness of the times, I heard, mingled with these sounds, also the shouts of laughter from some of the bystanders; and on turning to see from whence they came, I discovered that the man in the water had made a misstep, and had with his boy fallen backward into the water; I waved my hand, and all were quiet, but none seemed sorry.

We closed this year with a powerful union camp meeting. The preachers present were John Strange and James B. Finley, presiding elders; George Mallory, Thomas L. Hitt, and others. The Lord was present, and we felt his power to arouse sinners to conviction and to grant them pardoning mercy. The meeting proved a great blessing to the circuit.

Near the close of this year I was brought very low, by a violent attack of bilious fever; and when my life was despaired of I was visited by brother Strange, who prayed with us, and for me especially. I dated my recovery from that day; and when I met brother Strange at Madison, in the Conference room, he grasped my hand and said, "There is no man on the Conference floor whom it gives me greater joy to meet than you." It was no less a matter of rejoicing to me that I had been spared; that another year's labor had closed; that I had been faithful to my calling, in the midst of my trials and afflictions, and that I could yet look to Jesus for my exceeding great reward. Brother Roberts presided in his usual pleasant and agreeable manner, very much to the satisfaction of all present. In order to prepare us for our different fields of labor, he addressed us in a solemn and impressive manner, which I shall never forget. The whole Conference was in tears, and every man seemed ready for any field of labor' that, in God's good providence, might be assigned to him.

CHAPTER IX.

This year, 1829, I was sent to the Crawfordsville circuit, brother Strange presiding elder. I soon reached my field of labor, and commenced in truth to be a successful Methodist minister. I was alone in the work on a four weeks' circuit, which embraced the following towns, in the order given: Crawfordsville and Lafayette; from thence to Delphi and on to Logansport; once out to Fort Wayne, and back to Attica; then down to Portland and Covington. My general health was good, although I was confined for about three weeks in Crawfordsville with chills and fever. Lafayette was very new at that time, having only five brethren and a class of twenty members. We had several revivals, one especially in Crawfordsville, where I was assisted by brother James Armstrong.

This revival gave a new impetus to Methodism in that place, which was for some time afterward the prevailing denomination in the town. Our camp meeting was also a success. Strange, Armstrong, and others were present. The object of our preaching was to convert souls, and our brethren were mighty in prayer. The result was that convictions followed fast upon each other, till its close. I left in company with brother Armstrong on the way to Conference, which was to be held at Edwardsville, Madison county, Illinois, September 18, 1829. We soon met with other preachers, and before we reached Conference our company increased to twenty. We journeyed together three hundred miles on horseback, and enjoyed our ride very much. Traveling in those days had many pleasant features, but sometimes those which were not so pleasant.

At one place where we staid over night, our horses were fed upon oats, mixed with castor beans. The result was that several of them were sick and unfit for use the next morning. We hired what horses could be obtained, and used some of ours that were sick, and at last found ourselves at Conference safe, and in good time. We were very pleasantly entertained, and a more agreeable company of brethren I have seldom met than those at the Conference at Edwardsville; Bishop Soule presided, and did so most acceptably. On Sabbath morning he preached a very excellent sermon. John Strange and James Armstrong followed in the afternoon. Their efforts were attended with great power. While Strange was preaching, the congregation almost involuntarily arose to their feet, and shouted "Halleluiah!" till their deafening hosannas almost drowned the voice of the preacher. He was in turn affected by their enthusiasm, and sat down, shouting "Glory to God in the highest!" At this session a collection of one hundred dollars was taken up for superannuated preachers.

From this Conference I was sent to Logansport mission, embracing Lafayette, Delphi, and Logansport. With this charge I had an appropriation of fifty dollars missionary money. I remained here till the first quarterly meeting, and then my presiding elder, J. Strange, removed me to Bloomington circuit. I had Jesse Hale for my colleague. We had a prosperous year, and a number of conversions. We visited several camp meetings, every-where meeting with great success. It was a four weeks' circuit, and numbered seven hundred and eight members. We came nearer getting our quarterage than we ever had since I began my labor, each receiving one hundred dollars. We left here, I trust, with seals to our ministry and spiritual profit to our souls.

Our next Annual Conference was held at Vincennes. Bishop Roberts was taken sick at St. Louis. S. H. Thompson and Peter Cartwright were presidents *pro tem.* The Conference was very pleasant, and ended in a manner very satisfactory to all of the brethren. I was sent to the Tazewell circuit. After spending a few days with my parents I started for my circuit, in company with A. E. Phelps. Our circuits joined each other, and lay on the Sangamon River. We were in good time for our work, and during the year had several pleasant interviews. Mine was a four weeks' circuit, and very laborious. There were twenty-eight appointments, including a distance of more than three hundred miles travel. We had a most delightful Fall, which lasted till near Christmas.

The most prominent places were Peoria, Hollen's Grove, now Washington; Mud Creek, Walnut Grove, Mackinaw Town, Stout's Grove, Dry Grove, Blooming Grove, now Bloomington; Randolph Grove, Big Grove, Cherry Grove; from thence down Salt Creek to the Falling Timber country; brother Beck's on Sugar Creek, Hittle's Grove, and Dillon's, where I had two appointments; from there I went to Grand Prairie; from thence to several neighborhoods, and back to Peoria.

On Christmas eve there was a most fearful snow-storm. The snow fell to the depth of three feet, so that the remainder of the season my labors were confined to the western part of the circuit. In many places there were immense drifts, and the snow was so crusted that it was impassable. It was March before the snow went off, and then the heavy rains, added to the snow, caused such a freshet as had seldom been known in that region.

We had a few conversions during the Winter, and the members were much revived. This year was one of special interest to me. As usual, there was a young lady selected as suitable for the minister's wife, and such she proved in very truth. Brother William Heath, a brother-in-law of Rev. Samuel Hamilton, of the Ohio Conference, had lately settled in Hollen's Grove. It was to his daughter that my attention was directed. I brought her an undivided affection, for I had never proposed marriage before. I had traveled nine years on the circuit, and often in loneliness. She consented to share with me the toils of an itinerant life, and on the 1st day of September, 1831, we were joined in marriage by Rev. Jesse Hale.

It is a saying that "to every man there is one good woman." My wife has proved so to me. For thirty-five years we journeyed on life's pathway together, and each succeeding year grew happier in each other's love. I thank God for the helpmeet he gave me. Would that she had lived to bless all the remaining years of my life as she did those that are past! From the pleasant picture of home-life I must turn once more in my narrative—as I did in reality in the years gone by—to the scenes of my labors.

The year was a prosperous one. Our members numbered two hundred and fifty-two. Peter Cartwright was my presiding elder. We closed the year, as usual, with a camp meeting.

Mrs. Beggs accompanied me to Conference this year, which was held at Indianapolis. It was a long and tedious ride for a woman to perform on horseback, and we were also to ride one hundred miles beyond to visit at my father's. We remained there but a few days, and then started north-west for a three-hundred-mile ride to my father-in-law's, near Peoria. The evening before we arrived at Washington we had to cross Mackinaw River. Not having been apprised of its depth, we ventured in, and found ourselves in very deep water. It was up to the horse's back, and we were both thoroughly wetted. When we got to the opposite bank we found it to be about five feet high, and it was impossible for the horses to get up. I climbed up and secured a strong limb, which I placed along side the horse. My wife then reached me her hand, and, with my help, succeeded in climbing up this limb till she reached the bank. "Perils by sea and perils by land." I then led the horses some distance up the stream, till they could land. We remounted, and had before us a ride of fifteen miles ere we reached my father-in-law's. We arrived there wet and tired, yet thanked God that we were safe, and took courage for further efforts in this great cause.

This year I received my appointment to Chicago mission station. In July of the previous Summer I had attended two camp meetings—one at Cedar Point, and the other at Plainfield. They were both successful, the one at Plainfield especially so. From this latter place father Walker and myself started for Chicago, about forty miles distant. When we arrived brother Walker gave out an appointment for me to preach in the garrison, in old Dr. Harmon's room. After the sermon was over he gave it out that I was to preach again next morning at nine o'clock; and this was the beginning of a happy time here. I opened the door for the reception of members, and I think ten joined the Church. Among the number were brother Lee and wife, and Elijah

Wentworth, with his mother and two sisters. We formed a class of these few members, and it was this class, the first ever formed in Chicago, that now awaited me at my new appointment.

I commenced my work here alone, and the prospect seemed gloomy enough. The garrison consisted of two or three frame houses, and some huts occupied by the French and Indians. This, only about twenty-five years from the time I now write, was all that there was of our now mighty city. Some changes had taken place since the preceding Summer, and on my arrival I felt somewhat encouraged. Several families had moved in—father Nobles, with a wife and two daughters, Colonel Richard Hamilton and wife, and Dr. Harmon Irwin, a son of the above-mentioned, with his wife. There were six more members added to my class.

I remained here preaching nearly seven weeks before I could obtain any accommodations for my family, and then went back to my father-in-law's after Mrs. Beggs. It was the middle of January, 1832. It will be difficult to those of my readers who never braved the perils of pioneer life to realize how great were the hardships of the first settlers, and among these there were not many who passed through more toil and discomfort than the Methodist itinerant; and yet there are veterans in the cause who are still living, and rejoicing that God gave them the privilege, in their younger days, of laboring for him. Now that the fields are all white, and the harvest is ready, we forget past toils in the joyful present, and count ourselves blessed that we are still laborers.

But let me return to my perilous journey. It was just after the January thaw, and we had mud and ice, high waters and no bridges, and long distances between houses, which made my journey of one hundred and forty miles very tedious and difficult. I had traveled some distance, and was still thirty-five miles from Washington, now Magnolia. I had but two biscuits in my pocket, and, as the beginning of a hard day's journey, was obliged to swim Sandy Creek. My next obstruction was Crow Creek. At the old ford there was so much water and ice that I was obliged to ride up the stream for a number of miles over the open prairie. I crossed several of the largest branches, and was congratulating myself that I had conquered my greatest difficulties. I was shaping my course toward Washington, when I came to the main branch. Here the water was low, but it had frozen hard to the very bottom. The thaw had caused the water to overflow the ice to the depth of three feet. This water had also frozen over, but not hard enough to bear up my horse on the new-made ice. He broke through the ice at the top, and also at the bottom of the stream. After making several fruitless attempts to cross, I again rode out on the prairie. I rode on and on till I lost sight of timber and of my course, out on the sea of open prairie without a compass or a guide.

It was cloudy and cold, and near night. I must

either cross the river or lie out all night upon Grand Prairie. I chose the former, and attempted to cross at the risk of being swamped in the mud and ice. I broke the ice as well as I could to about the middle of the stream, when the under ice gave way, and down went my horse, throwing me off at one side. This broke the surface ice around the horse, and also in front of him; I then gave him the word, and he struggled nobly, bringing me out upon the right side without any serious injury. I was well drenched. I took off my boots, and emptied the water out of them, and wrung out my socks, and the skirts of my overcoat. It was very cold, yet I mounted my horse, thanked God for my safety, and took courage, although I still had great obstacles before me. It was still cloudy, and there was no road and no timber in sight. The sailor out of sight of land, with no compass, is no more at loss than is one on the open prairie where no shrub, or tree, or dim speck in the distant horizon is to be seen.

I was in greater straits than ever. I did not know what direction to take, and there was no time to be lost; I started, and soon found myself on a slight elevation of prairie; from this point I could at a great distance discover a patch of timber, and I directed my course toward it. After riding till a late hour in the night I reached the timber, and found there a small farm inclosed by a fence. I took down the rails and rode through, where I found stacks of wheat and straw. After vainly searching for more evidences of a human habitation, I concluded to make the best of my situation, and pass the night there with what comfort I could. I fed my horse some of the wheat, and in my frozen clothes lay down in the straw. I remained here but a short time, when I recollected the apostle's advice, that "bodily exercise is profitable." I resorted to violent exercise, in order to bring my blood into circulation, and then lay down in the straw again; I kept this up all night.

In the morning my prospects brightened; I heard some one calling hogs, and, homely as was the sound, it was a most welcome one. I saw some one on the opposite side of a creek, and called out to him. I learned that this stream was Panther Creek, and that I was twenty miles from Washington. He asked me where I had staid over night, and I told him, and also the liberty I had taken in feeding my horse. He said the stacks were his, and that it was "all right." He then told me that I must ride three miles up the creek, where I would find a bridge, and that by the time I came down again I would find some breakfast prepared for me. It was a welcome sound; for I had eaten nothing for twenty-four hours, except those two biscuits. My breakfast was a feast, for I brought to it the best of sauces as a relish—a good appetite. It was as great a joy to those early settlers to welcome a stranger to their board, was it as to the hungry traveler to partake of their hospitality. May God's blessing rest on him and his for his kindness that morning!

I thanked him, and attended morning devotions. The thanks and the prayers of the Methodist minister in those days always settled the reckoning with their hosts. I mounted my horse, who had also shared the hospitalities with me, and was soon well on my way to Washington. On reaching Walnut Creek I found I must swim it, and also many other smaller streams before I reached my father-in-law's. I was much comforted to find them all well, and Mrs. Beggs impatient to join me even in my arduous labors. I remained here but a few days, and had my scanty effects packed on a sled.

Having a good snow we reached the Big Vermilion late in the evening; it was too high to ford; and being nearly opposite the house of Martin Reynolds, I shouted at the top of my voice, till I made myself heard. He soon came down to our relief with his sled and horses. We traveled down the stream, he on one side and I on the other. At last we found a place on the ice, where we ventured to meet. With certain precautions we attempted to cross on the ice. I took the rails of our old-fashioned bedstead, and by walking on one while I shoved the other along in front of us, we at last found ourselves safely landed on the other side. After having a comfortable night's rest, we went back in the morning to see to the horses and look after my effects.

As we were crossing in a canoe, we came very near being capsized; and in case we had been, we should have been drowned. But God in his good providence saw fit to spare us for further labors. I took my goods back about five miles, and left them till the roads should become passable. I staid at brother Reynolds's a few days; and in the mean time walked over to Ottowa, a village about twelve miles distant, where I preached a sermon. After this I again went after my horses and goods, and brought them to the river-side once more, in hopes to get them across. We did so by making a bridge sixteen feet in length, which reached from the river's edge to the ice in the middle of the stream. I ran them across the ice by means of a hand-sled, and brother Reynolds with his team moved them up to Ottowa. Brother Green took them farther on the way to his house; and there they remained till the next Spring.

To give some idea how the early settlers lived, I will tell the reader of our fare while at brother Reynolds's, and how we obtained it. There was no flour to be had, and no mills for grinding. Our corn, of which we had great plenty, had to be pounded in a mortar. The only pestle we had was made by driving an iron wedge into a stick, which served for a handle.

While going from brother Green's to Plainfield we were overtaken by a storm of rain and sleet, which made the ground literally one sheet of ice. The horse which Mrs. Beggs rode had no shoes.

When we reached Platteville the creek was swollen so high that it could not be crossed at that point. Brother Reed, who was with us, managed to get across, but judged it was not safe for us to attémpt it. So we traveled, he on one side and ourselves on the other, some distance along the stream, till at last we found a crossing-place. The storm continued till we reached Plainfield. I was fearful the exposure would cost Mrs. Beggs her life. It was several weeks before she recovered, and then not entirely, from the effects of her stormy ride. There was yet no room to be had in Chicago, and it was thought best for my wife to remain at Plainfield till the ensuing Spring, while I kept up my appointments till May.

CHAPTER X.

JESSE WALKER was superintendent of the mission work from Peoria to Chicago, and also had a nominal appointment at Chicago. His labors, however, were so extensive that he preached here but a few times during the year. Brother Walker was not able to attend Conference, held in Indianapolis, in 1831. After consulting me, to know if I was willing to take charge of the mission at Chicago, to which I consented if Conference should so decide, he wrote to Bishop Roberts to appoint me to that work. So this was my home for the coming year, and I hastened to take charge of the little class I had formed a few months previous. I found them all standing fast in the liberty of the Gospel.

Our meetings were generally held in the fort, and they increased in interest till our first quarterly meeting, which was held in January, 1832. I had been helping brother Walker hold some meetings at Plainfield, and we left there on one of the coldest days of that Winter for my quarterly meeting at Chicago. It was thirty miles to the first house. Brother T. B. Clark started with us with an ox team, for the purpose of carrying provisions to help sustain the people in Chicago during the meeting. Provisions were very scarce here at that time. Late in the evening we became alarmed lest he had perished in the cold, and went out on a fruitless hunt after him. He arrived, at eleven o'clock that night, at our stopping-place. The next day saw us all safely in Chicago, where we met with a warm reception from brother Lee and family.

Here, to-day, amid the presence of this great and prosperous city, let us reconsider our humble beginnings. Thirty-six years ago a load of provisions was brought by an ox team from the village of Plainfield to sustain the friends that met here for a quarterly meeting! The meeting commenced with power, and increased in interest till Sunday morning. My first sermon was preached on Sabbath morning at ten o'clock, after which brother Walker invited the people around the sacramental board. It was a season long to be remembered. Every one seemed to be baptized and consecrated anew to the great work to be accomplished in the village that was destined to become a mighty city.

Jesse Walker was my successor in 1832. He moved his family up to Chicago as soon as possible, and set to work. I attended his first quarterly meeting; it was held in an old log school-house which served for a parsonage, parlor, kitchen, and audience-room. The furniture consisted of an old box stove, with one griddle, upon which we cooked. We boiled our tea-kettle, cooked what few vegetables we could get, and fried our meat, each in its turn. Our table was an old wooden chest; and when dinner was served up we surrounded the board and ate with good appetites, asking no questions for conscience' sake. Dyspepsia, that more modern refinement, had not found its way to our settlements. We were too earnest and active to indulge in such a luxury. Indeed, our long rides and arduous labors were no friends to such a visitant. This palatial residence, which served as the Chicago parsonage, was then situated between Randolph and Washington streets, the first block west of the river.

The Winter previous I had purchased a claim, the only title to be had. Then I paid three hundred dollars for a claim upon two hundred and forty acres, eighty of which was covered with timber land, portions of which to-day sell for one hundred dollars per acre. My aim then was to secure a home, when the time should come that I could no longer travel on the itinerant work, which I had laid out as the business of my life while health and strength remained. The Lord prospered me in my purchase. I was well paid for my land, for which blessing I am yet thankful, and trust that I shall ever be found a good steward of the manifold mercies of the Lord.

This year there were no returns of members. At this time a little incident occurred in the life of Jesse Walker worthy of note, as showing the intolerance we had sometimes to meet with, even in a new country. At an early day he was in the habit of holding meetings for the handful of Americans then in St. Louis. Finding that there was a need for regular appointments, he made them for once in four weeks. The Catholics hearing of this great outrage—that a Methodist was to preach regularly among them—went to their priest with a complaint against such presumption. "Never mind," said the priest, "they can't do much; if nothing else will do, we will starve them out." "Starve them out," said the complainant, "why, they will live where a dog would starve to death!" And it was through the untiring efforts of Walker that the foundations of Methodism were so deeply and broadly laid, that neither Catholicism nor the "Prince of the power of the air" has been able to withstand its growth. The handful of seed which he then planted has now become like the "Cedars of Lebanon." May we ever manifest his zeal in all good works which the Lord may appoint unto us!

Amid our other trials and hardship we suffered some from fear of the Indians. I had laid in my store of provisions for the coming Summer. It was during my absence that Mrs. Beggs was greatly annoyed by the Potawatomie Indians, who frequently brought rumors that the Black Hawks would kill us all that Spring. It was not long before the inhabitants came flying from Fox River, through great fear of their much-dreaded enemy. They came with their cattle and horses, some bareheaded and others barefooted, crying, "The Indians! the Indians!" Those that were able hurried on with all speed for Danville. All the inhabitants on

Hickory Creek and in Jackson Grove took fright also, and fled.

A few of the men only staid behind to arrange their temporal matters as best they could under the circumstances. In the mean time some friendly Indians who knew of their fright were coming to inform them that their dangers were not so great as they supposed. The men, seeing these, and supposing that they were hostile, mounted their horses and fled for life, before they could be informed of the friendly intentions of their visitors. The latter then tried to head them in, in order to correct their mistake. This, of course, only made matters worse; and the men hastened on with greater speed till they reached their families, who had by this time come to a halting place for the night. Their cattle and horses were turned out to feed and scattered over the surrounding country. They were making arrangements for supper—some of them having their meals prepared, others just commencing to prepare them—when here came those men, flying in hot haste, one of whom had lost a hat, and their horses jaded and worn, with a ten-mile race. When they told of their narrow escape, and how the Indians had tried to head them, there was confusion and dismay in the little camp.

It was urged that all should remain quiet till they could get their cattle and horses together; but there was too much "demoralization" for that. One team could not be found, and it was thought better to sacrifice one than that the whole should suffer. So it was decided that they should move off as silently as possible; yet there was one ungovernable person among them, who made noise enough in driving his oxen to have been heard a mile distant. Of course this was very annoying to the others, who felt the necessity of being quiet. The hatless man and one or two others found their way to Danville in advance of the rest, and told their fearful stories— how the Indians were killing and burning all before them, while at this time it is presumed that there was not a hostile Indian south of Desplains River. At Plainfield, however, the alarm was so great that it was thought best to make all possible efforts for a defense, in case of an attack.

My house was considered the most secure place. I had two log pens built up, one of which served for a barn and the other a shed. These were torn down, and the logs used to build up a breast-work around the house. All of the people living on Fox River who could not get farther away made my house a place of shelter. There were one hundred and twenty-five, old and young. We had four guns, some useless for shooting purposes. Ammunition was scarce. All of our pewter spoons, basins, and platters were soon molded by the women into bullets. As a next best means of defense, we got a good supply of axes, hoes, forks, sharp sticks, and clubs. Here we intended to stay till some relief could be obtained. This was on Thursday; and we remained here till the next Sabbath, when the people of Chicago, hearing of our distress, raised a company of twenty-five white men, and as many Indians, who came to our aid. They remained with us till the next morning, (Monday,) and then concluded to reconnoiter along Fox River.

The Indians, with Mr. Lorton at their head, were to go to Big Woods, (now Aurora,) and Gen. Brown, with Col. Hamilton and their men, were to visit Halderman's Grove, and then fix upon a place to meet in the evening, where they might spend the night together in safety. In the afternoon Mr. Lorton came back, with two or three of his Indians, and brought us fearful stories of how they had all been taken prisoners, and kept two or three hours; the Indians, however, being on good terms with Black Hawk, he had allowed him, with an escort, to have his liberty, in order to go up to Chicago, where he intended to take his family for safety. He must go that night, and had but a moment to warn us of our danger. He told us our fort would be attacked that night, or the next at the longest, and that if they could not storm the fort at first, they would continue the siege till they did. He advised us to fly to Ottowa or Chicago as soon as possible.

Such a scene as then took place at Fort Beggs was seldom witnessed, even in those perilous times. The stoutest hearts failed them, and strong men turned pale, while women and children wept and fainted, till it seemed hardly possible to restore them to life, and almost cruel for them to return from their quiet unconsciousness to a sense of their danger. It was no time to hesitate or deliberate. Immediate departure was the word; but they were divided as to the best means to be taken in finding a place of security; some wished to go to Chicago, others to Ottowa, while some proposed to separate and scatter for the woods. After several short and pithy speeches were made, James Walker was elected Captain, and formed us into a company. We were advised that Indians would never attack a fort, unless driven to it, and that it was safer to remain where we were, at least till we heard from the remaining men.

All possible preparations were then made for our defense, and we determined to sell our lives as dearly as we could. A long piece of fence was torn down and strewed about the fort. We set fire to these rails, so that we might see the Indians when they came for attack. We had several alarms; yet we remained here safe till Wednesday evening, and then every man was ordered to his post to prepare for an onset from the enemy. To our great joy the white men returned that evening; but they brought us news of the massacre of fifteen white inhabitants on Indian Creek; also that they were burning houses and killing cattle. They advised us to leave the fort at once, and go either to Ottowa or Chicago. We chose the latter course. One circumstance I had forgotten to mention. When the inhabitants fled from Fox River, there was one infirm old man who was confined to his bed with the rheumatism. He advised them to leave him, as he had not many days to live at all events. They left him, and it was several days before they ventured back to see what had become of him. They found him, and learned that the Indians had been there and brought him food. He was brought to our fort, and there was as much rejoicing as if one had been raised from the dead. It was decided that we should take him with us to Chicago. We spent the night in busy preparations for our departure the next day. In getting our oxen and horses together, it was found that we had only teams enough to carry the people. Nearly all of our effects had to be left behind; some of my iron-ware and bed-clothes I hid in hollow trees, in hopes of finding them again, should I ever return. I did return a long time after that. I had been detained by sickness, and found that my bed-clothes were nearly spoiled, and a great destruction of property besides, although no houses were burned.

We left our fort at seven o'clock on Thursday morning, with our company and the twenty-five Chicago men as guard; we made quite an imposing appearance. We arranged ourselves so as to cover near a mile in length on the road. It was afterward said that the Indians were watching us, and would have made an attack but for our formidable appearance and numbers. We traveled forty miles that day, and reached Chicago by sunset.

CHAPTER XI.

There was no extra room for us when we arrived in Chicago. Two or three families of our number were put into a room fifteen feet square with as many more families, and here we staid, crowding and jamming each other, for several days. One afternoon, as if to increase our misery, a thunder-storm came up, and the end of our room was broken in by a stroke of lightning while we were taking a lunch. None of us were hurt, but the lightning passed down the wall to the room below us, leaving a charred seam within a few inches of a keg of powder. But our room, which was in the second story, was filled with a distressing odor of sulphurous smoke, and the report was the loudest I ever heard. The next morning our first babe was born, and during our stay fifteen tender infants were added to our number. One may imagine the confusion of the scene—children were crying and women were complaining within doors, while without the tramp of soldiery, the rolling of drums, and the roar of cannon added to the din; and yet out of this confusion we tried to arrange order. The soldiery were drawn up in solid column near one of the houses, whose friendly steps were my only pulpit. Here I stood and pointed out to them the "Lamb of God, who taketh away the sins of the world."

In a few days the inhabitants of Walker's Grove, now Plainfield, returned to the fort with fifty men for a guard, and Captain Buckmaster in command. They were able to raise, that year, some buckwheat and a few potatoes. Mrs. Beggs was yet too delicate in health for me to think of leaving. She was still confined to her room, yet our stay here was of short duration. Major Whistler came on with his troops, and at the first roar of his cannon on the lake shore there was great rejoicing. But our joy was soon turned to heaviness. Instead of receiving protection, we were turned out of our shelter in order to give place to his men, who had been exposed to the rough winds on the lake. The order came for us to leave the garrison. We should have rebelled could it have been of any use, but there was no help for us but to obey. The Major and his family came into our room, and we were turned out into the pitiless rain-storm that afternoon. We found shelter in an open house, where, from the dampness and exposure, Mrs. Beggs and the child took a severe cold. Colonel Richard Hamilton then gave us the use of one of his small rooms. We made up our bed on the floor, where the cold and dampness caused both mother and child to take additional cold. I also became sick from the exposure, and matters indeed wore a gloomy look to us. I trust, however, that on the day of reckoning it will be said unto

Colonel Hamilton for his great kindness unto us,' "I was a stranger and ye took me in; enter thou into the joys of thy Lord."

I then proposed to Mrs. Beggs to go to Plainfield. She consented, saying it would be no better to die here than to be killed by the Indians on the road. Forty miles through the wilderness! Some had been killed but a few days before, although, happily for us, we did not know of it at that time. We started on our journey, our only defense being one loaded pistol, a strong faith in the living God, and the promise, "No harm shall befall thee." We reached the fort late in the day, quite safe, but much fatigued. I then decided to secure a guard to Ottowa, and to get Mrs. Beggs on to Washington to her mother's. There had been a company of men detached to go either to Ottowa or Chicago to draw rations for the soldiers. They decided to go to Chicago. They were to start the next morning. That afternoon, however, Colonel Owens, Indian agent, came down with the news that General Scott had come to Chicago with his men, and also brought the cholera, a worse-dreaded foe than the Indians. This decided the men to go to Ottowa for rations, and by that means we obtained a guard.

The drive to Ottowa through the hot sun and over the rough road came very near exhausting my wife and child, yet we ventured on to Washington alone. The Indian difficulties being by this time pretty much over, I concluded to return alone to the fort. In the mean time the inhabitants had fled from the cholera, leaving Chicago almost deserted. Some of them had come to our fort, while others went to Danville. Numbers died of the cholera, and General Scott's men had to remain till the epidemic had subsided. It was not long after this that General Scott gave chase to Black Hawk, and effectually drove the Indians away. We now had peace in all our borders. There was no hope now of my doing any thing in my station, so I concluded to go on a visit to my father's, in Clark county, Indiana. From this place I started again for Washington, a journey of three hundred miles, which cost me an outlay of six cents. I found my wife and child very much improved in health, which gave me renewed courage, and I thanked God for his great blessings.

After a few days' rest I started for Conference, which was held at Jacksonville, Illinois. Our members numbered ten, with Jesse Walker presiding elder. The Illinois Conference having been divided, there remained to us twenty-five preachers. The most prominent were M. Taylor, Peter Cartwright, Jesse Walker, J. Dew, S. H. Thompson, Simon Peter, and J. Sinclair. Bishop Soule presided, and we had a very pleasant session. There were only forty preachers, traveling and local, to supply the whole State of Illinois. I was sent to the Desplaines mission, with an apprppriation of two hundred dollars from the Missionary Society.

This year, 1833, my mission embraced the following appointments: Plainfield, Naperville, E. Scarriott's, (East Dupage,) Oswego, Halderman's Grove, John Green's, Ottawa, Martin Reynolds's, (twelve miles down the river,) Jackson's Grove, Reed's Grove, Hickory Creek, and Yankee Settlement. The prospects of peace, and the fact that we could return again to our worship, gave us many hearty amens from the brethren, especially at a camp meeting at Joliet, on the claim of brother Gongers, where the scattered inhabitants had but just returned from their flight from the Indians.

It was a year of hard labor; for I had a number of long rides. Then, too, came our first great sorrow. We lost our only child, Mary Ellen. We bowed our heads in submission, as we thought that "our loss was her gain." If the Lord had given her unto us, was it not meet that he should take her unto himself again? And we lived in the hope of one day being welcomed by her to our mansion in the skies. It is many years since she died, and her mother has now joined her across that Jordan of death, while I yet remain, after a conflict of near a half century, on the confines of that brighter world, faint, yet pressing onward, with the joyful prospect of their welcoming me to my home in heaven.

Desplaines returned thirty-four members. Jesse Walker was superintendent. In 1834 our Conference met at Union Grove, St. Clair county, Bishop Roberts presiding. Our business was dispatched with the usual satisfaction to all. I was reappointed to Desplaines mission, and I returned with renewed zeal, which in this case was the more necessary, as the rage for speculation was just commencing among both settlers and emigrants. It was an earnest struggle, and it sometimes seemed impossible to hold the attention of a sinner long enough to impress him with the great claims which the Gospel had upon him. Those who would not come out to church I followed to their houses, conversing with them on the highways and by the wayside. It was a doubtful struggle; but, by the help of the Lord and his efficient instruments, in the persons of brothers Walker, E. Scarriott, and F. Owens, I saw many souls converted and believers strengthened. I was enabled to form new classes, and our quarterly meetings, two days' meetings, and camp meetings were crowned with abundant success. Our numbers increased to fifty-seven, J. Sinclair our presiding elder.

My worldly goods increased, so that, if one could use the paradox, I was cursed with blessings. Three years before I owned a horse and sixty dollars. Now my farm of two hundred and forty acres was nearly paid for; and I had four horses, seven cows, and forty hogs. My farm also yielded bountifully; and now it had come to that, that I must either give up farming or the itinerancy. I chose to cling to the latter; for I remembered the solemn promise I had made at the time of my ordination, to give myself up wholly to the work of saving souls. Accordingly I sold out my stock, and with the proceeds built a barn; I then rented my farm for one year. I had made a sacrifice; yet I believe it worked together for good to me and mine; and, which was my higher aim, for the good of the cause. It is with the greatest pleasure that I now look back, and think that I have given up my best days to the service of the Lord; and I now call upon my soul, and all that is within me, to bless his holy name; and I pray that the "words of my mouth and the meditations of my heart may ever be acceptable in His sight."

The Conference was held at Union Grove, about three hundred miles distant; and I, in company with Rev. Z. Hall, rode to it on horseback, at the rate of fifty miles a day. Our stay at Conference rested us, and we returned to the moral conflict with renewed zeal. I was sent to the Bureau mission in 1835.

In the Summer of 1834 I accompanied John Sinclair, presiding elder, to his quarterly meeting at Galena. Barton Randle and J. T. Mitchell were laboring on that circuit. After a profitable and pleasant meeting we started for a camp meeting that was to be held near Princeton. The meeting was somewhat advanced, and there was prospect of a good work. Two Congregational ministers came to the camp-ground, and proposed to join us in our efforts. There was to be no doctrine preached, and at the close of the meeting the converts were to join where they pleased; to this our presiding elder strongly objected. He said he was a Methodist, and he must preach their doctrines, and that there could be no union on such terms. We had an unusually successful meeting, the fruits of which I trust will be seen in eternity; and from that time Methodism has taken deep root in that quarter, growing even till now.

When I arrived at my mission that year with my family, the only shelter I could get was a small log-house fourteen feet square. It had but one window, and that with four panes of glass. There were no shelves, and only a stick chimney. Most of our things had to be stowed away in boxes. To add to our discomfort the Winter was unusually severe. A sister of mine lived with us. A short time before our second child, James Williams, was born, I moved into a log-cabin, somewhat larger than the first, but little better in other respects. I had a large four weeks' circuit—Ottowa, Dayton; two appointments on Indian Creek, Pawpaw, Mulligan's Grove; three appointments on Bureau, and four miles to the west, Old Indiantown; then three appointments up at Peru, and one at Judge Strong's, five miles below Ottowa; and another at Troy Grove—making sixteen appointments in all; J. Sinclair presiding elder. This year we had a good revival; returned one hundred members; raised about eighty dollars for missions.

Our next Conference was held at Springfield; Bishop Roberts presided. Our number of preachers stationed was about sixty. There were several transferred—A. Brunson, W. B. Mack, W. Wigley, H. W. Reed, and S. F. Whitney. I was sent back to my mission of last year. There had been a new mission formed, which took off two of my appointments, namely, Indian Creek and Ottowa.

We had this year a glorious revival, much more extensive than last year. We also had an excellent camp meeting. A. E. Phelps was present, and preached with great liberty and with powerful effect. W. B. Mack followed with another very effective sermon, and the meeting closed with a number of conversions and accessions to our number; yet we received a blow this year that was greatly to the injury of Methodism. This was the downfall of our brother W. B. Mack; but the Lord overruled the affliction, and Methodism in that quarter yet lives. The number of members returned in 1836 was two hundred and thirty-one.

In the year 1837 Conference was held at Rushville, Illinois, Bishop Roberts presiding. It was a season long to be remembered, especially for a missionary meeting, a thing unheard of in that day. P. R. Borein spoke in favor of the missionary cause. His speech greatly moved his hearers, so much so that Bishop Roberts sat trembling in his chair, while the tears coursed rapidly down his cheeks. This speech was the beginning of Borein's brilliant career. John Clark had just come down from the Lake Superior mission, and presented the claims to education of two or three Indian boys for the mission field among the Indians. Great was the work and great the occasion, and our brother caught the inspiration, and his speech sent an electrifying thrill for the missionary cause through the whole Conference. The result was a very large collection for the work, many of the preachers paying their last dollar, and then having to borrow money to get home with.

This year I was sent to Joliet. My colleague was Matthew A. Turner, and presiding elder John Clark. My circuit embraced all the counties south of the Desplaines River. It was a glorious year to me. We had several conversions, with strong evidence of their being born into the kingdom; and especially at our camp meetings did the work of grace thrive.

One circumstance is worthy of note, as showing God's care over his children. We had two local preachers and two exhorters, and there being no presiding elder the charge of the meeting and preaching fell upon me. Brother Joseph Shoemaker gathered up his family and came up to the feast of the tabernacles, as was the custom in that day. Our aim was to get spiritual good to our souls, and to do good unto others. His wife had been a member of some years' standing, yet was not satisfied with her attainments, and throughout the whole meeting earnestly sought the blessing of acceptance. It was a time of melting power; yet sister Shoemaker left the meeting under great depression. They left, and on their way home they continued singing, shouting, and praying, brother Shoemaker having in charge a spirited team of horses. All at once there went up from the wagon a shout of "Glory to God!" and as it burst upon the ears of the driver, he let go his reins and fell back in the wagon, joining the general shout. Away went his horses, at the top of their speed, making a circuit of several miles. Some of the brethren who were behind caught the horses as they came in from their detour, and found all safe and still praising God, unconscious of all that had passed. God had watched over them, and given his angels charge concerning them, and how could harm befall them?

This year I commenced the first church in Joliet, and it was completed in time for our last quarterly meeting. I preached the first Methodist sermon in Joliet, with only the inmates of a private house for my congregation. There were but few present, and they were hardened in sin; but now, by the grace of God, the Church there numbers hundreds, and may the Lord prosper them unto the end!

Here I transcribe the inscription taken from the tombstone of Rev. Jesse Walker. It was written by Bishop Hamline, at my request. His remains lie in the Plainfield cemetery.

JESSE WALKER.

Died Oct. 4, 1835,

AGED SIXTY-NINE YEARS.

At the Rock River Conference, in 1850, his remains were removed to this place by his sons in the Gospel, who erect this stone to transmit his revered name to coming generations.

CHAPTER XII.

In the year 1837 I traveled the Forked Creek circuit, living at Wilmington. Our accommodations were very unpleasant, yet they were the best to be had. We lived in the second story. The weather was very hot, the season sickly, and the musketoes intolerable. I have frequently sat up all night to keep them off from those who slept.

There were some very sudden deaths among my flock, yet we had some reason to rejoice in the good work that I was still urging forward. Our quarterage was light, as we had but few members, and all were very poor. Yet they were the Lord's poor, and had large souls, and shared liberally with me of their scanty means. John Clark was presiding elder. We had a camp meeting at Reed's Grove, where we had such wonderful displays of God's power and glory, that it remains like a bright light in the memory of those who survive; and they speak of it as most triumphant and successful in its powerful conversions. When the meeting closed, and we had the last mourner down for prayers, there were but two unconverted souls left. There was one man, now brother Thomas Underwood, who called himself "a hard case." He came on the ground with many others, steeped in sin like himself. On

Sabbath, with others, he came forward for prayers. After a long struggle, and many prayers in his behalf, late in the evening he raised his head, and said, "I think I feel better." "Yes," said he, "I *do* feel better; I think I have got religion." Then he arose, and in the most earnest tones said, "Yes, I *have got* religion." One could almost see his face shine; and yet he so feared that others might doubt his sincerity, that he began exhorting sinners in the most earnest manner, pointing them to the Lamb of God as their all-sufficient Savior; and enforced the exhortation by alluding to himself as the most hardened of sinners. If God could save him, what might he not do for others if they would only repent? He then took hold of one hardened sinner that sat near him; said he, "You are going to get religion too." "No!" said the sinner, "I am not." "Do not say so," said he; "I once said so too; but I thank God that I have come here." He continued urging him for a long time; yet the man persisted in his refusal. At last he said, "O, do not say so; you will, you must come with us yet." The man turned pale, and down he came and commenced praying; soon Israel was victorious.

This man's efforts and success were so great that he had but to ask a sinner to yield, and he gave himself up to the Savior. When the invitation came for the young converts to come forward to join as probationers, he was the first to come. Seeing that others hesitated, he begged the privilege of helping them to take their final resolution. "O yes," said I, "bring them in by all means." By his persistent efforts he brought in several. One of them said to him, "You are going to heaven, brother Thomas." "Yes," said he, "I am going, if I have to go alone; still I am going." His face is yet Zionward, he is still on his way to heaven; but not alone. Some time after this, when, on being examined in class meeting, he was feeling very gloomy, he said he could best describe his condition by comparing himself to a pile of drift-wood, hedged in the swollen river, and to move forward was out of the question. The meeting went on, and it became a heavenly place in Christ Jesus. Brother Underwood arose and said, "Glory to God, brethren, I'm afloat."

At our present meeting J. Clark, presiding elder, came and preached once, and then left on a visit to his father's. William Crissey, Francis Owens, and some others composed the group of ministers. From among our brethren of the laity we had the Frazier's, Kelly's, and old brother Watkins. From Forked Creek we had brother Shoemaker, George Lyonbarger, and a few others. In those, days when I could get these lay brethren, and old brother F. Owens, we seldom failed of having a time of refreshing from the "presence of the Lord." This year was a great spiritual feast to my poor soul. The number of members returned was one hundred and ten.

From the Alton Conference, September 12,

1838, Bishop Soule presiding, I received my appointment to the Joliet circuit, with William S. Crissey, A. Chenoweth superintendent. This was brother Crissey's second year; and he was an indefatigable laborer, attending to all matters both small and great, and completing the churches that I had commenced two years before—one at Plainfield and another at Joliet; J. Clark was presiding elder. The number of members returned this year was one hundred and eighty-eight. This was my first experience under a superintendent. The circumstances and events of the relationship were any thing but pleasant; and I prayed to be delivered from the like again. I may appropriately introduce here a connected view of the work in the locality embracing Wilmington, Joliet, and Ottowa from its origin to a very recent date.

In 1832 I was appointed to the Desplaines mission, embracing all the settlements from twelve miles below Ottowa up to Oswego, Naperville, Plainfield, Yankee Settlement, (four miles east of Lockport,) Hickory Creek, Jackson's Grove, and Reed's Grove. This latter was at the limits of the white population, and the number of members was thirty-four. Jesse Walker was my presiding elder. In 1833 I was returned to the same charge—small congregations, reached by long, slow rides, by Indian trails, or over the trackless prairie. This was a hard year's labor, resulting in but little apparent good. This Fall the preachers met in Conference at brother

Padfield's, Union Grove, about twenty miles east of St. Louis—an account of which session is elsewhere given. David Blackwell was appointed to Desplaines mission, John Sinclair presiding elder. It embraced all the white settlements this side of Ottowa, except Chicago, extending south to Forked Creek. Blackwell formed the first class in the last-named locality in John Frazer's log-cabin, brother Frazer leader; members, Mrs. Frazer, John and Elizabeth Williams, Robert and Ann Watkins, James and Nancy Kelley, James Jordan and wife, John and Elizabeth Howell, and Hamilton and Martha Keeney. Number of members this year, fifty-seven. Blackwell was reappointed in 1835, Wilder B. Mack presiding elder. Number of members returned, one hundred and sixty. The following year, (1836,) myself and Matthew Turner were appointed on the Joliet circuit, brother Mack presiding elder. Number of members returned, two hundred and fifty-three. In 1837 I was appointed to Forked Creek, embracing Wilmington, John Clark presiding elder. William Creery was on Joliet circuit. There were numerous conversions on both charges; members returned, two hundred and eight. In 1838 Milton Bourne went to Wilmington, and William S. Crissey, Asbury Chenoweth and myself, to Joliet, John Clark presiding elder; members returned, one hundred and forty-eight. In 1839 William Vallette to Wilmington, and William Wigley to Joliet; John Sinclair presiding elder.

In 1840 the Rock River Conference was formed, Wigley being returned to Joliet, and Rufus Lumery going to Wilmington; number of members, one hundred and forty-eight. In 1841 Simon K. Lemon went to Wilmington; John Sinclair presiding elder— a good preacher and hard worker, whose labors were blessed with a revival; members returned, two hundred and seventy-six. Milton Bourne went to Joliet. In 1842 Joliet circuit embraced Wilmington; preachers, Elihu Springer and S. K. Lemon; membership, two hundred and eighty-four. In 1843 I was returned to Joliet circuit, Levi Jenks and James Leckenby, assistants; S. Stocking presiding elder; membership, five hundred and twenty-nine. In 1844 H. Minard to Joliet circuit, William Gaddis to Wilmington; James Mitchell presiding elder. In 1845 O. A. Walker and R. E. Thomas at Joliet, William Gaddis at Wilmington. In 1846 brother Walker was returned to Joliet; brother Mitchell presiding elder. In 1847 John Nason to Joliet, S. P. Burr to Wilmington; members returned, one hundred and fifty-three; Milton Bourne presiding elder. In 1848 to Joliet, O. W. Munger; to Wilmington, S. P. Burr; members returned, one hundred and fifty-three. In 1849 T. F. Deming to Joliet, C. Lazenby to Wilmington; A. L. Risley presiding elder. In 1850 James P. Vance to Joliet, O. W. Munger to Wilmington; O. A. Walker presiding elder. In 1851 B. C. Swartz to Joliet, (mission station); to Wilmington, brother Munger;

brother Walker presiding elder. In 1852 M. L. Read to Joliet, W. Fidler to Wilmington; brother Walker presiding elder. In 1853 brother Read to Joliet; Wilmington, A. Reker; brother Walker presiding elder. In 1854 to Joliet, J. Gibson; to Wilmington, C. Reeder. In 1855 brothers Gibson and Reeder were both returned.

In 1856, Joliet, Wm. Goodfellow; Wilmington, to be supplied; J. Gibson presiding elder; members returned, one hundred and sixty-seven and one hundred and seventy-one, respectively. In 1857 to Wilmington, F. P. Cleveland; members, one hundred and twenty; Joliet, J. Vincent; members returned, one hundred and fifty-eight; J. Gibson presiding elder. In 1858 to Joliet, N. B. Slaughter; members, two hundred and two; to Wilmington, Wm. Keegan; members, one hundred and fifty-three; J. Gibson presiding elder. In 1859 same preachers and presiding elder; members, Joliet, one hundred and eighty-seven; Wilmington, two hundred. In 1860 to Joliet, H. Crews; members, two hundred and twenty; to Wilmington, R. N. Morse; members, one hundred and thirty-three; S. A. W. Jewett presiding elder. In 1861 preachers and presiding elder returned; members at Joliet, two hundred and twenty-two; at Wilmington, one hundred and ninety-two. In 1862 to Joliet, S. G. Lathrop; members, two hundred and three; to Wilmington, S. Washburn; members, two hundred and seven; brother Jewett presiding elder. In 1863 to

Joliet, S. A. W. Jewett; members, two hundred and three; to Wilmington, R. R. Bibbens; members, two hundred and twenty; W. H. Glass presiding elder. In 1864 preachers and presiding elder returned; members, Joliet, two hundred; Wilmington, one hundred and ninety. In 1865 to Joliet, W. P. Gray; members, two hundred and seventy-one; to Wilmington, brother Crews; members, two hundred and sixteen; William F. Stewart presiding elder. In 1866 to Joliet, W. P. Gray; to Wilmington, W. H. Glass; brother Stewart presiding elder. In 1867 both preachers returned; increase of membership not reported.

CHAPTER XIII.

From the Bloomington Conference in 1839 I received my appointment for Peoria, at the hands of Bishop Morris. A brief history of Peoria may not come amiss here. It is the oldest settled town on the lake, west of the Alleghanies. In 1722 it was in the hands of Virginians; but it was first governed by the French.

The State of Illinois has been owned by four nations—the Indians, French, English, and Americans. East of the present city of Peoria, La Salle with his party made a small fort in 1680; and, to commemorate his hardships, called both it and the Lake "*Crave Cœur*," which means in our language "Broken Heart." The Indian traders and whites engaged in commerce with them, resided at the old fort from the year 1680 till 1781, when John Baptiste Maillet made a new location and village about a mile and a half west of the old village, at the outlet of the lake. This town was called La Ville de Maillet; that is, Maillet City. At the old fort there was no gardening or raising of vegetables; but the inhabitants depended mostly upon the Indians and the chase for support. But at the new settlement gardens were cultivated and fields of grain were raised.

In the year 1781 the Indians, under British influence, drove off the inhabitants from Peoria; but at the treaty of peace in 1783 they returned again. Then in 1812 Capt. Craig wantonly destroyed the village; but the city of Peoria now occupies the site of the village of Maillet, and bids fair to become one of the largest cities in Illinois.

At that time the whole frontier, from the Mississippi down to the Wabash and above Vincennes, increased rapidly every year. The interior also grew more dense and more wealthy. In 1820 Abner Gads, with others, settled in Peoria. Soon after, an Indian agency was established; William Holland was appointed Government blacksmith for the Indians. They were at that time very troublesome, and his family were at times in great peril; and yet he remained at his post of duty for several years. After the whites commenced settling in Peoria, it was selected by the commissioners, William Holland, Joseph Smith, and Nathan Dillon, as the county seat. James Latham obtained a floating claim, and laid it on the town site. After it had been a subject of litigation for some time the matter was compromised, and his claim was located at Peoria. The French had a claim in the upper part of the city, which was recognized by the Government. The claimants were Burboney, Beeso, Serett, and James Mutty, the latter being the interpreter. It is said that they realized but little for their claims.

At the time of my appointment Peoria was a station, and had a circuit connected with it. Brother E. Thompson was sent with me. He preached on the circuit while I remained at the station. I have been thinking lately how very great the contrast is in the managing of appointments now as compared with that time—how the preacher nowadays makes arrangements with the people for his next field of labor; how high salaries are offered as an inducement; and how the people's wishes are consulted in these matters. It was very different in those days. At the Bloomington Conference, Bishop Morris having heard that certain arrangements had been made, and some agreements entered into by the people of Peoria, for the purpose of securing the services of brother C., set his foot firmly down and said, "He shall not go."

This brother C., it seems, had a brother-in-law, Dr. M., at Peoria, who, together with himself, felt a strong interest in securing the station for him that year. The Doctor raised by subscription a sum of three hundred dollars, and promised to risk the rest of his support. A request was then sent in to Conference, which, as I have said, the Bishop peremptorily refused. I preached my first sermon here entirely ignorant of the state of feeling then existing. As I rode up to the place, on Sabbath morning, where I was to preach, I was met at the door and asked, "Where is brother C.? We sent for him, and we expect him." I knew nothing of the matter, and could only reply, "I am sent as your preacher." After the sermon I went home with brother Bristol to dinner. While there, Dr. M. came in to make inquiry about brother C. When he was told that brother C. was not coming he seemed much excited, and said, "That is the way they always serve us here. I raised three hundred dollars, and could have easily raised more, and now, to be put off in this way, it is really too bad. If brother C. had come he would have built us a church, and Methodism would have been something; but now we shall have nothing done." The Doctor felt badly at the prospect, but I do not think he felt worse than I did at the *welcome* I had received.

Entering upon my work under such a depression made me cling closer to the Lord for help. On Monday morning, before I left, I visited all the members in town, and then started after my family. I had to remove them one hundred and twenty miles, and begin another year's hard labor. When we got to Peoria the only house we could obtain was a dilapidated dwelling which had long been the abode of rats, whose rights to our home were pretty actively contested for three months. One day while I was absent from home Judge Parker, although not a member of our Church, nor even a professor of religion, went and rented a comfortable house on his own responsibility, and offered it to my family as a home. They were moved and comfortably settled before I came back. It was with no little satisfaction to myself and family that this change for a better home had been effected.

Our only place of worship was brother Bristol's carpenter-shop, and there I preached, among jack-planes and chisels. The shop was situated on an alley, but I had got, by this time, thoroughly and earnestly at work, and we had excellent meetings, many souls being born into the kingdom. One evening while holding meetings we had a crowded house, and many came who had to go away again. I proposed the building of a new church, and told them if they would be led by me they would soon have a new church to worship in. The next morning I was met on all sides by objections. It was out of the question, they said, to build a church, the times were so hard and money so scarce, as every one would agree who knew the gloomy prospect of '39 and '40; besides, what made matters more discouraging, was the fact that about two years previous an attempt had been made to build a frame church. It was decided by a reverend brother that a frame church would be a disgrace to Peoria, and they must have a brick church or none. The lumber which had then been collected was sold, and the money obtained for it pocketed by Mark Hiken, a steward, My informants were brothers Bristol and Markle, both members of the Official Board. In face of all these objections I was still decided that we could have a church. I said to them, "Well, now, let's decide upon a place; get your axes, and let's go into the woods, fell our own trees, haul them up on the snow, and we can score and hew our own logs. I will beg lumber at the different saw-mills to raise it, and we can have a house."

A majority fell in with my plans, and we went to work, and by the opening of Spring we had the timbers for all of the sills and plates. Then I made a "bee" to get the timbers hewed, and also secured the studding. One Sabbath, after service, I told the brethren that I wished to see them all on the ground the next morning, as I intended, by the next Saturday night, to have the timbers all framed and raised. The invitation was extended to all; every one that could bore with an auger or mortise a hole was urged to be on the ground. Next morning only four or five came in answer to the call. "Now," said brother Bristol, "where are your men? I felt exceedingly small when you were urging them to come out; you know so little of the amount of work necessary to be done. I thought, by the way you talked, that you expected to see all Peoria obedient to the call." Said I, "Brother Bristol, I appoint you foreman of the work. Only go at it and lay out the work, and I will have hands here yet." So he and those who were present went to work in good earnest. About noon our foreman was taken sick, but I soon found another, and the work went on. Every toper that I found in the village I urged into the work, and "their name was legion," because the stagnation was so great that, there was no work to be had. Still, up to this time, I had no foundation for my church. In circulating among the people I found one man who would donate brick, and seeing a friend in the street with his horses and wagon, I had but to ask and I received. He hauled in the brick. Then I came across some masons, who kindly offered to lay up the wall, and by twelve o'clock on Saturday afternoon I requested all the workmen to go about and invite every one they should meet to come and help raise the church that afternoon. They came pouring in from all quarters, and just as the sun was setting the frame of the first Methodist church ever built in Peoria was standing.

It was predicted, even after this effort, by all the other denominations, that our church would never be completed. Nothing more would be done, they said, and the timbers would rot down. The next step, and the hardest one, was to raise money. A plan was soon hit upon. I was to take my horse and buggy, and traverse the State. I was to ask each man for a dollar, and as much more as he would give. So off I started. My largest subscription was twenty-five dollars. I took a tour through Alton, St. Louis, and Belleville, and returned with sixty-five dollars. Then my next resort was to go to the saw-mills again. I was successful in begging flooring, siding, and sheeting. One friend gave me a large red oak tree; this was for the shingles. So the brethren went out and felled the tree, sawed it up, hauled it in, and hired some one to turn it into shingles. One of the brethren donated poles for rafters, which were carted four miles; another brother hewed, fitted, and put them up. Then I resorted to another "bee," in order to get the siding planed and put on. Into this siding I drove the first nail. I then pressed another brother into the good work, and he laid the floor. We were now ready for plastering, which brother Loomis agreed to do if some one would put on the lath. Another "bee," and another, till we had the building nearly complete. We put in a temporary pulpit and seats, and I held my last quarterly meeting in it. We were less than ten dollars in debt, and nearly all the money spent on it was raised on my tour South.

At our last love-feast, which was conducted with closed doors, I felt unusually liberal. I was doorkeeper, and I let in several without questions. Brother King, one of the official board, came to me and said, "Brother Beggs, what do you mean by letting in so many to our love-feast? You have even let in old Heaton." Said I, "I do n't know old Heaton; but go back, brother King, take your seat and pray on." He did so, and our meeting grew in interest, till I opened the door to receive members. The first man who presented himself was "old Heaton"—as they called him. He, with a number of others, joined our Church; and by this time the moral thermometer in Peoria stood at salvation heat; and the power of the Lord came down in such a wonderful manner that there was one general shout of

"Glory to God in the highest!" Our shouting was heard almost over the whole city, the church being nearly central. People had come in from every direction to see our new church, and it was not large enough to hold all that came. One of the local preachers got so filled with holy zeal that he ran out of doors and shouted at the top of his voice, "Glory to God in the highest!" They had not even ceased their manifestations of religious fervor and zeal when the hour arrived for preaching. This meeting closed up my Conference year. The Church had been much revived, and many members joined on probation. All seemed thankful to God, and took courage for the future; and from this time onward Methodism had a stronghold in that city. It is now the leading denomination. My presiding elder for that year was Newton Benjamin.

CHAPTER XIV.

Some years after I had the pleasure of being at the dedication of the new brick church in Peoria, and Bishop Janes preached the dedicatory sermon; after which Dr. M'Neal read the history of the Church. He spoke of Rev. Joseph Arington as having formed the first class in Peoria. I could not but smile at the misstatement. This was in 1834. Nine years before, in the year 1825, Jesse Walker formed a class of sixteen members. I give their names: Jesse Walker and wife; James Walker and wife; sister Dixon, the wife of the proprietor of Dixontown, on Rock River; sister Hamlin, and another sister, converts that Winter; Wm. Holland and wife; Wm.' Eads and wife; Wm. Blanchard, Rev. Reeves M'Cormick, and Mary Clark.

The next Summer he held a camp meeting one mile above Peoria, on the west side of the lake; Wm. Holland moved up an old log-cabin for his tent; and the old hero, Jesse Walker, had with him his son and others; Reeves M'Cormick also assisted.

Wm. Royal was T. Hall's predecessor in 1832. It was then called Fort Clark mission. The boundaries of Hall's mission in 1832 and '33 were as follows: Peoria, Lancaster, now La Salle Prairie; brother Jones's, on Snack River; Princeville, Essex school-house; Fraker's Grove, now Lafayette; thence to Princeton, some thirty miles distant; and thence to Troy Grove, twenty-five miles farther; brother Long's, near La Salle; and thence down the river to Miller's school-house, five miles below Peru. Then next to John Hall's, one hundred and fifty miles around. Some time in the Spring he formed a class of six or eight persons. Their names are as follows: Wm. Eads and wife, sister A. Hale, sister Waters, David Spencer, and some others, John Sinclair, presiding elder; members returned, forty-eight. Wm. See traveled the Peoria circuit in 1827, and Smith L. Robertson in 1828. It was then a large circuit, and he held a camp meeting three miles east of Peoria, on Farm Creek, Sam. H. Thompson presiding elder. Jesse Walker, and, I think, Wm. See, assisted. Gov. Edwards, the first Governor of the State, was then present.

They had a gracious time; yet even in that early day they were not free from disturbance. A certain individual was sent after whisky, and who, in going for it, had to pass the camp-ground. He stopped to hear the presiding elder's sermon. After its close a collection was taken up, and the money designed for whisky (fifty cents) was thrown into the hat. When he returned and was asked where his money was gone to replied, "O I thought the preacher needed it more than you did the whisky."

A. E. Phelps was my predecessor in the station, and sustained himself well. The court-house was occupied by a Unitarian preacher as well as himself. One day the former, in preaching on the Divinity of Christ, ran across the track of A. E. Phelps, and so he pitched into the Unitarian champion rough-shod, and so completely showed the fallacy of his doctrine that he had to leave, and A. E. Phelps had the house to himself. By this he rose fifty per cent. in the estimation of his hearers. Here commenced his brilliant career as a successful champion against Unitarians, Universalism, Deism, and Exclusive Immersionists, as practising the only mode of baptism. I do not think any one of his antagonists ever got the better of him. He excelled as a historian, and was truly an able defender of Methodism. He increased in usefulness till he was called from his labors to his long rest. In his footsteps follows a son that bids fair for a useful minister. What greater star could be added to the crown of glory of a departed saint than that his sons were following in his footsteps?

Jesse Walker was born in Virginia, Buckingham county, near James River, June 9, 1766. He was not blessed with religious parents, yet they were moral, and taught him to pray while yet in early life, and attend Divine worship regularly. Lying and profane language were strictly forbidden. His father was neither rich nor poor, and taught him to work. From his youth his education was very limited, his schooling, all told, consisting of but twenty days.

When he was nine years old his mother took him to a Baptist meeting; here, under the influence of the sermon, was his first awakening to his individual responsibility to God. After this he often reflected on the judgment-day, and the miseries of an interminable hell, till a trembling would seize him, and then would he begin to pray in earnest. Soon after this, he says: "I heard another preacher, who told me how to pray and exercise faith in believing on the Lord Jesus. The next morning, as I was walking along, the Lord gave me such a spirit of wrestling that my faith took hold on God; and, in a moment, such a light broke in upon my soul, and such beams of Divine love, that I praised his hallowed name for the unspeakable riches he had bestowed upon my poor soul. I enjoyed his presence for years; but no one having spoken to me about joining the Church, I consequently did not present myself. I soon began to mix with the wicked, and lost my enjoyment, backsliding from one thing to another till I became very wicked, and even doubted my conversion. Then, to quiet my conscience, I tried to believe the doctrines of Calvinism, besides going to every Baptist meeting to confirm myself in the dogma of fate. In my most solemn moments I could not believe these things myself, and yet I often labored hard to make others believe them. My besetting sin was profanity, which was often a great cause of grief to my mother and sister. The strivings of the Holy Spirit had left me and I often feared that my damnation was sealed, and that the earth would open and swallow me up. I thought men and devils had combined to take away the last vestige of comfort that was left me. At last I fell on my face, and, with all my guilt and weight of sin, hell seemed to move from beneath to meet me at my coming.

"But in my extreme anguish of spirit God showed himself unto me; and by faith I realized such a fullness in Jesus that I once more ventured out on his precious promises; and I found, of a truth, that the virtue of his blood shed for me had healed every wound that sin had made. Then I felt to exclaim, O loving Savior! blessed Jesus! I now consecrate my all to thee, for time and for eternity; thou art the one altogether lovely, and I will praise thee with all my powers. Then I went out to find a fellow Christian, that I might talk with him of my newly found happiness. It was on the Sabbath day; and I had barely commenced telling him, when he proposed to me to swap horses. I regret to say that this man was a member of the Baptist Church; but so it was, and it had the influence to turn me to seek some other denomination than that toward whose members I had always felt such a brotherly love. I remembered that there was a Methodist class meeting about twelve miles distant; and I turned my horse, in hopes of getting there before the meeting closed. I was too late; and I dismounted and knelt down and prayed for direction.

Then I remembered that the members were to return by a certain house, and I staid there and awaited their arrival. Their songs seemed so heavenly that they exceeded any thing that I had yet heard. When they began to talk on the subject of religion, I found that their experience was like my own, and that it was no more nor less than the love of God shed abroad in the heart. Then, when I began to tell them what God had done for me, the power of the Lord came down. While some prayed, others were praising and singing; and sinners began to cry for mercy. The meeting continued all night. In the morning I returned home, rejoicing on my way, and blessing God for what I had seen, and for what my poor soul had enjoyed. When I got home, and told them of God's goodness, they thought I was crazy; and my exhortations to them to seek the Lord were so strange to them that I feared that my message was as seed sown by the wayside.

"It was not long before I visited again my brethren in class, and I was called upon to lead the class. It was a great trial to me, and yet I bore the cross. During our exercises the Lord poured out his Spirit again. Some shouted aloud, and others cried for mercy, and such a time of power was it that it lasted till dawn of day. Such a meeting I had never witnessed before. Soon after this our new preacher came on from Conference. He preached with great power, and invited such as wished to join on trial to remain in class. I embraced this, my first opportunity, and joined the Church in July, 1786. I was appointed class-leader; and the burden of lost souls was so rolled upon me that I gave myself up wholly to the work. Seeing me such a laborer in the vineyard, the preachers soon wished me to accompany them on the circuit. My inability kept me back for some time; but at last I felt the command—'Go ye into all the world and preach the Gospel'—in such an imperious manner that I gave myself up to the great work. I offered myself, and was received on probation in 1804, and appointed, as the Minutes show, to the Red River circuit; in 1805 to Livingston; in 1806 to Hartford circuit, William M'Kendree presiding elder."

Thus far I have given the narrative as I found it in manuscript. I shall now complete it as I heard it from the lips of a third person. In the Spring of 1806 brother Walker accompanied William M'Kendree to Illinois to spy out the promised land. He found it so beautiful that he determined at once to come over and possess it, believing that here was to be a great moral conflict, and that he was to be the Joshua to lead on his spiritual Israel to possess it. On his return he continued to preach on his circuit till Conference, and then he was sent to Illinois. He hastened home to his family, and arrived there about twelve o'clock. He told them of his new field of labor, and, after some refreshment, commenced packing up for a removal. By ten o'clock the next morning he and his family were on their way to Illinois. Horses were their only means of conveyance—four in all—one for himself, and one for his wife and youngest daughter, who rode behind her; one for his eldest daughter, about eighteen years of age—now sister Everett, who gives me this interesting account of the early settling in the West—and a fourth for his library, or books which he had for sale.

It was one of the duties of preachers in those days to sell books to those among whom they labored, and it was one of the great means in distributing the truth and helping to build up the cause of Christ. The family had each but one change of apparel, and that they had spun and woven before they left home. They brought no furniture, not even a bed, but started for the wilderness with as few worldly goods as possible.

Soon after crossing the Ohio River he found himself and family fully entered into the Indian Territory. At this time a fearful rain-storm met them, and they were rejoiced at being able to take shelter in a deserted wigwam, even drenched with water, besides the discomforts of cold and hunger. They remained here three days, till the storm had subsided, and the streams had fallen a little. They then packed up and plunged again into the wilderness, to encounter much water and much hard labor, to endure hunger and long, wearisome rides, till they reached Turkey Hill, a settlement in Illinois, and their home in the West. Here they staid with brother William Scott and family, a whole-souled Methodist, and a fast friend ever after; yet here, with all their plainness of apparel, brother Walker and his daughter had to take a severe lecture from sister Scott, because the daughter had worn a dress with short sleeves, or those which came only to the elbows, as was the fashion in those days. They looked so unmethodistic to sister Scott that she could not forbear speaking to them of the sinfulness of such things.

The only house that could be obtained for the preacher and family was an old log-cabin belonging to brother Scott. It had a plank floor, and a stick chimney with a hole burned out in the back so large that a modern cooking-stove could be thrown through it, as sister Everett expressed it, and the hearth so low down that the edge of the floor made seats for the whole family around the fire; and this was the parsonage and Winter quarters of the old hero of Methodism in Illinois. Having got into his smoky house, he made some few repairs, and arranged themselves as well as their circumstances would permit; he entered upon his labors with Methodistic zeal, and soon the good work began, and souls were converted. As the New-Year drew nigh he gave out that he would hold a watch-night. It was a great question among them all, "What could he mean by watch-night?" And he replied that he was going to watch for the devil, and urged them all to come out. The result was a crowded house. At this meeting was held, also, the first love-feast. It was a successful one, and the beginning of better things. The next Spring following this watch-night, April, 1807, was held the first camp meeting in the State of Illinois.

To show to what rude means one had to resort at that time, we can relate an incident. One evening there were no lights to be had on the camp-ground, and it was also very windy. An old lady voluntered to meet the difficulty. Accordingly she stepped aside and doffed a white cotton skirt, which she had suspended as a lamp-shade. Then she caused it to be expanded by means of a twig bent in a circular form—a suggestion of hoops, which had not been thought of in that early day. Then, for the light, she scooped out a large turnip, which she filled with lard. She then twisted a wick of cotton, and rubbing it in the lard set fire to it after it had been suspended inside of the first hooped-skirt and lamp-shade ever used in Illinois. By this light Jesse Walker was able to preach that evening. The preachers present were Walker, Biggs, and Charles Mathew, exhorting and preaching alternately.

The following Spring another was held by brother Walker. The ground was selected in the following manner: One day while brother Walker was looking for a suitable place for holding the meeting, he came to where a tree had been torn down by lightning. Here, thought he, is a visible display of God's power; and why not select this, as we may have a display of his mighty power for the salvation of souls? and, as if inspiration rested on him for a moment, said, in a very impressive manner, "Here it shall be."

The usual preparations were soon made, log-pens thrown up and covered with clap-boards, conveniencies for fifty families. These tents or pens encircled a large space of ground, leaving only passage-ways out into the open forest. On Friday morning the meeting commenced, by the sounding of a horn as a signal to rise; then, at the second sounding, they were to assemble at the altar for prayer before breakfast. Having assembled, a hymn was first lined and then sung. Those assembled on this morning were very despondent, as the presiding elder, William M'Kendree, had not yet arrived. While they were yet singing, all of a sudden they heard at a distance the sound of voices as if joining in singing one of the sweet songs of Zion. They were welcome sounds as they came rolling on through the forest, and attracted the attention of all at the altar. And as they drew nearer, we caught the inspiration of the song, in which they were pouring out their voices, and joined in the melody. It was our elder, in company with a number of preachers; and the song or hymn was continued amidst hearty hand-shakings, tears and smiles, and shouting of hosannas, which continued fifteen or twenty minutes before the preachers could get off their horses. Soon breakfast was served up, and all thereafter were at the stand ready for worship.

William M'Kendree preached, and the work of the Lord commenced with great earnestness and zeal. Those who accompanied the presiding elder were Abbot Goddard, James Quinn, Rev. Killybrew, Thomas Lathley, and Charles Matheny. The meeting continued till Monday; great power was manifest, and many were brought into the kingdom, by the blood of sprinkling. One week after, another was held a few miles south of the present Edwardsville. The first camp-ground was called Shiloh; the second, Bethel, and the third, Eunice. Col. Shelby, of Kentucky, who was a warm personal friend of brother Walker, attended some of these meetings in company with the elder.

CHAPTER XV.

I SHALL devote the present chapter to statistics and reminiscences of the progress of Methodism in the Fox River locality.

In 1835 William Royal was appointed to Fox River mission, his associate being Samuel Pillsbury; Wilder B. Mack was presiding elder. Brother Royal formed, as well as traveled, this extensive and most laborious circuit. I give the preaching-places and the classes and class-leaders, so far as I have information:

1. Commencing at Millbrook, on the Fox River; a small class.
2. At brother Wells's, six miles south of Yorkville.
3. Daniel Pearce's, near Oswego; a small class.
4. Samuel M'Carty's, near Aurora; established in 1835.
5. Brother Hammer's, north-east of St. Charles; a small class.
6. Rev. Charles Geary's, six miles north of Naperville.
7. At Salt Creek; no class.
8. At Elk Grove, class formed in 1836; members' names: Rev. Caleph Lamb and wife, Seth Peck and wife, S. Wheeler (leader) and wife.

9. Wheeling—class-leader, brother Wissencroff; members, his wife, sister Filkins, and a few others.

10. Plum Grove; no class.

11. Alexander's; no class.

12. Father Noble's, on north branch of Chicago River; a small class.

13. Libertyville; a small class under brother Brooks.

14. Ladd's, near the State line, north.

15. Marsh's Grove; brother Russell's.

16. M'Lain's, at Deer Grove.

17. Dundee; a small class.

18. Crystal Lake.

19. Virginia.

20. Pleasant Grove; a class.

21. Marengo.

22. At Mason's, two miles below Belvidere.

23. Brother Enoch's, two miles north-east of Rockford.

24. At the mouth of the Kishwalky.

25. At brother Lee's; a class of six.

26. At Judge Daniel's; a small class under brother White.

At the request of the presiding elder I assisted brother Royal in holding his fourth quarterly meeting at the last-named place; the first ever held near Sycamore, or that far north. This was in 1836. About one hundred were present on the Sabbath. The meeting was very successful, and from that time the work has gone steadily on. Each successive minister has had new zeal and new success, so that Methodism is now the leading denomination in that section. Monday morning, on our return to Millcreek, brother Royal had two appointments— one at Squaw Grove, the 27th, on his round. From here we went on immediately to Samanauk, the 28th preaching-place on the four weeks' circuit, requiring preaching every day. I preached here after having ridden thirty miles on Monday, at brother Hough's, the class-leader's, and after preaching four times at the quarterly meeting.

In 1837 W. Clark was appointed to Du Page circuit, which was a part of Fox River mission. That Fall, brother Wilcox formed the first class in Aurora. He preached at first in Samuel M'Carty's house; afterward in a small school-house. The first class consisted of brother M'Carty and his sister, now sister Hill, and a few others. The first church edifice in Aurora was built in 1843, the membership numbering from thirty to forty. The Board of Trustees consisted of brother M'Carty, C. H. Goodwin, P. Brown, C. E. Goodwin, and John Gibson. The building was enlarged by the addition of twenty feet in 1852. Brother Wilcox was a fine preacher, an excellent pastor, very punctual in all his duties. In 1838 he was returned, William Gaddis being his assistant. He formed the first class in Plum Grove, consisting of brother Smith and wife, Joseph Smith and wife, and Seth Peck and wife.

In 1839 William Kimball and William Gaddis were the preachers, John Clark presiding elder. In 1840 William Kimball returned to Du Page circuit, John T. Mitchell presiding elder. In 1841 John Nason and Seymour Stover were the preachers, John Sinclair presiding elder. They were returned in 1842, Levi Jenks assistant preacher. In 1843 E. Springer and M. L. Noble were the preachers, S. H. Stocking presiding elder. In 1844 the name was changed to St. Charles circuit, E. Springer and William Gaddis preachers, J. R. Goodrich presiding elder. In 1845 Solomon Stebbins and L. A. Chapin, James Mitchell presiding elder. In 1846 S. Stebbins returned. In 1847 S. Bolles and C. Lazenby, John Chandler presiding elder. In 1848 B. Lowe and W. J. Smith, M. Bourne presiding elder. In 1849 F. Harvey, H. Minard, A. L. Risley presiding elder. In 1850 T. Hall, S. Guyer, J. Baume, L. Hitchcock presiding elder. In 1851 R. A. Blanchard, L. Hitchcock presiding elder. In 1852 E. H. Gammon, L. Hitchcock presiding elder. In 1853 S. Serl, S. P. Keyes presiding elder. In 1854 E. Brown, S. P. Keyes presiding elder. In 1856 Aurora was made a station under charge of J. C. Sanford, E. H. Gammon presiding elder. This year Aurora enjoyed a gracious revival, the fruit, under God, of one of brother Sanford's most earnest and faithful efforts.

In 1859 I visited Aurora, and going to church on Sunday morning discovered brother Sanford in the pulpit. He urged me to preach on recognizing me, but I preferred to hear, and enjoyed one of the most charming discourses that I ever heard. Accompanying him home to dinner, we received a call from the priest of the parish, who wished to ask some questions if I felt free to answer. He wanted to know, in the first place, whether there was any difference between the Methodism of fifty years ago and the present. I thought I could point out some differences. To begin with, I had traveled nine years before I saw a Methodist preacher use notes in speaking. Moreover, I thought that not one-half, perhaps not one-quarter of the Methodists of those days could have got into love-feast had the sisters then dressed as they do now. Members of both sects could be recognized as such almost as far as they could be seen. I related an anecdote, in illustration of this, of a girl under conviction, who, hearing of a Methodist meeting fifteen miles distant, started on foot to go to it. Arriving near the church, she came to where two roads met. Uncertain which to take, she concluded to sit down till the people should come along, and follow those wearing plain coats and bonnets. I thought that Methodists might still be known by their dress, since now they dressed so much finer than many other people. That reminded the priest of a little occurrence. He took his daughter, a few days before, to a milliner to purchase a bonnet. After looking at several, which were thought too gay, he asked what kind of bonnet the Methodist ladies wore. "O," replied the milliner, "they are the most fashionable people in Aurora."

When I entered the church in the morning I had noticed that brother Sanford appeared very much puzzled. He explained the matter as follows: "I had," he said, "prepared full notes for one of my best sermons; but to have you in the pulpit and see me use them would spoil all. Not to ask you, an old minister, into the pulpit, I should feel to be unkind. So, after revolving the matter over, I determined to ask you, and if you would not preach, I would take a text and preach off-hand." "Bless the Lord!" said brother Jenks, "I have not heard you preach so good a sermon since you have been on the station; and if brother Beggs's presence will continue to add so much to your efforts, I hope he will favor us with it every Sabbath."

The second quarterly in Ottowa was held in 1833, on which occasion I formed the first class. In the Winter of 1834 our quarterly meeting was held at the house of sister Pembrook. The people came from a distance of ten miles. Brother Olmsted, a new-comer to the State, and living some distance up the Illinois River, heard of the meeting and came; and sister Pittzer came from a distance up Fox River. The love-feast Sunday morning was attended with great power. The preachers present were, John Sinclair presiding elder, William Royal, and myself. Sister Pittzer became very happy, and, though sixty years of age, seemed to renew her youth under Divine influences. Her loud shouts of "Glory to God!" alarmed a sister of another denomination, who thought a word of caution necessary. Taking the arm of the old sister she said, "Do thyself no harm." "Bless the Lord!" exclaimed the good sister, "religion never harmed any body yet!" Brother Sinclair and I preached alternately; each taking his turn at exhorting. Brother Royal was mighty in prayer. Brother Olmstead was so delighted with his first quarterly meeting that he told a brother that if he only had brother Beggs to preach, brother Sinclair to exhort—for he was mighty therein—and brother Royal to pray, he wanted no more.

In 1847 Du Page circuit was changed to Naperville. I give the subsequent statistics: In 1847 J. S. Best preacher, J. Chandler presiding elder; members, 276. In 1848 S. R. Beggs and C. Batchelor preachers, M. Bourne presiding elder; members, 270. In 1849 O. A. Munger preacher, A. L. Risley presiding elder; members, 270. In 1850 J. C. Stoughton preacher, A. L. Risley presiding elder; members, 186. In 1851 J. L. Jenkins preacher, John Sinclair presiding elder; members, 189. In 1852 J. P. Vance and A. Holcomb preachers, John Sinclair presiding elder; members, 184. In 1853 R. Beatty preacher, S. P. Keyes presiding elder; members, 273. In 1854 O. House preacher; S. P. Keyes presiding elder; members,

206. In 1855 O. House preacher, J. Flowers presiding elder; members, 214. In 1856 B. Close preacher, J. W. Agard presiding elder; members, 192. In 1857 both returned; members, 192. In 1858—Downer's Grove embraced—J. Note preacher, J. W. Agood presiding elder; members, 174. In 1859 E. Stone preacher, L. Hitchcock presiding elder; members, 172. In 1860 S. Burdock preacher, E. M. Boring presiding elder; members, 142. In 1861 both returned; members, 144. In 1862 J. T. Hannah preacher, E. M. Boring presiding elder; members, 120. In 1863 both returned; members, 120. Methodism has always had up-hill work on this charge, and so have other denominations, except the Evangelical Germans and the Catholics; nor does the prospect seem more flattering.

CHAPTER XVI.

The present chapter contains statistics and reminiscences of the early days of Methodism in Illinois at large, and especially in Wabash River and middle localities of the State, with a historical sketch of early explorations in localities embraced in the narrative.

The first Methodist preacher in Illinois was Joseph Lillard. He was admitted on trial in Kentucky in 1790, in which year he traveled the Limestone circuit, traveling the Salt River circuit in 1791. The next we hear of him is in 1793, in Illinois. It is claimed that he formed the first class in this State in that year, in New Design settlement, some distance south from Salem meeting-house, Captain Joseph Ogel leader. The next regular preacher was Hosea Riggs. He arrived in 1796, and his useful labors continued uninterrupted till 1841, in which year, at the age of eighty-one years, he died at his home, a few miles east of Belleville.

In the year 1804 Benjamin Young came to Illinois as a traveling preacher on the missionary work. Lewis Garrett was presiding elder. Governor Reynolds states, in his history of Illinois, that Young frequently preached at his father's house, in Randolph county, and was the first preacher he remembers hearing. He traveled over the entire American settlements. Subsequently, in 1805, brother Riggs preached at his father's house. These were the first religious meetings ever held in Randolph county. Rev. Thomas Harrison emigrated to Illinois in 1804, and continued to preach the Gospel, more or less, during the subsequent half century. In 1805 Joseph Oglesby traveled the Illinois circuit—a good preacher, who labored with marked success. I heard him in 1820. He stood full six feet, very straight, had dark hair, a penetrating eye beneath a prominent forehead, and a thin, tapering face. His manner was very dignified, and his gestures very correct, and his whole manner impressive. The effect of his discourse was sometimes overwhelming. He once preached at my camp meeting on the Vincennes circuit, from the text, "The Master is come, and calleth for thee." The audience, saint and sinner, was completely carried away, and I was so overcome that I did not feel that I could preach for a week afterward.

The first settlement in Edgar county was made in the Spring of 1817, on the arm of Grand Prairie, by John Stratton, Wm. Whitley, Blackman, and a few others. Col. Jonathan Mayo came in the Fall of the same year. This territory was then within the bounds of Edwards county. Illinois did not become a State till the following year. Terre Haute, Indiana, was laid out, and a few lots sold in 1816. Government land was entered at that time at two dollars per acre, one-fourth down, and the balance in two, three, and four years. The Vermilion circuit was the first formed in this region, in the Fall of 1823; H. Vredenburg preacher, S. H. Thompson presiding elder. The circuit embraced Edgar, Clark, and Vermilion counties, in Illinois, and Vermilion and Vigo counties in Indiana—that portion of the latter lying west of the Wabash River. The appointments ran thus: Mount Carmel, Wm. M'Reynolds; Wabash and Mount Vinnonia, W. H. Smith and C. Riddle; Kaskaskia, T. B. Leach; Illinois, John Dew and O. Fisher; Cash River, Joseph Patterson; Shoal Creek, John Davis and Jesse Green; Sangamon, John Miller; Mississippi, Isaac Piggott; Vermilion, H. Vredenburg and R. Delap.

The first class formed in this section was in 1819, in the house of Jonathan Mayo, on the north arm of Grand Prairie, by Joseph Curtis, who had just emigrated from Ohio; a worthy and efficient local preacher. The first quarterly meeting conference was on the same prairie, at the house of Rev. John M'Reynolds; Col. J. Mayo was recording steward; H. Vredenburg was preacher in charge; S. H. Thompson presiding elder. The Illinois Conference embraced Indiana also—two districts in each—John Strange and James Armstrong presiding elders in Indiana, and Charles Holliday and S. H. Thompson in Illinois.

These two States had 13,042 members, and forty-four traveling preachers. Not one of these is now a member of the Illinois Conference except the noble-hearted, iron-framed pioneer, Peter Cartwright. Prominent among the preachers of that day was John Fox, of precious memory—neat in person and attire, correct in his preaching, diligent in pastoral visitation, strict in administration of discipline, and powerful in prayer—his labors never failing to result in the salvation of souls. This year closed the labors of Rev. C. Holliday as presiding elder. He was my elder when I was on the Vincennes circuit, and few men ever proved a greater blessing to me. The precision and directness of the appeals in his edifying, soul-stirring sermons, produced effects which remained fresh and powerful for weeks. In 1833 James M'Kean and T. Files were appointed to Paris circuit, both men of great service to the Church. Brother Files has a son still living in Clark county, a worthy and efficient steward in the Church. Rev. H. Crews and G. W. Robbins were very successful presiding elders on the Danville district. The latter was somewhat slow of speech, but always paid his hearers for waiting. Brother Crews, now of Rock River Conference—of whom a biography is given in another chapter—is among the most popular and useful of those occupying the same responsible position in his Conference. In Edgar county the Methodist Church still maintains its original position in advance of other denominations.

Brother Exum Evans was one of a large family that moved from North Carolina with their father, and settled in Clark county in 1812. His parents were Quakers, after the "most straitest" of which sect the children were all raised. They made their home in the midst of a large Quaker settlement near York, not far from the line of Crawford county. They held their meetings in a small log school-house, and strictly forbade their children going to the Methodist meetings. Brother Exum did not, therefore, hear a Methodist preacher till he was fifteen years old. When on a visit to his uncle's, Rev. brother Stewart held a two days' meeting, assisted by brother Hearn. Exum Evans heard Stewart here, who, as he describes, preached with such power and assurance that his message seemed to come from God. Such preaching he had never heard before. When brother Hearn, whose appearance was not so prepossessing as some, arose to follow Stewart, Exum was afraid he would spoil all that had been said; but to his astonishment the stream of eloquence deepened and widened, till it became overwhelming and irresistible, and great power of the Spirit attended the Word.

The meeting, says Exum, greatly prepossessed us in favor of Methodism. It took place at the log-cabin of brother Isaac Snipes, who was the leader of the first class ever formed in that section. It consisted of brother J. Snipes and Nancy his wife, Archibald Comstock and Charity his wife, and Sally Millard and Elizabeth Park. It was held about three miles south of York.

Some fifteen years after this, Rev. Wm. Crissey came upon this circuit, and held a protracted meeting in a school-house in the same neighborhood. It continued till there were about eighty converted, one-half of whom were Quakers, young and old. Brother Exum was among nine children who embraced religion and joined our Church, as did also his brother before his death. Mr. Maffitt, in describing the Eastern preachers, spoke of their method as being as a general rule systematic and phlegmatic; but the Western preachers—their voice was like a mountain horn. Our camp meetings were peculiarly the school of this style, in which the appeals had all the freedom of the open air and the winds, and the directness and speed of the lightning. I attended such a meeting at Mount Carmel in 1825, over which S. H. Thompson, presiding elder, presided. The converts in those days were born strong into the kingdom, and entered it shouting. Charles Slocomb, who labored in the Wabash region, was such a preacher as I have described—a local preacher, yet his ministrations invariably attended with great power.

At the above camp meeting a most hardened sinner was forced to cry for mercy, under one of his powerful discourses. He was portraying the misery of the damned, when this man, an old Revolutionary soldier who had been standing on the outskirts of the throng, came rushing toward the altar, crying at the top of his voice, "Quarter! quarter!" Falling on his knees he exclaimed, "I am an old soldier;

I fought through the Revolutionary war; I have heard the cannon roar in battle, and seen the blood pour forth in streams; but since God made me, I have never heard such cannonading as this. I yield! I yield!"

I add, as appropriate in this connection, brief reminiscences of early Methodism in Sangamon county. Sangamon, in the Pottawotamie language, means a plenty to eat; or, expressed in Scripture parlance, a land flowing with milk and honey. But, in fact, about all of Illinois is as good as Sangamon, and equally attractive. In June, 1822, a colony of six families moved into this county from Kentucky, and settled on Nigger Creek. They were Methodists, and brought with them tracts and Testaments. They at once formed a Sabbath school, M. Conover superintendent. It soon numbered thirty-five scholars and four teachers, mostly Presbyterians and Baptists—some beginning with the alphabet and learning to read the New Testament.

Sister Catherine C. Rucker, from whom I received this information, stated that one old Baptist was so afraid of Sabbath schools that, when solicited to send his children, he replied that he would as soon send them to a horse-race. But he was finally induced to send them; and he was so pleased with their progress that he gave liberally toward the purchase of more books. The first camp meeting in Sangamon county was held in the Fall of 1823, or 1824, at Rock Creek, Gorden Prairie. There were about nine tents, and a congregation of perhaps eight hundred on the Sabbath. James Simms conducted it. He was a powerful preacher. The meeting continued three or four days.

As soon as the State Government was established, emigration began to increase, and there continued to flow in a more wealthy and permanent population. The State purchased land and made better settlements, schools were established, and houses of worship were erected in many colonies. The farmers raised a surplus of produce, mills were built, and considerable was exported; commerce began to assume a regularity which is necessary to its permanence and success. The people were greatly in debt, however, and the dearth of currency retarded the prosperity of the new State in a great measure, yet not entirely. In April, 1829, Abner Eads, J. Hervey, and some others, left St. Clair county, and located in Peoria. This was the first settlement of this city by Americans.

A few years after our Indian agency was established here, Marquette, and Joliet, of Quebec, with others, in 1671, determined to explore the land toward the setting sun and the father of waters, the Mississippi. On the 13th of May, 1673, a little band of seven left with two bark canoes, in which they carried a scanty store of provision, bound they knew not where. After reaching Green Bay they entered Fox River, and in their ascent endured much hard labor and suffering. They reached the

Kickapoos and Miamies' village, beyond which point no white man had ever traveled. The natives were astonished at their daring and enterprise, and on the 10th of June they left their village with two braves to guide and assist them through the Sac nation and the marshes of that region to a navigable point on Wisconsin River.

After praying fervently to the mother of Jesus for protection, they committed themselves to the vast flowing river, till upon the 17th of June they entered the Mississippi. Marquette says of this, "It is impossible to express the joy which I felt when I first found myself on the bosom of this mighty river. The abundance of birds and fishes and their tameness was astonishing to me. A large fish came near breaking our canoe in pieces." Their voyage was increased in pleasantness in their reception, by a tribe of Indians, the Illinois. After many complimentary speeches and presents, a great feast was given to the Europeans, consisting of honey, fish, and roast dog. After the feast they were paraded through the town with great ceremony and speech-making, and escorted to their canoes by six hundred people.

The rolling tide soon bore them to the Pekitanoni, or Missouri; thence passing a dangerous rock in the river, came to the Ohio, a stream which makes but a small figure in Father Marquette's map. At the mouth of the Arkansas they were attacked by some warriors, and had nearly lost their lives; but

Marquette resolutely presented the pipe of peace, and this softened the hearts of the old men. They were permitted to go on their journey. After some difficulty they reached the Illinois River, through which they sailed up to the lake. "No where on my journey," says Marquette, "did I see such grounds, meadows, and forests as on this river—the abundance of game, buffalo, deer, wild-cats, bustards, swans, ducks, and beavers."

In September the party, without loss or injury, reached Green Bay, and reported their discoveries; an important one in that day, but of which we have no record save the brief narrative of M. Joliet. These were the first Europeans that passed through our State. La Salle was their successor.

The Roman Catholics were the first to plant the standard of the Cross in the Mississippi Valley. From Canada to New Orleans they labored to Christianize the savage and the scattered white population; but, after all, what has Jesuitism done to Christianize this great valley compared with the results of evangelical efforts? The State and river takes its name from a tribe of Indians called the Illinois. The word is a mixture of French and Indian.

CHAPTER XVII.

In 1828 Jesse Walker was superintendent of Fox River mission, John Dew presiding elder. In 1829 the name changed to Salem mission. Peter Cartwright was then presiding elder, and Isaac Scarritt preacher in charge. Jesse Walker was sent to Desplaines mission, and the same year he formed a class at Walker's Grove. This, I think, was the first class in the bounds of the Rock River Conference, but as soon as the mission was abandoned the class was given up. This same year Jesse Walker settled in Walker's Grove, now Plainfield. The names of the above class were as follows: Jesse Walker and Susannah his wife, James Walker and wife, brother Fisk and wife, Timothy B. Clark and wife, brother Weed and wife—about twelve in all.

This same year there was a class formed in Galena by John Dew; yet when I examine closely I have to decide in favor of Plainfield's being the first permanent class. In the year 1833 I succeeded Jesse Walker, commencing in the Fall of 1832. I took charge of Desplaines mission, Jesse Walker presiding elder. In the Winter of 1833 the first temperance meeting was held in this upper country. The speakers were Mr. Arnold, James Walker, and myself. We made considerable effort, which was productive of some good; yet we were partially shorn of our strength, there being a small store in the place, where, among other things, whisky was kept for sale, and as the firm, two of the leading men present, would not sign the pledge, it kept many others back. Yet those who did sign stood firm, and we have continued to battle for the cause of temperance ever since.

We then raised, by the assistance of brother Ross, a permanent fund of $15,000, by means of which we drove the last doggery from Plainfield. These same efforts might be made in other places were they to continue unitedly and perseveringly. May the Lord pity the faint-hearted, and make them more than ever bold and able advocates of this great cause! This year was closed with some conversions; members returned, thirty-four.

In the Fall of 1833 I was returned to Desplaines mission. This was the year when the tide of speculation rolled in upon us of which I have before made mention. The year closed with a membership of fifty-seven, J. Sinclair presiding elder. In the Fall of 1834 David Blackwell was my successor—a fine young preacher and a good pastor. He was on the ground to receive all emigrants, who, by this time, were very numerous, both from the East and South. The year closed with a good camp meeting. The members returned numbered one hundred and seventeen, J. Sinclair presiding elder. He was returned in the Fall of 1835, with W. B. Mack presiding elder. He had a pleasant year, with some increase; members returned, one hundred and sixty.

In the Fall of 1836 the name was changed to Joliet circuit, and I was appointed here, with M. Turner for my colleague, W. B. Mack presiding elder. This year hard riding, much labor, and great success; members returned, two hundred and fifty-three, embracing Plainfield. In this year I got up a subscription to build a church in Plainfield. It was soon under way, and finished before the hard times set in, but it was a long time before we paid off its debt. The Baptists built one also, about the same time, and we soon had two churches to worship in, and a glorious revival was the result. In 1837, on my return to Joliet, I got up a subscription, and a church was commenced which William Crissey, my successor, finished the next year. He was a good preacher, a faithful pastor, and possessed a good business tact. He had a good revival, and a return of two hundred and thirty-seven members. The decrease is accounted for by a division of the work.

Forked Creek circuit was formed in 1838. William Crissey, A. Chenoweth, and myself as supernumerary, were the preachers. This year our labors were so successful that our members numbered one hundred and eighty-eight. In 1839 a new circuit was formed called Milford, Elihu Springer preacher in charge, and J. Sinclair presiding elder. This circuit embraced all east of Fox River, with Oswego and Plainfield. The same preachers and presiding elder were returned in 1840, and a gracious revival was experienced, especially in Plainfield. Such a time of confession and humiliation on the part of the members of all denominations had never been witnessed, and the result was the conversion of sinners and the building up of membership of all Churches. Dr. Comstock's labors were greatly blessed. He had but few equals in preaching, and the Word came with power and full of the Holy Ghost. This year he returned two hundred and four members.

In 1841 the Conference appointed Rufus Lummery and H. Hadley, with J. Sinclair presiding elder. This year Rufus Lummery became dissatisfied with Methodist customs and left, taking as many with him as he could persuade to follow his example, and joined the Wesleyans. Members returned, two hundred and fifty. In 1842 Wesley Batchelor and R. R. Wood preachers, J. Sinclair presiding elder. A good year and labors blest; members returned, two hundred and sixty-four. In 1843 S. F. Denning, S. H. Stocking presiding elder; faithful in their labors; yet hard work and poor pay. Number returned, two hundred and sixty-four. In 1844 S. R. Beggs and John Hewter, Luke Hitchcock presiding elder. We had at Plainfield a good revival and a number added at other points, embracing Morris, Conger's, and Gleason's Ridge; number returned, three hundred and thirty-five. In 1845 Levi Jenks and James W. Burton, L. Hitchcock presiding elder. The preachers were much beloved, and kept the work in a healthy condition; number returned, three hundred and twenty-nine. In 1846 John Agard and W. B. Atkinson, M. Bourne presiding elder; number returned, three hundred and sixty-six. In 1847 A. Wolliscraft and J. Lazenby, M. Bourne presiding elder; number returned, three hundred and fifty-seven. Had a good revival at Lisbon and Plainfield.

In 1848 Plainfield was made a station, Jonathan Stoughton preacher, M. Bourne presiding elder. Some extensive revivals. Both men returned in 1849. Conference held at Plainfield this year. In 1850 S. Stover, one of our best preachers, a strict disciplinarian; members returned, one hundred and forty-seven. In 1851 S. Stover was returned. He labored faithfully as preacher and pastor, with more pruning of unprofitable members. Our condition as a Church might be better to-day, if more members were lopped off. Yet we had additions, however, to keep up our number, one hundred and forty-seven. Quarterage light. How much the Church still owes to her faithful preachers! Their untiring labors can never be repaid this side heaven. In 1852 David Cassiday was appointed at Plainfield. The way was prepared for a good work, and he commenced in earnest. His labors were greatly blest, O. A. Walker presiding elder; number returned, one hundred and eighty-nine. In 1853 he was returned and had another prosperous year, O. A. Walker presiding elder. A number of conversions; members returned, three hundred and sixteen. In 1854 O. A. Walker and M. L. Reed; Plainfield and Lockport united; J. W. Flowers presiding elder; members returned, two hundred and fourteen. In 1855 S. A. W. Jewett, O. A. Walker presiding elder. In 1855 he was returned. In 1857 Robert Betty, a good preacher, and one who attended to all the wants of the Church, both small and great; J. Gibson presiding elder; number of members, one hundred and ninety-five. In 1858 Robert Betty was returned, and left the station in a healthy state; number of members, one hundred and ninety-five.

In 1859 A. W. Page preached well and visited the membership. We had this year the most extensive revival that we had ever enjoyed—convictions pungent, conversions strong and clear; and before the meeting closed there had been about two hundred forward for prayer, and one hundred had joined the Church; members returned, three hundred. In 1860 he was returned, J. Gibson presiding elder; more pruning, and strict discipline; number of members, two hundred and forty-four. In 1861 Robert K. Bibbins; membership diminished by pruning, removals, and deaths, to one hundred and ninety-four; J. Gibson presiding elder. In 1862 he was returned; had some conversions and additions; he was respected and beloved, yet was not fully appreciated; number of members, one hundred and ninety-seven. In 1863 C. C. Best. He requested a change, owing to many obstacles in the way of his getting to Plainfield, and brother M'Reading was supplied. He was a fine preacher and a good pastor, and had some conversions; number of members, two hundred. In 1864 Isaac Lyonbarger entered on the work with great zeal, both in preaching and visiting; and through his efforts the Sabbath school interest was greatly blessed. During his stay we had a revival equal to brother Page's, in 1859, perhaps greater. Some valuable and steadfast accessions were made; yet, during his stay, there was some falling off; presiding elders were, first, H. Crews, and, last, brother Stewart. In 1867 M. Smith, a good preacher, powerful in exhortation and prayer. We had a number of conversions, forty additions, and a donation of two hundred and seventy-five dollars.

In the presence of Bishop Roberts and myself Dr. Cartwright related the following anecdote: At one of the Annual Conferences the Bishop was detained on account of sickness, and R. R. Roberts was elected Chairman to fill his place. The place was filled so much to the satisfaction of the Conference that they determined to elect him Bishop at the next General Conference. The first morning after they had all collected, Dr. Cartwright looked across the room and saw a fine, portly looking man, and asked a brother who that was? Said he, "That is Robert R. Roberts"—he was so active and expert in business, and withal so pleasant, that he was admired by all the Conference.

When the time for the election of Bishops came he cast in his vote, so mirthful and so jovial as if all was going on to his greatest satisfaction. When the votes were counted, and it was found that Roberts came near being elected Bishop, the responsibility, in view of so great an office, seemed to overcome him and he was entirely unmanned. He left the room and sought a retired place outside in the grounds, where he paced back and forth in the greatest perturbation, and it seemed that he would sink under the responsibility. I have seen but few men that I thought were possessed of more excellent traits of character than Bishop Roberts.

CHAPTER XVIII.

During the great rebellion in the South I had a great anxiety to participate in our struggle for liberty; but there was no opportunity till September 14, 1864, when the way opened for me to spend six weeks in the work of the Christian Commission. Leaving home I arrived at St. Louis at the above date. As I could not get passage on a boat for two days, I entered immediately on my work there, by distributing books and papers among the sick in the hospitals. In Hickory-Street Hospital I conversed with about thirty members on the subject of religion; and held a class meeting, inquiring into their spiritual condition, encouraging, reproving, and exhorting throughout the entire hospital. I never knew before how peculiarly adapted to hospital visiting our class meetings were.

I also visited Jefferson Barracks, and preached to some of the most hardened men. I do not think I should have succeeded in getting them together had it not been for one of their number, who, although somewhat under the influence of liquor, said, "Boys, be still, he is an old man, and he must and shall have a hearing." He then made them all sit down, and he assisted me in singing. After prayers I preached and distributed some papers and books among them, exhorting each one to prepare to meet his God. On Monday morning I went on board the steamboat Post Boy. The water was low, which made our passage somewhat slow. We had a mixed company on board of professors and irreligious; yet I preached to a very attentive audience, and prayed that it might bring forth fruit abundantly. I distributed books to the soldiers on board. We stopped a short time at Cairo, and then set sail for Memphis, where were the rooms of the Christian Commission, to which I was bound.

My field of labor was assigned me at Memphis and vicinity. I visited all the hospitals, and also the prisons, preaching, praying, and conversing with all, both sick and well. I believe I never gave my time up more fully to the work than I did during the two months that I spent on this mission. I generally preached three times on the Sabbath, and several times through the week. Once, as I was preaching to the prisoners, some sitting, some standing, and others lying down, one of the soldiers slipped a pack of cards into my pocket. I had three more appointments on that day, and seven miles to travel. For fear of having them seen I slipped them into another pocket, and forgot the circumstance till some one called on me for a Testament. I drew out the pack of cards, supposing I had found one. Judge of my surprise and mortification as I handed them out in presence of quite a number of persons. I explained the matter, however, and said that I was taking them back to commit to the fire for safe-keeping.

On my return I was invited to preach at Hawley Springs by a brother of another denomination, who was preaching and teaching in the colored Baptist church. I consented to go the next Sabbath in the afternoon. I had to preach at half-past nine on an iron-clad gun-boat. After the morning service I walked three miles to my appointment. I took dinner with the high-priest of the parish, and was accompanied to the church by him and two colored brethren, all of whom sat in the pulpit. When I got about half through, the darkey burst into a prolonged roar or shout, which so drowned my voice that I stopped, when they commenced shaking hands and shouting the louder, till one, in passing the pulpit, reached me his hand, shouting, "Glory to God for de true Gospel!" The shouting then subsided, and I finished my sermon with an invitation for all who wished an interest in our prayers to rise up; and not a few did so. I dismissed the meeting with a farewell till we should meet above.

During my stay I visited the monument of Andrew Jackson, and found the following inscription recorded upon it:

ANDREW JACKSON,
THE SEVENTH PRESIDENT OF THE UNITED STATES.
Inaugurated Jan. 8, 1859.
THE FEDERAL UNION MUST BE PRESERVED.
Honor and gratitude to those who have filled the measures of their country's glory.
Erected in the City Court Square.

The second line, "The Federal Union," etc., had been partly chiseled out by the rebel soldiers.

My time having expired I packed up my effects, and was soon on board the steamer and breasting a heavy current of the Father of Waters. Some time in the evening our boat struck a snag, and tore out the wheel-house and some of the paddles of the wheel, which disabled us, and we were obliged to cast anchor till morning; then we made our way back to Memphis as best we could, and the next evening we started on another boat. We were forty miles up the stream when one of the passengers wished the Captain to land his boat and take on some fruit, assuring him that there was no danger of rebels, as there were two fires—the signal of safety—to be seen burning on shore. He landed, and about twenty-five hands went on shore to assist in bringing in the fruit, when the rebels commenced firing with small arms, and poured a volley of lead into our boat. Some of them came on board and demanded a surrender, and threatened the engineer if he did not surrender they would blow out his brains. They were told to go to the pilot. They then ran into his cabin, crying, "Surrender, surrender." Major Smith, one of our paymasters, said to them: "Do not be in a hurry." The rebels replied by shooting him through the breast, and he fell to the floor. Major Beler ran down on the bow of the boat, and met one of the rebels; both fired, and both were killed.

This attack commenced about midnight. Another rebel was shot in the breast, and when we reached Cairo he was yet alive. One negro was badly wounded. I was in bed, and, hearing the noise, it was some moments before I realized what was going on. The roar of guns, the cry of don't surrender, intermingled with oaths, aroused me to a sense of our danger. Hastily dressing, and putting my money in the bottom of my socks, anticipating the plunder of my boots, I went out. The balls were yet pouring into the sides of the boat, and most of the passengers lying flat on the boat to escape the shots. The table at which there had been card-playing was upside down, the players having left it in some haste. Those having money were proposing to give the women half if they would secure it. Every one seemed panic-struck, from the Colonel down to the private. A number of soldiers were on board, but mostly those who were on a furlough, having left their arms, and only a few had revolvers. By this time the boat was getting out from shore, and the rebels, finding some of their number killed, jumped overboard. It is doubtful whether they reached the shore; and those who had gone on shore for the fruit were probably taken prisoners. The rebel that was killed proved to be a sergeant whose family lived in Iowa, as some of his papers showed. We were told that the man who persuaded the captain to land had laid this plot before leaving Memphis. After this we went on pleasantly till we reached Cairo, and here we assisted some sick soldiers on board the cars, making them as comfortable as we could.

I left for St. Louis, and arriving there late in the afternoon on Saturday, I spent the Sabbath again in Jefferson Barracks. I preached at half-past ten to a very attentive audience, and with some liberty. They had a Methodist chaplain. He had an appointment at two o'clock in the chapel, and requested me to preach. We had a full house, and all attentive. The audience was made up of some of several denominations, and some hardened old sinners. Before I got through the power of the Lord was manifest among them. There were earnest inquirers after everlasting life, and shouting and amens came near drowning my voice.

After the meeting closed I was introduced to the chaplain who was to preach in the evening—a brother Ives, of the Baptist persuasion. I found that I had known him favorably at Plainfield. He urged me to preach again in the evening, till finally I consented. The house was full, and our meeting was more powerful than in the afternoon. It was then proposed that I should remain there a week holding meetings, but I would not consent to this, having made my arrangements to be at home. Accordingly I left on Monday morning, greatly delighted at having been able to do something in behalf of those who were doing so much for their country.

CHAPTER XIX.

EXTRACTS FROM METHODISM IN CHICAGO, GIVEN BY GRANT GOODRICH.

THE first quarterly meeting in Chicago was held by Jesse Walker, and John Sinclair presiding elder. There were present at that communion, William Lee, a local preacher, and wife; Charles Wisencraft and wife; Henry Whitehead, Mrs. R. J. Hamilton, and Hannah Harmon. Some of them are still living. The meeting was held in Watkins's schoolhouse, on the north side of the river. It was at this meeting that Rev. Henry Whitehead received license to preach. This and the old log school-house, in which I formed the first class, were used as places of public worship by the Methodists; and when the tide of emigration poured in so rapidly, they found themselves straitened for room. Early in the Spring of 1834 brother Whitehead and Mr. Stewart contracted to build a small but comfortable house of worship, on the north side of the river, on the corner of North Water and Clark streets. It was pushed forward with great energy to an early completion. Jesse Walker preached here every Sabbath, being a stationed preacher, and was assisted in preaching, praying, and exhortation by the local preachers.

From this time Methodism began to flourish; and its proportion to other denominations, was as five to seven till near 1850. In 1834 John Sinclair, our present veteran and presiding elder, was in charge of the district extending from Salt Creek, east to the Wabash and west to the Mississippi, and all north of Rock Island to the last white man's cabin; embracing a larger territory than the present Rock River Conference. Finding that wherever he had been, Walker had been there before him, and being ambitious to preach Christ first to some of the new-comers, he heard of a family that had just settled at Root River—now Racine—and made all haste to bear them the offer of eternal life. Coming by the way of Chicago, he met brother Walker; inquiring after his health, he was told that he (Walker) was well, but very tired, as he had just been to look after a family recently settled at Root River. In despair Sinclair gave up the hope of the honor he had counted upon as unattainable.

To the zeal and efficiency of John T. Mitchell, Chicago Methodism is greatly indebted. He gave to the Church a thorough organization, and laid the foundations of her future usefulness and stability. At the Conference of 1836 Rev. Otis T. Curtis succeeded him—a quiet, amiable, and pious man, but wanting in that controlling energy and efficiency demanded by the circumstances and the times. In the general commercial crash which succeeded, few of the members escaped. There were some who were so grieved at the loss of their wealth that they turned their back on God, despising the treasures at his right hand. The integrity of others was not proof against the sore trials of the times; but especially sad was the ignominious fall of our presiding elder, W. B. Mack. The outbreaking crimes and scandalous conduct of some of our members, who had been active and prominent in the Church, fell in quick succession with crushing weight upon the faithful few, and with our pecuniary embarrassments, threatened to overwhelm and scatter them with shame and confusion.

There has never been a time in the history of Methodism in Chicago when false brethren, wicked men, and tempting devils seemed so near the accomplishment of its destruction as at this period. We felt that we were the scoff and scorn of the wicked and the reproach of the good. By the standard-bearers of our beloved Church the cause of God had been deeply, foully dishonored. Deep was the humility to which God brought his children for their want of fidelity against the allurements of worldly wealth. He took his fan in his hand—blessed be his name!—not to sweep away, but to purge and purify his Church.

Still there were faithful ones who survived, ornaments to the religion of Christ, who remember with trembling and holy gratitude those dark and terrible days when the death-agonies seemed upon our mangled and bleeding Zion, and how the few that yet remained faithful, with sad hearts and bowed heads, gathered around their almost forsaken altars, and humbling themselves before God with tears and agonizing prayers, besought the world's Redeemer for mercy and for help.

At the Conference of 1837, in answer to the prayers of His children for a Joshua to lead them out of the wilderness, God sent Rev. Peter R. Borein, of blessed memory, whose name never falls on my ear, who never rises to my thoughts but a holy influence comes, and an impulse toward heaven, whither he has gone; and there comes, too, that last injunction which fell from his lips as the waters of Jordan were closing over him, "Be faithful; be faithful unto death." He came in the fullness of the Gospel, *burdened* with the love of Christ to dying men. He gathered his feeble flock around him and breathed into them something of his own mighty faith, and with them at the feet of the Redeemer cried for help, till salvation was poured as in a mighty torrent upon the people.

During the Winter of 1837–8 quite a number were converted, some of whom are still living; but compared with the work of the succeeding year the revival was quite limited.

At the Conference of 1838 Borein was returned; and owing to the poverty of his charge a missionary appropriation was obtained for that year by the presiding elder, Rev. John Clark. The little church building was removed from the north side to Clark-street, the site of the present church, and was enlarged to twice its size.

In December a revival commenced, deep, widespread, and powerful. From this time till April brother Borein held meetings every night, and frequently during the day. Night after night, with tireless zeal, he poured forth the arrows of God's truth; he followed the smitten sinner into his home, into his shop, and even pursued him to the haunts of dissipation; and, with pleadings and entreaties that seemed almost resistless, besought him to be reconciled to God. The house, from first to last, was crowded to its utmost capacity, and the altar was thronged with penitent souls. Concern for the soul seemed to swallow up every other; more than three hundred were converted, most of whom united with the Church, comprising about one-tenth of the whole population. But the Master had determined to call his faithful servant home; he was ripe for heaven, he had kept the faith, his course was finished, and his crown was ready.

Those who heard his last sermon will never forget it. It was the vision of the dying Stephen: "But he being full of the Holy Ghost, looked up steadfastly into heaven, and saw the glory of God, and Jesus standing on the right hand of God." As he spoke of the beatific sight which burst upon the vision of the dying martyr, he seemed himself to catch a glimpse of the glories which Stephen saw; there seemed a radiance upon his countenance, and a prophetic fire burning upon his lips. God, he said, "had not seen fit to reveal to us a material idea of heaven, but every one had some mental conceptions of it and its inhabitants." He believed that in the next, as in this world, there were degrees in Christian attainments, and that in the land of glory some would occupy higher positions than others; that sometimes his imagination had pictured heaven as a vast amphitheater, whose seats rose tier above tier, up to the very throne itself; and when, from the lower seats, the white-robed struck the exultant song of redemption, it was caught up from rank to rank, growing louder and sweeter as it rose, while in unison the angel choir struck their lyres, and from every golden harp-string of saint, angel, cherubim and seraphim, was poured the rapturous, jubilant, adoring song, and heaven was filled with an atmosphere of melody.

Who shall dare to say that God in that hour did not permit his soul to catch some strain of that heavenly music, in which he was soon to join? A day or two after he was laid on his dying bed, his work was done, and God took him. None knew him but to love him. As an effective preacher he had but few equals. He had that moving, winning power, that seized at once the conviction and the heart, and made them willing captives; and that earnestness, that yearning tenderness was his, that made his hearers feel that his heart would break under a sense of their danger, if they refused to come to Christ and be saved. His hearers felt that he was truly an embassador for God, in Christ's stead. It is said that he was converted at about thirteen years of age, that he did not then know his letters; but feeling that he was called of God to carry truths to. his fellow-man, he commenced to acquire that knowledge which he deemed so indispensable to his great mission. He was two years at the Illinois College, at Jacksonville.

In the September previous to his death he commenced the study of Hebrew, conscious, as he said, that there was a depth of meaning and beauty in the original, especially in Isaiah and the Psalms, which the translation could never convey, and which he longed to know and feel; and, notwithstanding he held meetings every evening, and many times in the day, from December to April, he was able before his death to read a chapter in the Hebrew Bible with only occasional reference to his lexicon. To-day he sings a sweeter, nobler song, in heaven, than David ever sang on earth. May it be our unceasing efforts, and that of our children, to follow him as he followed Christ!

CHAPTER XX.

At the Conference in 1839 Rev. S. Stocking was appointed to this Church. The difficulties of following such a man as his predecessor can be well appreciated. Peace, however, prevailed, and there were quite a number of conversions. In 1840–41 Rev. H. Crews was stationed here. Prosperity and conversions attended both years of his administration. The house again became too small, and was enlarged to nearly double its former capacity. In 1842 Rev. N. P. Cunningham was transferred from the Illinois Conference and appointed preacher in charge. He, too, has since been removed, as we trust, to our Father's kingdom on high. He was an earnest, laborious man, and as a doctrinal preacher had few equals. He had some peculiarities not the most pleasing, but was sincere and zealous, and did much good.

The house was again becoming too small for the increasing congregation, and it was resolved to colonize in some other part of the city the next year. With this view, in 1843, Rev. Luke Hitchcock was appointed preacher in charge, and Rev. Abram Hanson assistant. The lot on which Canal-Street Church stood was purchased, and a church erected. During the Winter the health of brother Hitchcock failed, and he was compelled to leave his charge. The presiding elder, H. Crews, then residing at Southport, removed to Chicago, and, with brother Hanson, supplied the two congregations. About seventy-five members went to Canal-Street, but it was determined that the two societies should constitute but one charge, and the leaders and stewards meet in one board. The finances were, however, kept separate, each society paying a specific amount, and the preachers supplying each Church alternately.

At the Conference of 1844, under the same arrangement, Rev. William M. D. Ryan was transferred from Ohio and made preacher in charge, and Rev. Warren Oliver was appointed assistant. Under this arrangement harmony prevailed, and both societies were blessed with prosperity. During the following Winter a very general revival occurred, and a large number were added to the Church. Clark-Street became crowded beyond the convenient capacity of the house. It had been enlarged and patched up so many times there was almost danger that it might fall down. Brother Ryan urged the necessity of building a permanent house of worship of sufficient capacity to accommodate the congregation, and infusing something of his own energy into the Church, it was resolved to attempt the erection of a large building. It was undertaken with much trembling, and with many forebodings of the result. It is due to him to say that few men possessed the energy and tact which could have inspired the Church with the requisite spirit and liberality to carry on the enterprise to a successful termination.

It was proposed to make the seats free, provided six thousand dollars could be raised to be paid before the completion. About four thousand dollars, however, was all that could be obtained. It was clear the enterprise must be abandoned, or some plan devised to increase the subscriptions. It was finally resolved to sell a sufficient number of seats to cover the cost of the house, at the appraisal of the trustees—all subscriptions paid, to be received in payment. Several persons offering to increase their subscription, and others who had refused to subscribe offering to give liberally under this arrangement, six thousand dollars were soon raised, and the trustees contracted for the erection of the building and finishing of all but the basement—this amount payable on the completion of the building, and the balance in one year. The house was ninety-eight feet six inches by sixty-six feet. The old church was removed to the lot on the corner of Dearborn and Madison streets, and occupied till the erection of the new building.

In November, 1845, the house was dedicated. From the amount raised at the dedication, the sale of the seats, and other means, the trustees were able to meet present demands on the contract, and the Church felt greatly relieved. Had it not been the first large house of worship built in the city, and one of the most prosperous business years, it is feared that the society would have been crushed in the undertaking. But a gracious Providence favored us on every hand. A necessity for the basement and class-rooms was now felt; and although all had given so liberally, yet they had been so blessed in what they had done, that almost with one accord they declared their willingness to give more. In one evening the funds necessary to finish the basement were raised; and though it was Winter the work was pushed rapidly to completion. The first Sabbath after the house was completed was a day of great rejoicing; when with gratitude and praise they lifted up their hearts to God for the goodly heritage he had given them. There was in their case a literal fulfillment of the declaration of Holy Writ, "There is that scattereth, and yet increaseth." When the debt was paid, it is believed that all were pecuniarily richer than when it was contracted. Providence seemed to have been well pleased with his stewards, and richly verified his promises in them. The whole cost was about twelve thousand dollars, and it was all paid as it became due. During the Winter God also blessed his children by the conversion of a number of souls, and adding them to his Church.

In 1845 Canal-Street Church was separated from us, and Rev. Silas Bolles appointed to it; brother Ryan was returned to Clark-Street. At the Conference of 1846 Rev. Chauncey Hobart was transferred from the Illinois Conference, and stationed at

Clark-Street, and Silas Bolles reappointed to Canal-Street. Among the events of this and the succeeding year was a most unhappy controversy with Rev. James Mitchell, the presiding elder, which shook the Church nearly to disruption. Circumstances transpired which satisfied the great majority of Clark-Street Church, that the well-being of Zion forbade the return of elder Mitchell to this district. At the session of the Conference of 1847 a representation of this matter was made to the Bishop by nearly all of the official board. Some of the brethren in Clark-Street Church, and also in Canal-Street as well as at other points on the district, were of a different opinion. Such action was taken by elder Mitchell in Conference as forced those opposed to his return to prefer charges against him, instead of leaving the matter in the hands of the Bishop. A part of the charges only were disposed of by the Conference. Elder Mitchell was not returned to the district, but was ordered to be reproved in open Conference by the Bishop, and allowed a superannuated relation. The charges undisposed of were determined at the Conference in 1848, and the occasion of the trouble went out from among us.

Previous to the Conference of 1847 a number of members determined to form another Church on the north side of the river. They purchased two lots on Indiana-street, built a neat chapel, and solicited a preacher at the ensuing Conference. At the Conference of 1847 Rev. Philip Jackson was sent to the Clark-Street Church. His prudence and steady firmness did much to preserve the integrity of the Church. Rev. O. Bronson was stationed at Canal-Street; but his health failed before the end of the year, and he was forced to retire from his work. Rev. Freeborn Haney was appointed to Indiana-Street. This year a Church on Indiana-street was commenced for the German brethren, which is still in a flourishing condition. In 1848 Rev. Richard Haney was sent to Clark-Street, Rev. R. A. Blanchard was sent to Canal-Street, and Rev. John F. Devore to Indiana-Street.

In 1849 the two former were reappointed to Clark and Canal Streets, and Rev. Zadok Hall to Indiana-Street. During this year earnest prayer was made to the Most High that he would water his thirsty Zion. In answer, his children were revived, and a goodly number were converted. Other Churches shared also in the reviving influence. At the Conference of 1850 Rev. S. P. Keys was sent to Clark-Street, Rev. W. Palmer to Canal-Street, and Rev. Boyd Low to Indiana-Street. During this year, through the liberality of brother Orrington Lunt, an opportunity was offered of obtaining a lot on the corner of State and Harrison streets for another church. A Sunday School Union was also formed among various Churches, for the establishment of Sunday schools and the extension of church-building, under whose supervision a small chapel was built on Clinton-street for Sunday school and preaching purposes, and where preaching was had every Sabbath by some of the local preachers. A building formerly occupied by the Presbyterians was purchased and moved on to the State-street lot, fitted up in a neat and convenient manner, and a Sunday school organized.

In 1851 Rev. N. P. Heath was sent as a missionary to occupy it and organize a society. He entered with great zeal upon his work, and a number of members united there, and a Church was organized under the most flattering prospects. At the same Conference brother Keys was returned to Clark-Street, Palmer to Canal-Street, and Rev. J. W. Agard to Indiana-Street. In January, 1852, brother Palmer took his departure to the spirit-world. He was a devoted minister, and had been blessed with great success in winning souls to Christ. Rev. J. E. Wilson was appointed by the presiding elder to take charge of the Canal-Street Church the remainder of the year. During this Winter a revival occurred. Since the great revival of 1838–9 there had been none which gave so fair promise of permanent good. Its subjects were mostly young men and women, the children of pious parents, who had been trained and nurtured in the lap of the Church. It is to be hoped that these and such as these will fill the places that we shall soon leave vacant. God help them to act well their part.

At the General Conference a book depository and the North-Western Christian Advocate were authorized to be established in the city. The Depository has been for several years in successful operation, and will no doubt be the means of a general diffusion of our Church literature throughout the West. The Advocate was placed under the charge of Rev. J. V. Watson, who proved himself an able and accomplished editor for a number of years. The necessity for such a paper had long been felt, and the placing of brother Watson at its head insured the interest of a large circle of devoted and loving friends to the cause. He was one of the great lights of the Church; but he has long since gone to his rest, and we can not forbear paying that tribute to his memory which he so richly deserved.

At our last Conference in 1852 Rev. John Clark was transferred from the Troy Conference and appointed to Clark-Street. He was presiding elder on the same district from October, 1836, to October, 1840; and in 1841 was transferred to Texas, and in 1844 from Texas to Troy Conference. N. P. Heath was returned to State-Street; J. E. Wilson to Canal-Street, with William Kegan as his assistant, with which Church the Owen-Street charge was connected. Silas Bolles was appointed to Indiana-Street, and Philip Barth to the Indiana-Street German Church. Another German Church was organized on the south side of the river, and Rev. Augustus Kellner appointed preacher in charge. He procured a lot on the corner of Van Buren and Griswold streets, where another church was built.

Great efforts were made to secure lots and establish Churches in other localities, which by the energy and liberality of the various members of already formed Churches, have since been rendered successful. A plan was formed and put into execution for bringing into efficient action the talents of local preachers. A circuit was formed, embracing Cross Point, Clinton-Street Chapel, Hamilton's School-House, the Car Factory School-House, Jackson's Ridge, and Cleaverville, where preaching was expected at least once on every Sabbath.

CHAPTER XXI.

In the evening of the 7th of April, 1812, the children of Mr. Kinzie were dancing before the fire to the music of their father's violin. The tea-table was spread, and they were awaiting the return of their mother, who had gone to visit a sick neighbor. Suddenly the door was thrown open, and Mrs. Kinzie rushed in, pale with terror, and scarcely able to articulate. It was with difficulty that she composed herself sufficiently to give the necessary information that the Indians were up at Lee's place, killing and scalping all before them, and that while she was at Burns's a man and boy were seen running on the opposite side of the river with all speed, and called across to give notice to Burns's people to save themselves, for the Indians were already at Lee's place, from which they had escaped. Having given this terrible news, they had made all possible speed for the fort, which was on the same side of the river.

All was now consternation and dismay. The family were hurried into two old pirogues that were moored near the house, and hastened across the river, to take refuge in the fort. The man and boy, on arriving at the fort, were scarce able to give a coherent account of the scene of action; but in order to render their story more intelligible, we will describe Lee's place, since known by the name of Hardscrabble. It was a farm intersected by the Chicago River, about four miles from its mouth. The farm-house stood on the western bank of the south branch of this river. On the same side of the main stream, but quite near its junction with Lake Michigan, stood the dwelling-house and trading establishment of Mr. Kinzie.

The fort was situated on the southern bank, directly opposite. This fort was differently constructed from the one erected on the same site in 1816. It had two block-houses on the southern side, and on the northern a sally-port, or a subterranean passage from the parade-ground to the river. This was designed as a means of escape in case of danger, or that the garrison might be supplied with water during a siege. The officers were Capt. Heald, Lieut. H., the son-in-law of Mr. Kinzie, and Ensign Konan—the two last very young men—the Surgeon, Dr. Van Voorhies, and seventy-five men, very few of whom were effective.

In the Spring preceding the destruction of the fort, two Indians of the Calumet band came to the fort on a visit to the commanding officer. As they passed through the quarters, they saw Mrs. Heald and another lady, wives of the officers, playing at battledore. Turning to the interpreter, one of them, Nanmongee, said: "The white chiefs' wives are amusing themselves very much; it will not be long before they are hoeing in our cornfields." This was considered, at the time, an idle threat—a mere ebullition of jealous feeling at the contrast between the situation of their own women and those of the white people.

Some months afterward how bitterly was this remembered!

In the afternoon of the day on which this narrative commences, a party of ten or twelve Indians, dressed and painted, arrived at the house, and, according to the custom among savages, entered and seated themselves without ceremony. Something in their appearance and manner excited the suspicion of one of the family, a Frenchman, who remarked: "I do not like their appearance; they are none of our folks; I know by their dress and paint, they are not Pottawotamies." Another of the family, a discharged soldier, then said to the boy who was present: "If that is the case, we had better get away from here if we can. Say nothing, but do as you see me do." The soldier then walked leisurely toward the canoes, which were tied near the bank.

An Indian asked where he was going. He pointed to the cattle and some stacks of hay which were standing on the opposite side of the stream, and made signs that he must go and fodder the cattle, and afterward they would return and get their supper. He got into one canoe and the boy into the other, and they were soon across. They pulled some hay for the cattle, and made a show of collecting the cattle by a gradual circuit, till their movements were concealed by the hay-stacks, and then ran for the woods, which were close at hand. They had run only about a quarter of a mile, when they heard the discharge of two guns, which they supposed had been leveled at those they had left behind. They hastened on with all speed till they arrived opposite the house of Mr. Burns, where, as before stated, they called across the stream to warn the family of their danger. When these two arrived at the fort some of the soldiers were absent, having had leave that afternoon to go out on a fishing excursion. The commanding officer immediately ordered a cannon to be fired, that they might be warned of their danger. The soldiers were at this time two miles above Lee's place. Hearing the signal, they immediately put out their torches, for it was now dark, and dropped down the river toward the garrison as silently as possible. As they passed Lee's place it was proposed that they should go in and tell the family that the signal from the fort meant danger. Every thing was still as death; they groped their way along, and as one of them jumped into the small inclosure that surrounded the house he placed his hand on the dead body of a man. By passing his hand over the head he ascertained that it had been scalped.

They then hastened back to their canoes, and reached the fort unmolested. The next morning it was proposed at the fort that a body of men, soldiers and citizens, should go to Lee's place to learn the fate of its occupants. The two men were found dead and much mutilated, with their faithful dogs beside them. Their bodies were brought to the fort and buried. The inmates at the fort received no further alarm for several weeks.

It was on the afternoon of the 7th of August that a Pottawotamie chief arrived at the fort, bringing dispatches from General Hull, announcing the declaration of war between the United States and Great Britain, that General Hull was at the head of our army at Detroit, and that the island of Mackinaw had fallen into the hands of the British. Captain Heald was ordered to evacuate the fort, if practicable, and in that event to distribute all the United States property in and around the fort among the Indians in the immediate neighborhood.

After the Indian had done his errand, he requested a private interview with Mr. Kinzie, who had taken up his residence at the fort. The Indian wished him to ascertain if it was Captain Heald's purpose to leave the fort, and strongly advised against any such measure, proposing that they remain till a reenforcement would be sent to their assistance; and at the same time, should they conclude to go, advising the best route and offering what help he could. Mr. Kinzie immediately acquainted Capt. Heald with the Indian's friendly communication, also throwing in the weight of his own advice to remain at the fort, inasmuch as they were supplied with provisions and ammunition for six months.

Capt. Heald replied that he should obey orders and evacuate the fort; but since he must divide the United States property, he should remain there till he had called the Indians together and made an equitable division among them. The Indian chief then suggested the expediency of marching out and leaving all things standing as they were; and that possibly while the Indians were engaged in the dividing of the spoils, the troops might effect their retreat unmolested. This advice was strongly seconded by Mr. Kinzie, but did not meet the approbation of the commanding officer.

However, as it was highly improbable that the command would be permitted to pass through the country in safety to Fort Wayne; and their march must be slow to accommodate the helplessness of the women and children—some of the soldiers being superannuated and others invalid; and since the order was left discretionary, it was the unanimous advice to remain where they were, and fortify themselves as best they could. It was further argued that aid might arrive from the other side of the peninsula before they could be attacked by the British from Mackinaw; and even should it not come, it was better to fall into their hands than to become victims to the savages. Capt. Heald replied that a special order had been issued by the War Department that no post should be surrendered without battle having been given; that his force was totally inadequate to an engagement, and that he should unquestionably be censured for remaining, when there appeared a prospect of a safe march through; upon the whole, he deemed it expedient to assemble the Indians, distribute the property among them, and ask them for an escort to Fort Wayne, with a promise of a considerable reward upon their safe arrival—adding that he had full confidence in the friendly professions of the Indians.

From this time, the other officers held themselves aloof, and spoke but little upon the subject, although they considered the project of Capt. Heald as little short of madness. This dissatisfaction among the soldiers hourly increased, till it reached a high pitch of insubordination. The Indians now became daily more unruly, entering the fort in defiance of the sentinels; making their way without ceremony into the officers' quarters; showing in many ways open defiance.

Thus passed the time till the 12th of August, on the afternoon of which day, the Indians having assembled from the neighboring villages, a council was held. Capt. Heald only attended; his officers declining his request for them to accompany him, as they had been secretly informed that it was the intention of the young chiefs to fall upon the officers and kill them while in council. Capt. Heald could not be persuaded that this was true. The officers only waited till he in company with Mr. Kinzie had left the garrison, and then they took command of the block-house which overlooked the esplanade on which the council was held. They opened the portholes, and pointed the cannon so as to command the whole assembly. By this means the lives of the whites in council were probably preserved.

In council Capt. Heald told the Indians that the goods at the factory, and also the provisions and ammunition, were to be distributed among them the next day. He then requested an escort of the Pottawotamies to Fort Wayne, offering them liberal rewards when they arrived there, and making many professions of kindness and good-will toward them. The savages promised all he required; but Mr. Kinzie, who understood their character well, still advised the Captain to remain, and used every effort to open his eyes to the bad state of feeling that really existed among the Indians.

He reminded him that since the troubles with the Indians on the Wabash, there had been a settled purpose of hostilities toward the whites, in consequence of which it had been the policy of Americans to withhold all fire-arms and ammunition, or whatever would enable them to carry on their warfare upon the defenseless inhabitants on the frontier. Capt. Heald now seemed to consider that he was furnishing the enemy with arms against himself, and determined to destroy all the ammunition except what should be necessary for the use of his own troops. The Indians suspected what was going on, and crept stealthily as near the scene of action as possible; but a vigilant watch was kept up, and no one was suffered to approach except those who were engaged in the affair. On the 14th of August some relief to the general despondency was afforded by the arrival of Captain Wells with fifteen friendly Miamis. He had at Fort Wayne heard of the order for evacuating the fort at Chicago, and knowing the hostile determination of the Pottawotamies, had made a rapid march across the country to prevent the exposure of his relative, Captain Heald, and his troops to certain destruction. But he came too late. When he reached the post he found that the ammunition had been destroyed and the provisions given to the Indians. Captain Wells, when a boy, was stolen by the Indians from the family of Hon. Nathaniel Pope, in Kentucky. Although recovered by them some time after, he preferred to return and live among the Indians. He married a Miami woman, and became chief of that nation. He was the father of the late Mrs. Judge Wolcott, Maumee, Ohio.

CHAPTER XXII.

EVERY preparation was made for the march of the troops on the following morning, but, notwithstanding the precautions that had been taken to preserve secrecy, the noise made in knocking in the heads of the barrels had betrayed their operations. So great was the quantity of liquor thrown into the river that the taste of the water next morning was, as one expressed it, like strong grog. Among the chiefs, although they shared in the general hostile feelings of the tribe toward Americans, there remained a strong personal regard for the troops at this fort and a few white citizens of the place. These chiefs used their utmost influence to allay the revengeful feelings of the young men, and to avert their bloody designs, but without effect.

On the evening after the council Black Partridge, a conspicuous chief, entered the quarters of the commanding officer. "Father," said he, "I come to deliver up to you the medal I wear. It was given me by your people. I have long worn it as a token of our mutual friendship, but our young men are resolved to imbrue their hands in the blood of the whites. I can not restrain them, and I will not wear a token of peace while I am compelled to act as an enemy." Had further evidence been wanting, this would have been sufficient to have warranted the most dismal forebodings. There were not wanting, however, a few gallant hearts who strove to encourage the desponding company. There had been reserved but twenty-five rounds of ammunition and one box of cartridges, which must, under any circumstances of danger, have proved insufficient; but the prospect of a fatiguing march forbade the troops embarrassing themselves with a larger quantity.

The morning of the 14th all things were in readiness. Nine o'clock was the hour fixed upon for starting. Mr. Kinzie had volunteered to accompany the troops in their march, and had intrusted his family to the care of some friendly Indians, who had promised to convey them in a boat around the head of Lake Michigan to a point in St. Joseph's River, there to be joined by the troops, should the prosecution of their march be permitted. Early in the morning, Mr. Kinzie had received a message from To-pee-mee-bee, a chief of the St. Joseph's band, informing him that mischief was intended by the Pottawotamies, who had engaged to escort the detachment, urging him to relinquish his design of accompanying the troops by land, and also promising him that the boat containing himself and family should be permitted to pass in safety to St. Joseph. Mr. Kinzie declined, as he believed his presence might act as a restraint upon the fury of the savages, so warmly were they attached to him and his family. The party in the boat consisted of Mrs. Kinzie and her four younger children, the nurse, a clerk of Mr. Kinzie's, two servants, and the boatmen, besides two Indians who acted as their protectors. The boat started, but scarce had they reached the mouth of the river, a half mile below the fort, when another messenger arrived from To-pee-mee-bee to detain them where they were. In breathless expectation sat the wife and mother. She was a woman of uncommon energy and strength of character, yet her heart died within her as she folded her arms around her helpless infants, and gazed upon the march of her husband and child to certain death.

As the troops left the fort, the band struck up the dead march. On they came in military style, but with solemn mien. Capt. Wells took the lead at the head of his little band of Miamis. He had blackened his face before leaving the garrison, in token of his impending fate. They took the road along the Lake shore, and when they reached the point where commences the range of sand hills intervening between the prairie and the beach, the escort of the Pottawotamies, a number of about five hundred, kept the level of the prairie instead of continuing along the beach with the troops and Miamis. The troops had marched perhaps a mile and a half, when Capt. Wells, who had kept somewhat in advance with his band, came riding furiously back, shouting: "They are about to attack us; form instantly and charge upon them!" Scarcely were the words uttered, when a volley was showered from among the sand hills.

The troops were hastily brought into line, and charged up the bank. One man, a veteran of seventy Winters, fell as they ascended.

The remainder of the scene is best described by an eye-witness, and a participator in the tragedy—the wife of Lieut. Helm. She says: "After we had left the bank, the firing became general; the Miamis fled at the outset. Their chief rode up to the Pottawotamies, and said, 'You have deceived the troops and us; you have done a bad action;' and, brandishing his tomahawk, continued, 'I will be the first to return and punish your treachery.' He then galloped after his companions, who were now scouring across the prairie. The troops behaved most gallantly. They were but a handful; but they resolved to sell their lives most dearly. Our horses pranced and bounded, and could hardly be restrained as the balls whistled among them. I drew off a little and gazed upon my husband and father, who were yet unharmed. I felt that my hour had come, and endeavored to forget those I loved, and prepared myself for my approaching fate.

"While I was thus engaged, the surgeon, Dr. Van Voorhees, came up. His horse had been shot under him, and he had received a ball in his leg. Every muscle of his face was quivering with the agony of terror. He said to me, 'Do you think they will take our lives? I am badly wounded, but not mortally; perhaps we might purchase our lives by promising them a large reward. Do you think there is any chance?' 'Dr. Van Voorhees,' said I, 'do not let us waste the moments that yet remain to us in such vain hopes. Our fate is inevitable; in a few moments we must appear before the bar of God. Let us make what preparations are in our power.' 'O, I can not die,' exclaimed he, 'I am not fit to die. If I had only a short time to prepare! Death is awful!' I pointed to Ensign Konan, who, though mortally wounded and nearly down, was still fighting with desperation on one knee. 'Look at that man,' said I; 'at least he dies like a soldier.' 'Yes,' replied the unfortunate man, with a convulsive gasp; 'but he has no terrors of the future. He does not believe there is one.' At this moment a young Indian raised his tomahawk at me; by springing aside I avoided the blow, which was intended for my skull, but which alighted on my shoulder. I seized him around the neck; and, while exerting my utmost efforts to get possession of his scalping-knife, which hung in a scabbard over his breast, I was dragged from his grasp by another and an older Indian. The latter bore me struggling and resisting toward the lake.

"Notwithstanding the rapidity with which I was hurried along, I recognized as I passed the lifeless remains of the surgeon. Some murderous tomahawk had stretched him upon the very spot where I had last seen him. I was immediately plunged into the water and held there. As I resisted, however, I soon perceived that the object of my captor was not to drown me, for he held me firmly in such a position as to keep my head above the water. This reassured me; and, looking at him closely, I soon recognized, in spite of the paint by which he was disguised, the Black Partridge. When the firing had nearly subsided, my preserver took me from the water, and led me up the sand-bank. It was a burning August morning, and walking through the sand, in my drenched condition, was inexpressibly painful and fatiguing. I stooped and took off my shoes to clear them from the sand, when a squaw seized and carried them off. I was placed upon a horse without any saddle; but finding the motion unendurable, I sprang off.

"Partly supported by my kind conductor, Black Partridge, and partly by another Indian, who held dangling in his hand a scalp which I recognized as that of Captain Wells, I dragged my panting steps to one of the wigwams. The wife of Waw-bee-mee-mah was standing near, and seeing my fainting condition, she seized a kettle, dipped up some water from a stream that flowed near, threw in some maple sugar, and stirring it with her hand, gave me to drink. This act of kindness, in the midst of so many horrors, touched me most sensibly; but my attention was soon diverted to other objects. This work of butchery had commenced just as we were leaving the fort. I can not describe the horrible scene which ensued as the wounded and dying were dragged into camp. An old squaw, infuriated by the loss of friends, or excited by the bloody scenes around her, seemed possessed with a demoniac fury. She seized a stable fork, and assaulted one miserable victim who lay groaning and writhing in the agony of his wounds.

"With a delicacy of feeling scarcely to be expected, Waw-bee-mee-mah stretched a mat across two poles between me and this dreadful scene, although I could still hear the groans of the sufferers. On the following night five more wounded prisoners were tomahawked. Those of the troops who had escaped surrendered, after a loss of about two-thirds of the party. They had stipulated, by means of an interpreter, for the lives of those remaining and those who remained of the women and children, but the wounded were not included. They were to be delivered at some of the British ports, unless ransomed by traders. The Americans, after their first attack, charged upon those who were concealed in a sort of ravine intervening between the sand-banks and the prairie. The Indians gathered themselves into a body, and after some hard fighting, in which the number of whites had been reduced to twenty-eight, this small band succeeded in breaking through the enemy and gaining a rising ground not far from the oak woods."

The contest now seemed hopeless, and Lieutenant Helm sent Perest Leclerc, a half-breed boy in the service of Mr. Kinzie, who had accompanied the detachment and fought manfully, as interpreter, to propose terms of capitulation. It was stipulated that the lives of all the survivors should be spared, and a ransom permitted as soon as practicable. But in the mean time a horrible scene had been enacted. A young savage had climbed into the baggage-wagon containing the children of the whites, twelve in number, and tomahawked the entire group. When Captain Wells saw this he exclaimed, "Is that their game? Then I will kill, too." So saying, he turned his horse's head and started for the Indian camp. Several Indians pursued him, and as he galloped along he laid himself flat on his horse to escape their shots. They took effect, however, at last, killing his horse and severely wounding him. At that moment he was met by a friendly Indian, who tried to save him from the savages, who had now overtaken him. As he was being supported by his friend, he received his death-blow from a savage who stabbed him in the back. Those of the family of Mr. Kinzie who had remained in the boat near the mouth of the river were carefully guarded by the Indians. They had seen the smoke and the blaze, and immediately after the report of the first tremendous discharge.

Some time afterward they saw an Indian coming toward them, leading a horse on which sat Mrs. Heald. "Run," cried Mrs. Kinzie; "that Indian will kill her. Run; take the mule, which is tied to a tree, and offer it to her captor as a ransom for her life." The Indian was by this time in the act of removing her bonnet, that he might scalp her. The servant ran up with the mule, and by that, and the offer of ten bottles of whisky, effected her release. "But," said the Indian, "she is wounded; she will die; will you then give me the whisky." It was promised him. The savage then took Mrs. Heald's bonnet, placing it on his own head, and, after an ineffectual attempt on the part of some squaws to rob her of her stockings, she was brought on board the boat, suffering great agony from the many bullet-wounds she had received. The boat was at length permitted to return to Mr. Kinzie's home, where Mrs. Heald was properly cared for. Mr. Kinzie soon after returned. The family were closely guarded by their Indian friends, whose intention it was to carry them to Detroit for security. The rest of the prisoners remained at the wigwams of their captors.

The next morning, after plundering the fort, the Indians set fire to it. Black Partridge, with several others of his tribe, established themselves in the porch of the building as sentinels, to protect the family. Soon after the fire a party of Wabash Indians made their appearance. They were the most hostile of all the tribes of the Pottawotamies. Being more remote, they had shared less in the kindness of Mr. Kinzie and his family. On arriving at Chicago they had blackened their faces, and they now proceeded toward the dwelling of Mr. Kinzie. From his station on the piazza Black Partridge had watched their approach. His fears were for the safety of Mrs. Helm, Mr. Kinzie's step-daughter. By his advice she was made to assume the dress of a French woman of the country; namely, a short gown and petticoat, with a blue cotton handkerchief wrapped around her head. In this disguise she was conducted by Black Partridge to the house of Ouilmette, a Frenchman, with a half-breed wife, who formed a part of the establishment of Mr. Kinzie, and whose house was close at hand. It happened that the Indians came first to this house in their search for prisoners.

As they approached, the inmates, fearful that the fair complexion of Mrs. Helm might betray her, raised a large feather-bed, and placed her under the edge of it upon the bedstead, with her face to the wall. Mrs. Bisson, the sister of Ouilmette's wife, then seated herself with her sewing on the foreside of the bed. It was a hot day in August, and the feverish excitement of fear, together with her position and wounds, became so intolerable that Mrs. Helm begged to be released and given up to the Indians. "I can but die," said she; "let them put an end to my misery at once." Mrs. Bisson replied, " Your death would be the destruction of us all. Black Partridge has resolved that if one drop of the blood of your family is spilled, he will take the lives of all concerned in it, even his nearest friends; and if the work of slaughter once commences, there will be no end to it, so long as there remains one white person or half-breed in the country." This nerved

Mrs. Helm with fresh resolution. The Indians entered, and she could occasionally see them from her hiding-place gliding about and inspecting every part of the house, till, apparently satisfied that there was no one concealed, they left.

All this time Mrs. Bisson had kept her seat on the side of the bed, calmly sorting and arranging the patchwork of a quilt, and preserving the appearance of the utmost tranquillity, although she knew not but at any moment the tomahawk might aim a fatal blow at herself. Her self-command unquestionably saved the lives of all present. From Ouilmette's the party of Indians proceeded to Mr. Kinzie's. They entered the parlor, in which the family were assembled with their faithful protector, and seated themselves in silence. Black Partridge perceived from their moody and revengeful looks what was passing in their minds; but he dared not remonstrate with them, but observed in a low tone to one of the friendly Indians, "We have endeavored to save your friends, but it is in vain; nothing will save them now."

At this moment a friendly whoop was heard from a party of new-comers on the opposite side of the river. Black Partridge sprang to meet them as their canoes touched the bank near the house. "Who are you?" demanded he. "A man." "Who are you?" "A man like yourself." "But tell me *who* you are?"—meaning, tell me your disposition, and which side you are for. "I am the San-ga-nash," replied the stranger. "Then make all possible speed into the house; your friend is in danger, and you alone can save him." Billy Caldwell—for it was he—a man well known to the tribes for his never-failing help to them in their need—then entered the parlor with a calm step, and without a trace of agitation in his manner. He deliberately took off his accouterments, placed them with his rifle behind the door, and then saluted the hostile savages: "How now, my friends? a good day to you. I was told there were enemies here; but I am glad to find only friends. Why have you blackened your faces? Is it that you are mourning your friends lost in battle?" purposely misunderstanding this token of evil design, "or is it that you are fasting? If so, ask our friend here, and he will give you to eat; he is the Indians' friend, and never yet refused what they had need of."

Thus taken by surprise, the savages were ashamed to acknowledge their bloody purpose. They therefore said, modestly, that they came to beg white cotton of their friends, in which to wrap their dead. This was given them with some other presents, and they took their departure peaceably. On the third day after the battle, the family of Mr. Kinzie, with the clerks of the establishment, were put into a boat under the care of a half-breed interpreter, and conveyed to St. Joseph's, where they remained till the following November under the protection of To-pee-mee-bee's band. They were then conducted to Detroit, under the escort of two of their trusty Indian friends, and delivered up as prisoners of war to Col. M'Kee, the British Indian Agent.

CHAPTER XXIII.

WHENEVER the Indian came among us, my ideas of what should be due unto woman, and my sense of the elevation to which Christianity assigns her, was often greatly shocked by the inhuman manner in which the Indian treats his squaw. She is little better than a beast of burden. It is no' uncommon sight to see the woman laden with mats and the poles, with which the lodge is built, upon her shoulders; her papoose, if she has any; her kettles, sacks of corn, wild rice; and not unfrequently the household dog perched upon the top of all. If there is a horse or pony among the list of domestic possessions, the man rides, while the squaw trudges along with her heavy burdens on foot. It is the instinct of the sex to keep up the idea of their supposed superiority, by asserting it on every and even the slightest occasion. But, for the sake of humanity, we must say of the Indian, that whenever he is out of sight of others, and there is no danger of compromising his own dignity, the husband is willing enough to relieve his wife of some of the heavy burdens which custom imposes on her, by sharing her labors and hardships.

I think the picture is not altogether an unknown

one, in some domestic arrangements of civilized life. Even in their dances, the squaws, who stand a little apart and mingle their discordant voices with the music of the instruments, rarely participate in the dance. Occasionally, however, when excited by the general gayety, a few of them will form a circle outside, and perform a sort of ungraceful up-and-down movement, which has no merit save the perfect time that is kept, and for which the Indians without exception seem to possess a natural gift. The rhythm of nature to which their ears are constantly inclined, has the effect of introducing at least one element of order in these barbaric souls. O, how much civilization owes to the influence of the Bible! how it has exalted man, and woman along with him! What heart can ever express becoming gratitude to God for his inestimable gift of the Bible! In the Christian rites, in the soul's salvation, woman is raised to a level with man; and in and through these has she now her exalted position over that of her sisters of the primeval forest.

I have frequently been asked the cause of the Sauk war, and have been able to answer only from the impressions I received and my own observations, or information furnished at that time. I think it but justice to Black Hawk and his party to insert the following account, preserved among the manuscripts of the late Thomas Forsythe, Esq., of St. Louis, who, after residing among the Indians many years as a trader, was, till the year 1830, the agent of the Sauks and Foxes. The manuscript was written in 1832, while Black Hawk and his compatriots were in prison at Jefferson Barracks. It is an extract from the "Life of Mrs. J. H. Kinzie:"

"The United States troops arrived at St. Louis and took possession of this country in the month of February, 1804. In the Spring of that year a white person was murdered in one of the settlements by a Sauk Indian. Some time in the Summer following the State troops were sent up to the Sauk village, on Rock River, and a demand was made of the Sauk chief for the murderer. The chief delivered him up without hesitation to the commander of the troops, who brought him down and handed him over to the civil authorities at St. Louis.

"During the ensuing Autumn some Sauk and Fox Indians came to St. Louis and had a consultation with General Harrison, Governor of Indiana Territory, on the liberation of their relative, the murderer, then in prison. Quash Quam, a Sauk chief, who was the head man of the party, repeatedly said that 'Mr. Pierre Chowteau, sen., came several times to my camp and told me that Governor Harrison would liberate my relative, the murderer, if I would sell the lands on the east side of the Mississippi River. At last I agreed to sell the land from the mouth of the Illinois River as high up as Rocky River—now Rock River—and east of the ridge that divides the waters of the Mississippi and Illinois Rivers. This was all the land that I sold him on those conditions.' Quash Quam also told the same story to Governor Edwards, Governor Clark, and Mr. Auguste Chowteau, commissioners appointed to treat with the Indian tribes of the Illinois River, in the Summer of 1816, for lands on the west side of this river. Quash Quam said: 'You white men may put what you please on paper, but I tell you again that I never sold any lands higher up the Mississippi River than the mouth of Rocky River.'*

"In the treaty first mentioned the line commences opposite the mouth of the Gasconade River, and runs to the head-waters of Jefferson River,* and thence down to the Mississippi; from thence up the Mississippi River to the mouth of the Ouisconsin River, and up this river thirty-six miles; from this point in a direct line to a little lake in Fox River of the Illinois; down Fox River to Illinois River, and down this latter to its mouth; from that point down the Mississippi to the mouth of the Missouri, and from thence to the place of beginning.† The Foxes and Sauks were never consulted, nor had any knowledge of this treaty—that is, the tribes at large. It was made and signed by two Sauk chiefs, one Fox chief, and one warrior. The annuity to be paid in accordance with treaty was $1,000. This payment was always made in goods sent from Georgetown, D. C. They were poor articles of merchandise, not at all suitable for the Indians,

---

* There is no such stream as Jefferson River.
† See treaty dated at St. Louis, November 4, 1804.

and very often damaged. The Indians received these goods, supposing they were presents made by the Government, and not payments upon land, till I, as their agent, convinced them to the contrary.

"In the Summer of 1818, when the Indians heard that the goods delivered to them were annuities for land sold by them to the United States, they were astonished, and refused to accept the goods, denying that they had ever sold lands as stated by me, their agent. Black Hawk in particular, who was present at this time, made a great noise about this land, and would never receive any part of the annuities from that time forward. He denied the authority of Quash Quam to sell any part of the land, and forbade the Indians receiving any part of the annuities from any American, otherwise their lands would be claimed at some future day. As the United States do insist on retaining lands according to the treaty of November 4, 1804, why do they not fulfill their part of that treaty with the Indians as equity demands? The Sauk and Fox Indians are, according to that treaty, allowed to live and hunt on the lands as long as the aforesaid lands belong to the United States. In the Spring of 1827, about twelve or fifteen families of squatters arrived and took possession of the Sauk village, near the mouth of Rocky River. They immediately commenced destroying the bark boats belonging to the Indians; and when the Indians made complaint at the village of the destruction of their property, they were abused by the squatters.

"When they made complaint to me as their agent, I wrote to Gen. Clark, Superintendent of Indian Affairs, at St. Louis, stating to him, from time to time, what had happened, and giving a minute detail of every thing that passed between the squatters and the Indians. The squatters insisted that the Indians should be removed from their village, saying that as soon as the land was brought into market they would buy it all. It was useless for me to show them the treaty and urge upon them the right that the Indians had to remain upon their land. They tried every method to annoy the Indians, by shooting their dogs, claiming their horses when they break into their poorly protected cornfields, selling them whisky contrary to the wishes and oft-expressed requests of their chiefs, particularly of Black Hawk, who both solicited and threatened them; but all to no purpose.

"When these lands were sold in the Autumn of 1828, there were about twenty families of squatters at and in the vicinity of the old Sauk village, most of whom attended the sale. There was but one family able to purchase a quarter section, unless we except George Davenport, a trader, who lived in Rock Island. To the land remaining unsold the Indians, of course, had still a right by treaty. This right, however, was not allowed, and they were ordered to move off. In 1830 the principal chiefs and others among the Sauk and Fox Indians, informed me that they would move to their village on Iowa River. The chiefs advised me to write to General

Clark at St. Louis, asking him to send up a few of the militia; so that Black Hawk and his followers would see that every thing was in earnest, and would move to the west side of the Mississippi to their own lands. I wrote as advised, but General Clark did not think proper to comply.

"In the Spring of 1831 Black Hawk and his party were joined by many Indians from the Iowa River. Then Gen. Gaines came on with a company of militia and regulars, and compelled them to remove to the west side of the Mississippi. When Black Hawk recrossed the river, in 1832, with a party of Indians, who numbered in all three hundred and sixty-eight, they brought with them all their women and children, showing that they had no intention of making war. Gen. Stillman's detachment, however, saw fit to attack them, and there was nothing left for them but to defend themselves. The war ended in their defeat, and some of the principal Indians were put in chains and in prison at Jefferson Barracks. It is very well known by those acquainted with Black Hawk, that he ever sustained the character of a friend to the whites. Often has he taken into his lodge the wearied white man, given him food to eat and a blanket to sleep on before the fire. Many a good meal has the Prophet given to the traveler passing through his native village. He has recovered the horses of the white man from the Indian, and restored them to their rightful owner without asking compensation.

What right have we to tell any people, you shall not cross the Mississippi or any other boundary? Should the Indian wish to return and revisit the land where once he roamed in freedom, sole possessor of the land, shall we meet him in the deadly array of battle, simply because we have the power?"

In the above extracts many occasional comments upon the ruling powers have been omitted. There is every reason to believe that, had the suggestions of Thomas Forsythe been listened to, the sad record of this unhappy war might never have been, and that of the untimely fate of some of our countrymen, who fell victims to their exasperated fury at Kellogg's Grove, soon after the commencement of the campaign.

CHAPTER XXIV.

In 1833 the last Indian tribe of the Pottawotamies sold all their lands in the north-eastern section of the State to the General Government, and bid a long farewell to the graves of their fathers. This cession being made and the public lands surveyed, the country was settled up in a few years.

The Indian has some noteworthy traits of character, as some of the following anecdotes will show:

Several years since the Sac Indians killed some of the Iowa tribe, and a demand was made for the murderers. By compromise, the demand was reduced to one Sac, and the tribe agreed that the murderer should be given up to death. The Indian on whom this sentence fell was, at the time, too sick to travel. A brother of the sick man volunteered to die in his stead, and marched with the Sac chief to the Iowas, and cheerfully gave himself up to be executed. This noble act of the young Indian, who was so brave and generous as to suffer death in the place of his brother, softened the hearts of the Iowas, and they restored the young Sac with honor to his nation.

In the Fall of the year 1833, Mr. George E. Walker, Sheriff of La Salle county, had, in his official capacity, a singular transaction with a young Pottawotamie. Walker was a backwoods man, a man of great ability, and keen insight into the Indian character. This gave him great influence over the Indians. Two Indians had been concerned in the massacre of the whites in the Black Hawk war the previous year. They had been indicted for murder, and had appeared at the time the circuit court was to be held; but the term of the court was changed, and they were not tried. The Indians, supposing that the whites did not want them any longer, went with the rest of their tribe over to the west side of the Mississippi. Walker and other securities were responsible for the appearance of the prisoners. It was just after the close of the Black Hawk war, and angry feelings existed between the Indians and whites, yet Walker proposed to go alone among the Indians and bring back the prisoners. He went single-handed into the heart of the enemy's country, two or three hundred miles from any settlement, and in the midst of a tribe who were exasperated against the whites.

He called a council of chiefs, and it was agreed that the two young Indians should return with Walker, the chiefs being certain, as well as the young Indians, that they were to be hung. They also felt an extreme dislike to the ignoble manner in which they were to die. To be shot would have been more honorable; but still they went. Walker and the Indians bade a long farewell to the tribe, and started for Ottowa, where the court was to be held. They traveled, camped, and slept together till they came to Rock Island. At that time there were many Indians collected together there on a trading expedition. The prisoners had a strong dislike to being seen under guard, and requested the privilege of going alone through the settlement. Walker, who understood their character and language equally well, readily consented to their request. They said they could die like men, but that they could not endure the dishonor of being led like dogs, under the power of Walker, among the whites and Indians at the Island. They went on alone, and met Walker at the place agreed on, on the opposite side. Walker had with him a horse, whose services he shared in turn with each Indian. Sometimes one of the Indians would ride on ahead and prepare camp for the travelers as they came up. Walker never held out the least inducement to them that they would be acquitted. One night they encamped at an old Sac encampment, by the request of the Indians, where they found good water and groves.

Here Walker was entirely at their mercy. His horse ran away, and one of the Indians went in search of it, traveling ten or twelve miles before he found it, and returned with it to its owner. Indeed, he was in their power for many nights, when they might have killed him and returned to their tribe without again being sought for. For these traits of honor the Government procured able counsel to defend the Indians. Colonel William S. Hamilton was employed, and this gentleman, having great influence with both whites and Indians, the Indians were acquitted, and returned safely to their nation.

Another affair will show how they respected Walker, and how much influence and power he had over them. On Peoria Lake, about seventy miles below Ottowa, a young chief, Senacherine, found an Indian who had murdered another Indian. The chief brought him to Ottowa, and desired Walker to hang him. Senacherine said that Walker was a great man among the Indians, and, should he hang the Indian, it would do more to prevent crime than for his warriors to shoot him. Walker was not at home, and his father met the Indians, was kind and civil to them, and all the time in great anxiety as to how his son would extricate himself from the dilemma in which he would find himself on his return.

On Walker's return, the young chief at once made known his business. Walker agreed to hang the prisoner, but said he was hungry and must have some dinner. While Walker was eating, he gave the young chief and those with him some brandy, and ate very slowly, that he might reflect. Walker was a large trader with the Indians, and, therefore, did not wish to displease the chief. At length, when his meal was finished, the brandy had had the desired effect in making the chief relax somewhat in his desire to have the man hung, as the prisoner himself had killed the other in a drunken frolic, and was totally unconscious of the enormity of his crime. When the chief had become sufficiently mellowed by the brandy, Walker got a rope as if preparing to hang the prisoner, and said, "I will hang the prisoner now, if you desire it; but in a few months, when all the Indians will be at Chicago to receive their annuities, it will be more effectual in preventing crime among your tribe, to hang him in public before all the Indians. However, I will hang him now, if you say so." The chief decided to postpone the hanging, and before the time came the affair was settled among themselves.

Another time, when the Indians were at Chicago to receive their annuities, a drunken Indian who had been on a frolic for several days, and was entirely covered, face and all, with mud and dirt, came up to Walker and desired to kiss him. Walker replied that it was Sunday—a holiday with the Americans; but that if he would come to-morrow, he might then kiss him. But the Indian became sober and forgot the matter.

Once, on a steamboat on the Illinois River, a young clergyman from one of the Eastern colleges, being very desirous of getting information concerning the Indian character and peculiarities, Walker was pointed out to him by some wag as a half-breed who could give him all the information he wished. Walker's appearance favored the joke, as he had a dark complexion and exceedingly black eyes, and also spoke the Indian language fluently. Walker gave the clergyman all the information he desired, and the young man finished his questions by asking Walker about his Indian parentage. Walker carried out the joke without explaining, and the whole conversation was published in one of the Eastern papers as information coming from a half-breed.

CHAPTER XXV.

The origin of the name Chicago has been much discussed. Some of the Indians are said to derive it from the name of the fitch, or polecat; others from that of the wild onion, with which the woods formerly abounded. All agree that the place was named after an old chief who was drowned in the stream bearing his name. This event must have been very remote. An old French manuscript brought by General Cass from France, purporting to be a letter from M. de Ligney, at Green Bay, to M. de Siette, among the Illinois, bearing date 1726, designates the place as "Chicaugoux." This orthography is also found in old family letters written at the beginning of the present century. In giving the history of the place the Indians are reported as saying that the first white man who settled here was a negro.

In an early day, when General Cass was appointed Governor of Michigan Territory, he made a visit, with his family, to Chicago. Public houses were then scarce on the Lake Shore. As a gentleman informs me, the Governor called at a Frenchman's of the name of Byee, and inquired if they could get dinner and have his horse fed. The Frenchman replied in the affirmative. The Governor sat for some time looking at the landlord, waiting for an invitation to dismount, and the landlord, in like manner, looked silently at him. At length the guest said, "I suppose you do not know who I am." The Frenchman said he did not. "Well," said he, "I am Governor of Michigan." "O, be sure; we are all governors here. There is the stable, and there is the crib; just go and help yourself." The Governor did as he was bid. After dinner he did likewise; and went on his way rejoicing, having learned that there were more governors in the country besides himself.

Among the landmarks of Chicago is Mr. Peck's building, which stands on the south-east corner of La Salle and South Water streets. It was finished and occupied by him in 1833, being built of oak and black walnut lumber, which were hauled from Walker's mills—now Plainfield—forty miles southwest from Chicago. He bought his lot of W. F. Walker for $80, now—1855—valued at $42,500, and the largest part of it sold. In 1831 the story goes that gamblers would stake a quart of brandy against some Chicago lot near the court-house, and the brandy was esteemed the greater loss of the two. The best lots on Lake-street sold for from $30 to $100. On the 26th of November of this year the first newspaper was published in Chicago by John Calhoun. On the first of October, 1835, Colonel Russell started with two hundred ox teams to move the baggage with the last of the Indians, about 1,500 in all. It took forty days to reach their destination west of the Missouri. It is less than forty years since Chicago was surrounded by Pottawotamies. The first census of Chicago was taken in 1837— whites, 4,099; colored, 71: total, 4,170. The Illinois and Michigan canal was begun in 1836, ground being broken at Bridgeport on the fourth of July. The Legislature of that year appropriated a half million of dollars for its construction. There was not, in 1831, a canal, railroad, or plank road leading out of the city. Three years previously there was but one mail from the East each week, and that was brought from Niles on horseback.

Mrs. Kinzie relates how once, upon Sunday, they rowed up to the point to attend service conducted by Rev. Mr. See, or father See, as he was more familiarly called. I knew him well, and as a good preacher, and if he "got into the brush," as the pioneers used to say when one was at a loss how to go on in his sermon, it was no more than others did who made pretensions to greater advantages when trying to preach without a manuscript, and at last did not get the brush cleared away, after all, as well as did father See. Indeed, I have often thought of the story of one of the "regular succession," who, while preaching, suddenly discovered that "thirdly" had been blown out of the window, by means of which he lost the thread of his ideas, and came to a full stop.

Father See, a blacksmith by trade, was poor, but he was one of the "Lord's poor." If his hands were dingy, what else could be expected? It showed that he was willing to labor six days in the week for his own sustenance, and give God the fruits of his heartiest labors on the Sabbath, expecting nothing again, and that he thought more of the salvation of souls than of personal display. Mrs. Kinzie says:

"We saw a tall, slender man dressed in a green frock coat, from the sleeves of which dangled a pair of hands giving abundant evidence, together with the rest of his dress, that he placed small faith in the axiom, 'Cleanliness is next to godliness.' He stepped briskly upon the platform, behind a table, and commenced his discourse. His subject was 'The fear of God.' There was a kind of fear, he told us, that was nearly akin to love—so near that it was not worth while splitting hairs for the difference. He then went on to describe this kind of fear. He grew more and more involved as he proceeded with his description, till at length, quite bewildered, he paused and exclaimed, 'Come, let us stop a little while and clear away the brush.' He unraveled, as well as he was able, the tangled thread of his ideas, and went on with his subject. But soon again he lost his way, and came a second time to a halt. 'Now,' said he, at the same time wiping the perspiration from his forehead with a red cotton handkerchief which was many degrees from clean, 'now suppose we draw back a little piece.' Then he recapitulated what he wished to impress upon us of the necessity of cherishing a fear that was unto salvation, 'which fear,' said he, 'may we all enjoy, that together we may soar away on the rolling clouds of ether to a boundless and happy eternity, which is the wish of your humble servant,' and flourishing abroad his hands with an indescribable gesture, he took his seat. It will be readily imagined that we felt our own religious exercises at home to be more edifying than this, and that we confined ourselves to them thereafter." Mrs. Kinzie again speaks of him in another part of her book, and says: "There was also a Mr. See, lately come into the country, living at the point, who sometimes held forth in the little school-house on Sunday, less to the edification of his hearers than to the unmerciful slaughter of the 'King's English,'" to which I can add that I thank God he slaughtered sin also, and this is saying much more for him than can be said in justice of some who are wiser in their own conceit than was he.

The following is extracted from a letter of Rev. Isaac Scarrit, to whom reference is elsewhere made: "On reading the 'Rise and Progress of Methodism in Chicago,' by Grant Goodrich, Esq., I feel somewhat inclined to form a kind of appendix to that narrative by giving some reminiscence of my own. In 1828 I succeeded Rev. Jesse Walker as superintendent of the Fox River mission. At that time James Walker was living where Ottawa now stands; Pierce Hawley, Edmund Weed, and J. Beresford lived at what was afterward called Holderman's

Grove. These, with my own family at the mission, constituted the whole of the American population on the north-west side of the Illinois River, and between that and Chicago. The whole region, except a strip along the river, was Indian country. While here I planned a trip to Chicago, distant some seventy or eighty miles, and about midsummer, with George Furkee, a half-breed Indian who resided at the mission, for my guide, I set out on my adventure.

"The first night we lodged at an Indian village near to where Plainfield now stands. The next evening we entered Chicago, which, in addition to the buildings constituting Fort Dearborn, contained the old Kinzie house, a new house of Colonel Hamilton's, with, perhaps, one or two others in that quarter, and those of J. Kinzie and J. Miller up at 'the point.' The latter two gentlemen seemed to be upon a strife with each other which should excel in honor and popularity whereby to promote their individual interests. I took up my residence at Miller's, who, with laudable generosity, undertook to administer to my comfort and further my views. The next day was the Sabbath, and I sent word to Lieutenant ———, that if it were his wish the superintendent of the Indian mission would preach to the soldiers and others at such place and hour as he might appoint. Answer was returned that he should not *forbid* the preaching, but that he should neither authorize nor make any arrangements for it. Not to be outdone by the honorable lieutenant on the point of independence, I declined going to the garrison under such circumstances, and made an appointment for preaching at Miller's at night. Most of the citizens and some of the soldiers were present, and gave respectful attention; but in the matter of congregation we received rather more than we bargained for. During religious service a gang of boatmen, with their vociferous yo-he's, commenced landing and rolling up barrels, etc., near to the door. This was a trick of Kinzie's, so Miller said, out of spite to him for having the honor of entertaining the missionary, and for the agency he took in promoting the religion of the place. Some murmurs were uttered on the desecration of the Sabbath, and of disturbing a congregation in the quiet performance of religious worship, and what redress the laws of the land provided; but it was finally concluded that the laws did allow ships' and boats' crews to land their cargoes on the Sabbath, and so the good people, after having manifested to the missionary a laudable regard for the sacredness of the Sabbath and the rights of religious worship, let the subject pass without further ado, and retired satisfied, no doubt, with the respect they had shown so rare a personage as a preacher of the Gospel.

"I can not say that this was the first sermon, or even the first *Methodist sermon*, that was ever preached in Chicago, but I may say that there were neither intimations or indications of its ever having been preceded; the whole movement, from first to last, bore the appearance of a new measure in that place.

"But, whatever numerical rank that sermon may claim, there is one consideration that renders it a subject of serious reflection to me. In years long gone by I had read of the massacre at Chicago, a place somewhere upon this mundane sphere, but upon what locality of our earth I was altogether ignorant. My impression was that it was somewhere among the antipodes, but a deep feeling of sympathy for the slaughtered victims took possession of my mind. Could any thing short of Omniscience, then, have divined that the same sympathizing, ignorant individual would one day stand on the very ground, and to some of the identical persons connected with the scenes of that fearful day should proclaim the message of 'Peace on earth and goodwill to men.' But so it was, and such has ever been the dealing of God toward me. He has led me in paths I had not known, and I trust he will still lead me, and bring me unto his heavenly kingdom."

I might here throw in the weight of my testimony as to whether this sermon of Rev. J. Scarritt's on his first visit to Chicago was in reality the first Methodist sermon ever preached there. Rev. Jesse Walker, and also Mrs. John Hamline, of Peoria, told me that in the Spring of 1826 father Walker went up on his boat from Peoria to Chicago. He had all the hands on board cease work till they could attend prayers, and all joined in singing, and then a fervent prayer was offered up in their behalf, asking the merciful protection of a Divine Providence throughout the day. I have no recollection that either of them told me that he preached during his stay in Chicago; but, if he did not, I presume it was the first time he ever went to a strange place, remaining as long as he did at Chicago, without preaching; and, as that was his errand up there, I have little doubt that he improved the opportunity he sought. He was at Chicago during his stay at Fox River mission, and if any chance offered he would not hesitate to improve it.

CHAPTER XXVI.

The present chapter is devoted to the publishing interests of the Methodist Episcopal Church, and is taken from an article written by Rev. E. H. Waring, and published in the North-Western Christian Advocate:

"In the providence of God the proclamation of the 'glad tidings' was accomplished for many centuries solely by the tongue and the pen. But when the Reformation was about to unchain the Word and send it forth untrammeled by Popish restraints, God added to these original agencies the mighty agency of the press, which was consecrated to Christianity by being first employed to print the Holy Scriptures in the language of the people. This invention has given a great impulse to the spread of knowledge, for it secures the rapid multiplication of books at rates of cost which place them within reach of all classes of the population.

"Wesley, distinguished for his practical sense, availed himself extensively of this means of disseminating his teachings, and for some length of time his press supplied the Methodists of England and America with Methodist literature.

"At length Providence opened the way for the establishment of a Methodist publishing house in the

United States. The business was commenced under the superintendence of Rev. John Dickins, in Philadelphia, in 1789. The capital of the infant 'Concern' amounted to only six hundred dollars, which was borrowed from the 'book steward' himself. The first book printed was Thomas a Kempis's 'Imitation of Christ,' followed shortly by the 'Arminian Magazine,' the Hymn-Book, the Discipline, the 'Saint's Rest,' and 'Primitive Physic.' Mr. Dickins continued to manage the business, with great fidelity and prudence, till 1798, when he died. He united in himself the offices of pastor, book steward, editor, and clerk.

"We can not, for want of space and information, enumerate all the changes which have occurred in the management and progress of the business during the seventy-four years of its existence. In 1804 the establishment was removed to New York, which city possessed the greatest facilities for the successful prosecution of the business. In 1808 the agents were released from pastoral duty, and were required to occupy themselves entirely with the duties of their office. Up to 1822 all the printing and binding was done by the job, in private establishments in the city. In that year a bindery was established in a building rented for the purpose, in Crosby-street, and the building referred to was purchased and a printing office set in it in September, 1824. This building, with additions made from time to time, being insufficient to accommodate the growing business, the present site on Mulberry-street was purchased in 1832, and new buildings were erected for the Concern, into which it was removed in September, 1833. These buildings, with an immense amount of stock and material, were destroyed by fire in February, 1836, involving a loss of $250,000. To replace the Concern and renew the business $88,346.09 was received in subscriptions and collections made throughout the Church, and $25,000 from insurance. With these means the agents proceeded to erect the buildings which are still occupied by the Concern, and the business went forward once more.

"The Concern at Cincinnati was established in 1820, under the direction of the late lamented Martin Ruter, who continued in its management till 1832.

"It is to be regretted that full information respecting the progress of the publishing business of the Church is not within general reach. The exhibits of the agents have not been published with the papers of the General Conference, excepting those presented at the last two sessions, and we can not find any satisfactory account of the early history of the Western Book Concern. Whoever will gather all the available information respecting our publishing interests, East and West, and publish it for the benefit of the public, will do a good service to the Church.

"Respecting the early history of the General Book Concern at New York, Ezekiel Cooper, who succeeded

Mr. Dickins in the agency, and managed the business from 1798 to 1808, in his letter of resignation to the General Conference of 1808 says that the total assets of the Concern in 1799 were only $4,000, and the net capital only $1,000; but at the close of his term he reported the aggregate capital to be $45,000. The following exhibit shows the state of the Concern at the periods specified:

	Aggregate Capital.	Net Capital.
1789	$600 00	
1799	4,000 00	$1,000 00
1808	45,000 00	
1816	147,133 99	80,000 00
1824	270,002 28	221,459 78
1832	448,745 70	413,566 93
1845	645,879 46	641,283 32
1856	738,977 36	568,272 65
1860	714,963 63	540,721 80
1863	526,650 02	496,968 14
1867	645,324 14	590,571 70

"The reduction in the capital at New York since 1856 has resulted, as we understand, from the heavy payments made to the Church South, and the sale of old stock at reduced values, rather than from any real falling off in the business of the Concern.

"Respecting the early condition of the Western Book Concern I have no information. The agents reported in 1856 that if it had not been for the reduction of their assets by the dividends paid to the Church South, and by other payments, they would have had at that time a net capital of $250,816.62. Their report for that year was:

	Aggregate Capital.	Net Capital.
1856	$234,026 84	$150,405 74
1863	329,398 10	263,112 24
1867	571,989 32	460,374 47

"According to the above showing the aggregate capital of the two Concerns amounted, January, 1868, to $1,217,813.46, and the net capital to $1,050,946.17.

"The reports show that the sales of books and periodicals have amounted, during the quadrennial terms specified, to the following amounts:

	New York Book Concern.	Western Book Concern.
1844—1848	$487,222 04	$125,413 65
1848—1852	653,190 78	200,829 53
1852—1856	1,000,734 18	649,840 73
1856—1860	1,175,867 29	1,127,851 00
Total since 1844	$3,317,014 29	$2,203,932 91

Total Sales of both Concerns from 1844 to 1860..$5,520,947 20

"The above showings are significant as exhibiting, first, the steady growth of the business as a whole, and, second, its large proportionate increase in the West. A few years more at the same rate of progress and the old New York Book Concern will have to yield the palm to her enterprising daughter of the West. So mote it be."

CHAPTER XXVII.

The first Baptist Church in Plainfield was organized in October, 1834. A list of the persons forming the Church, and officers, is here given: Rev. Joshua E. Ambrose, Moderator; members—Leonard Morse, Elizabeth Morse, Rebecca Carmon, Thomas Rickey, (elected Clerk,) Jane Rickey, Alfred B. Hubbard. The first church edifice was built in 1836. Elder and deacon Ashley came to this place in 1837. The new church, which was built in 1857 and dedicated in 1858, cost $4,100. The membership was one hundred and twenty-five. There was a defect in the Church management in supplying the pulpit, which prevented a greater prosperity. When the Church became dissatisfied with their preacher, or the preacher sought for a more congenial place of usefulness, this Church would be without a preacher sometimes for several months, and they were obliged to depend on a preacher from some other denomination—some transient•one—or do without any; and our Congregational brethren were oftentimes submitted to a like inconvenience.

The pulpit of the Methodist Episcopal Church has always been continually supplied, so that there was no break or want of a preacher to promulgate our doctrine of a full and a free salvation. This, together with our excellent Church government, and a membership that are to be co-workers together with God, has greatly contributed to the building up of the Methodist Episcopal Church in Plainfield, so that it almost doubles every other denomination at the present time.

A few months since a Baptist deacon from Joliet inquired of me how the Baptist cause was prospering in Plainfield. I replied that I did not know exactly, but that I had understood they were without a preacher, and, of course, they could not expect to flourish under such circumstances. After speaking rather despondingly of their want of zeal and derangement, he abruptly changed the subject, and asked how the Methodists were prospering with their new stone church. I replied that they had got the main building up so that it would soon be ready for the roof. He paused for a moment, and then said, in a very emphatic way, "What the Methodists can not do no one else needs try."

I think that there are but few places of the same age and population in the State that have had so many powerful conversions as Plainfield. Some have gone home to heaven, many have gone widely astray, yet on our Church records are now two hundred and fifty names. In 1820 the Methodists of America were 13,000 less in the number of communicants than its elder sister, the Baptist Church, which dates its American origin a hundred and twenty-five years earlier than ours. Ten years later the

Methodists were nearly one hundred thousand in advance of them. Great as that success appears, it is small compared with the statistics of the Centenary jubilee in 1866, when the Church numbered a full million of communicants, and her congregations a little less than four millions.

The Church is now divided into several bands, yet all identical, save in some points of Church government. Our design is to reach all of our population, from the northernmost inhabitant of Canada to the Gulf of Mexico, and from the Atlantic to the Pacific, and thence, by missionary effort, to plant the standard of the Cross and the liberty of the Gospel, as Methodism interprets it, to the uttermost verge of our green earth. These different bands of the Church number now about two million communicants. We probably owe the success of the Church, in a great measure, to its Arminian doctrines of regeneration, the witness of the Spirit, and sanctification, together with its systematic organization of a Church government, so perfectly adapted to the wants of a ruined world; and, above all, added to this is the blessing of God which we so earnestly seek to have bestowed upon all our labors. In no other sense can we accept the saying of the Baptist deacon, "What the Methodist Episcopal Church can not do no one else needs try."

In the growth of our village, as with all other Western towns, there came a time when the temperance cause needed greatly to be agitated. So a time was fixed upon, about the year 1833-34, I think. Our circuit preacher was William Cravens, and Samuel Hamilton our presiding elder. It was decided that there should be a pitched battle against whisky. The habit of using it in the harvest field and in all places of public gathering had become so prevalent that many of our members had been led off by its baneful influence. So it was resolved that at a certain quarterly meeting in the region of the Wabash William Cravens was to begin the attack, and Rev. S. Hamilton was to follow. William Cravens was not easily beaten in his strong arguments against the use of intoxicating drinks, and always went in for the teetotal system. When it came the turn for the presiding elder to speak the ground had been so well covered by the first speaker, and so well-toned and convincing were all his arguments that there seemed but little left for him to say, yet his happy and masterly descriptive powers were such that he soon held the attention of the congregation while he portrayed the drunkard's god and its worshipers. He said the god dwelt a long way up in a great hollow, with a bald head, and a long, crooked nose, and its worshipers' would come and sacrifice their corn, their rye, and their barley, and by and by would come and drink down of his spirits, and become so lost that their hats would fly in the air, and they would shout like devils. The faithful, fearless, unflinching testimony that the preachers gave that day could not but have a salutary effect.

But—to come from this to personal matters—I also had it to contend with, though not in quite so dignified a way. In an early day I rented my farm to a Mr. B., and was obliged, for a time, to reside in the same house with him. I was, of course, necessarily away from home a great deal while traveling on my circuit. Mr. B. had hands at work for him who loved a dram as well as himself. It was very annoying to the women, both Mrs. B. and my wife, that during my absence the jug of whisky was kept in the house and handed round freely before them. Immediately on my return it was concealed in the barn, and our tenant would become suddenly quite religious in his talk and professions. The women resolved to put a stop to this, and, taking their own way, recourse was had to a large dose of salts. Mrs. B. hesitated, but Mrs. Beggs, who had faced the dangers of Indian warfare, told Mrs. B. that the responsibility might rest on her shoulders. So one day just before the men came in at noon for their regular dram a large dose of salts was put into the jug. It had the desired effect, and the jug was removed to the barn for the remainder of our stay.

The new stone church in Plainfield was commenced in 1867, and completed the next year. It cost about $14,000. It was a great undertaking for Plainfield, but, all lending a helping hand, it came to a completion. The building committee were John Sheffler, E. I. Wood, and E. M'Closky. John Sheffler was superintendent. He paid more than any two of us, besides the use of his team and hired man. It is a beautiful church, fifty-two feet by seventy, the tower and spire together one hundred and twenty feet high. It is handsomely and tastefully finished off, with a singers' gallery, large enough for twelve or fifteen persons, in the rear of the pulpit. In the basement we have three class-rooms, besides a convenient lecture-room, with its door entering through the tower. There have been partly or wholly built this Summer, three or four other churches—the Baptist, Congregational, Evangelical, and Universalist. I think I am safe in saying that there are more persons in Plainfield, in proportion to its inhabitants, who come out on the Sabbath than in any other town in the State. As to the Evangelical Church in Plainfield, it now ranks second in the number of members in this place. The first class was formed by Rev. George H. Blank, and Simon Tolies presiding elder, Peter Burket class-leader. There were twenty-nine members, one local preacher—George Motuger—and one exhorter—J. Dillman. They have been favored with a number of revivals, and many powerful conversions. They have, perhaps, never had a more powerful revival and general ingathering than when under the two years' pastoral and ministerial care of Rev. Daniel D. Byers. They now number one hundred and fifty members. They have a good church and bell. It was commenced in 1854, and finished and dedicated the next year. This denomination has here located its college, and it has been in successful operation, with President Smith at its head, and an able faculty to assist him.

The following notice of the life and death of my wife, Elizabeth L. Beggs, is from the pen of Rev. W. F. Stewart:

"She was born in Muskingum county, Ohio, December 27, 1813, and died in Plainfield, Ill., August 7, 1866. She was the daughter of William and Susan Heath; was converted, and joined the Methodist Episcopal Church in Zanesville, Ohio, under the labors of Rev. Joseph Carper, in the year 1827. In the year 1830 she removed, with her parents, to the vicinity of Washington, in Tazewell county, Ill. In the year 1831 she was married to Rev. S. R. Beggs. To marry a Methodist traveling preacher, in that day, in Illinois, gave but little promise of ease or temporal comfort. True, their first appointment after marriage was to the 'eye of the North-West,' the embryo city of Chicago. But Chicago was a frontier mission station, from which the wild Indian had hardly taken his departure. There was no richly endowed Church corporation on Clark-street, or any wealthy membership to welcome and support the preacher and his family. They, however, endured hardness as good soldiers, did the work of evangelists, and had the honor of making to the next session of the Illinois Conference the first return of members from Chicago. For years they did emphatically pioneer work, and, when there was no prospect of support from the Church, sister Beggs would say to her husband, 'Go and preach, and I will manage to provide for the children.' With excellent talent for domestic economy, and great energy and perseverance, she always managed to keep the wolf from the door, and to extend hospitality to the itinerant and the emigrant who might call upon them. By the blessing of God, in after years, when they were compelled to retire from the regular work, they had a very comfortable home at Plainfield. Here, resting from their labors, they rejoiced to watch the growth and prosperity of the Church which they had assisted to plant.

"For a year previous to her death, as sister Beggs approached the confines of the other world, she showed how calmly and cheerfully a Christian can march forward to meet the last enemy. She made all her arrangements, temporal and spiritual, and when, at last, the summons came, she fell asleep in Jesus without a struggle or a groan. A large concourse of friends and neighbors followed her remains to the grave, weeping on account of their loss, but inspired with the hope of meeting her again in the resurrection of the just."

CHAPTER XXVIII.

A SHORT sketch of Methodism in Lockport, Ill., may not come amiss in this work. Lockport was laid out in 1830, and a sale of lots in the Fall of 1837 paved the way for the settlement of the town. In 1838 William Crissey was appointed to the Joliet circuit, at the Illinois Conference, with John Clark presiding elder. This circuit embraced Lockport. In the Winter of 1838 William Crissey formed the first class, consisting of the following members: Brother G. L. Works, class-leader, and wife, D. Breesee and wife, M. Brooks, R. Lowrie, Polly M'Millen, Dira Manning, A. Heath, and Julia Reed, with some others not known. Brother S. Vandecar was second class-leader. In the Spring of 1842 Colonel Joel Manning joined on probation, and was appointed class-leader, and continued in this office for nearly fifteen years. It is due to his labors, together with the aid of Dr. Wicks and other brethren, that Methodism lives and now numbers more than any other denomination in Lockport. In 1839 William Crissey and A. Chenoweth, with S. R. Beggs, supernumerary for the Lockport district. In Ottowa district, John Sinclair presiding elder, a good year, with a number of conversions. In 1840 W. Wigley. This year Rock River Conference was formed, and Lockport was left in Joliet circuit. In 1841 W. Wigley; he left, however, before the year closed, and brother Bachelor was supplied. In 1842, Joliet circuit, E. Springer. In 1843 S. R. Beggs, Levi Jenks, and James Leckenby. In 1844 brother Minord, and S. Stocking presiding elder. In 1845 O. H. Walker and E. R. Thomas. In 1846 O. H. Walker and brother Ellis. In 1847 John Nason. In 1848 O. A. Munger. In 1849 L. F. Dering, and the same in 1850. In 1851 A. L. Adams. In 1852 brother Stockdale, and Lockport was made a station. In 1853 brother Roe. In 1854 O. H. Walker and M. Read, Plainfield and Lockport being united. In 1855 M. Read. In 1856 brother Wright. In 1857 brother Williams. In 1858–59 brother Baume. In 1861 S. Davidson. In 1852 B. T. Stover. In 1863 J. Vincent. In 1864–65 J. Lineberger. In 1866–67 J. L. Harris. In 1868 W. H. Fisher.

In the year 1854–55, during M. Read's administration, the Lockport church was commenced and finished at a cost of about $7,000, which, perhaps, all things considered, no other minister in the Conference could have done. When all other resources failed, he pressed some of the most able brethren to the utmost of their ability, as he seemed determined to complete the church before he left the station. The church has proved one of the greatest blessings to the membership, and, no doubt, will continue to do so to generations yet unborn. A second parsonage was also built in 1867, costing about $3,000, on a beautiful lot opposite the church, well arranged and well finished, with the preacher and his family settled in it. The cost of this, as well as of the church, fell on a few of the more wealthy members. The Methodists are now the leading denomination of Lockport.

On Tazewell circuit, in 1830, it took four weeks to make the round. Peter Cartwright was presiding elder. The first quarterly meeting was held at George Hand's, December 17th. The brethren present were Jesse Frankebarger, Thomas Savery—local preachers—and myself. The exhorters were William Goodhart and John Dixon, stewards, and George Hand. The usual questions being asked and answered, at last came that, "What has been collected for quarterage?" The answer, eleven dollars; traveling expenses, one dollar. The second quarterly meeting was held at Eads' school-house, March 19, 1831. The following brethren were present: S. R. Beggs, preacher in charge; exhorter, William Heath; steward, John Johnston; class-leaders, William Eads, R. Wixam. Quarterage received, sixteen dollars and ten cents.

The third quarterly meeting was held at Dillen's settlement, and a camp meeting was also held on June 15, 1831. Members present: Peter Cartwright, presiding elder; S. R. Beggs, preacher in charge; William Brown, local preacher; stewards, Gideon Holly, John Johnston, Thomas Snell, Abner

Carpenter, R. Wixam, and James Latty. Quarterage, nine dollars and seventy-five cents; traveling expenses, fifty cents for Peter Cartwright, and one dollar and thirty-three and one-third cents for S. R. Beggs. The fourth quarterly meeting, and also a camp meeting, were held at Randolph's Grove, on the 10th of September, 1831. Preachers, Peter Cartwright and S. R. Beggs. The following brethren were examined and approved: Jesse Frankebarger, T. Savery, William Brown, Gabriel Watt, Thomas Davis, C. M'Cord, S. Stringfield, and J. Lathy. Exhorters: William Goodhart, John Dixon, William Heath, Robert Coper, Dudley Richards, and David Trimmer. The stewards were John Johnston, John Dixon, William Heath, George Hand, William Hodge, and William Eads. Gideon Holly, recording steward; James Lathy, secretary. After all, expenses deducted, there was left for me as quarterage fifty-five dollars and sixteen cents.

On the Tazewell circuit, in 1831, there was no church, nor towns, save Peoria and Pekin. There were four American families in the former, and six in the latter, and a membership of two hundred and fifty-two in all its boundaries. Look now at the cities and towns, its population and institutions of learning, its internal improvements, the number of preachers and presiding elders, its churches and comfortable parsonages, its thousands of membership, and their multiplied conversions annually.

The first class and first quarterly meeting in

South Ottowa was formed and held by myself. In 1833 I formed the class, and in the Winter of 1834 we held our first quarterly meeting at sister Pembrook's, John Sinclair presiding elder. The brethren and sisters from a distance came in—sister Pitzer from about eight miles up Fox River, and brother Olmstead nearly the same distance up the Illinois River. They were strangers, having but just moved into the country. I have given a particular account of this meeting elsewhere.

At our Conference in Rockford, in 1849, where Bishop Janes presided, business was dispatched with great rapidity, and very much to the satisfaction of the Conference. When the time came for fixing a place to hold the next Conference, several preachers claimed that their stations had the preference. James Stoten presented Plainfield as being the most desirable. To this it was objected that it would not be possible to accommodate all the preachers. This, of course, called forth a short speech from myself. I said that all those whom the brethren and friends could not entertain could find accommodations at the hotels, there being two excellent ones in the place, and I would foot the bills myself. As the result, when the vote was put Plainfield was fixed upon, July 17, 1850.

The time soon rolled round, and our little village witnessed its first Conference. The weather was extremely warm, and Bishop Hamline, who presided, felt its effects very much in his feeble state of health.

Still he labored unremittingly, and preached a powerful sermon on the Sabbath, which came near prostrating him. Our love-feast, as usual, was appointed at nine o'clock on Sabbath morning. All wished to enjoy it, and the consequence was that the church was very much crowded, and when it was time for love-feast to commence the Bishop asked the pastor if our rules had been obeyed in admitting persons into love-feast that morning. He said they had not. The Bishop then said, "I can not consent to relate my experience before this mixed assemblage, and we will change it into a social meeting of singing and prayer." During this Conference I boarded ten preachers, and one day while at dinner one of the brethren wondered why it was that I succeeded in gaining so much more of this world's goods than the rest of the preachers. Brother R. Haney said, "I can tell you. While you are roasting your shins around the fire he has been at work." At that time brother L. Swormstedt was Book Agent, and not finding a suitable room for settling up his periodical accounts, he inquired after that man who had promised at the Rockford Conference to furnish suitable accommodations or foot the bill. As I had a small account to settle with him, I made my way up, and told him my errand, and gave him my name. He looked astonished, and asked if I was the man who was to foot the bill. I told him that I was, and he replied, "When I heard of you down in Cincinnati, and of your promise, I took you to be some old Revolutionary soldier." I said no, but that I had been in the Black Hawk War, and that my house had been made a fort where fifty men were stationed.

It was at this Conference that we resolved to remove the remains of Jesse Walker from their obscure resting-place, one mile south of our cemetery. I think it was in the Fall of 1834 that I performed the marriage ceremony which united him to his second wife. He had then served two years in the Chicago mission station, after which he sustained a superannuated relation, and settled on a small farm about twelve miles west of Chicago, on the Desplaines River, and there he remained till he changed the cross for the crown, and earth for heaven, on the 5th of October, 1835. He was buried in Plainfield, and there rested till his sons in the Gospel resolved to remove his remains to their present resting-place. When the hour arrived for the interment the Conference adjourned, and marched in solemn procession to the grave. The remains of his first wife had also been disinterred, and brought to be buried with him. In one large coffin the bones were placed, and laid as nearly in their natural order as possible.

It was a season of great solemnity, both to our village and to the members of Conference. It had been arranged that there should be several speakers to bear testimony to the zeal of this untiring servant in the work of the Lord before the coffin was concealed forever from our sight. As I had known him personally longer than any other one present, I was to lead in the remarks. After singing and prayer, I proceeded to give a concise history of his arrival in this State as missionary, in the Fall of 1805, his extensive and different fields of labor, and especially our labors in the Central and Rock River Conferences. When I recounted our labors and sufferings in this new and uncultivated region together in the Lord's vineyard, my heart was too full for utterance, and I closed by adding, "For all this I shall be well rewarded if, at last, I can lie down by his side in this beautiful resting-place of the dead." Rev. J. Scarritt, who followed, was very happy in his remarks in portraying the untiring labors, great usefulness, and happy death of this unexcelled missionary. There were several others who made a few remarks, and upon our memories were forever engraved the solemnities of the occasion. The Conference proceeded forthwith to raise a subscription, that a suitable headstone might be placed to mark his sainted grave. I was appointed as a committee to procure it, and have made mention of it elsewhere.

In 1831, or near this time, there was a call made for missionaries to go to Oregon, among the Flatheads. By some means this tribe heard that the white man toward the setting sun had a big book that told all about the Great Spirit, and their anxiety to hear of him was so great that they called a council, and dispatched a delegation of six Indians to travel east till they came to the white man's wigwam, that they might know what the book taught concerning the Great Spirit. As General Clarke, of St. Louis, was well known among them, they went to him as the one most likely to give them reliable information. When he learned their errand he gave them a Bible, and explained to them the white man's beliefs of the creation, fall, and restoration through Christ—that we, through him, might, upon the conditions of repentance and faith, be fit to enter heaven. Getting what further information they could, they started back to publish the glad news of salvation to their brethren, and what they had learned of the Great Spirit. It was reported that but few of them ever reached their home; most of them fell in the wilderness before they had the happiness of pointing their friends to the Lamb of God, who taketh away the sins of the world.

Their solicitations for missionaries were so urgent that Bangs and Fisk advocated their new claim upon the civilized world, through the columns of the Advocate, with great earnestness and ability, till there came up an enthusiastic response to the call. Jason and Daniel Lee and Cyrus Shepherd were sent out as missionaries to this new field of labor. Bangs says that this had a most happy effect upon the missionary cause generally. Heretofore the entire fund raised for that purpose had not exceeded eighteen hundred dollars a year. The Macedonian cry was responded to throughout the entire Church by doubling the amount raised the year of their departure. The mission formed by these men, Stevens says, has since become the nucleus of Christianity and civilization of the new and important State which has since arisen on the north Pacific coast.

In the Fall of 1838, when our Conference was in session at Alton, in the midst of business, Jason Lee stepped into the Conference room, after seven years of absence. His long exposure to sun and rain, camping out nights, besides afflictions in the loss of his dear companion—a wife and mother—all pressing and wearing upon him amid his untiring labors, were as so many chapters of untold suffering; and yet, in his countenance, there was a heavenly resignation, and a mute expression which seemed to say, "Not my will, but thine be done." Our astonishment was increased when he introduced as his traveling companions two or three of the natives from the tribe of the Flathead Indians. It was very curious to see these Indians, with their heads perfectly flat from the nose upward to the crown, tapering all the way. I suppose that at the present time this practice of wearing a board while quite young in order to bring the head to this peculiar shape is very well known, yet it would, no doubt, surprise us now to see suddenly coming into a large audience these singular children of the forest. They had made considerable progress in learning, and had beautiful voices for singing, and sang several Methodist hymns in their own language. Some of them professed religion, and were members of the Church. Mr. Lee's design in bringing them here was to educate them and send them back as missionaries to Oregon.

The foregoing is the most reliable information that I could get respecting the Oregon mission. I presume the sermon that General Clarke preached to the Flatheads was the first and the last orthodox sermon he ever preached. He died in St. Louis, on the 1st of September, 1838. He had been Governor from 1813 to 1820, and Superintendent of Indian Affairs till his death. In 1803 he explored the Pacific coast, and through this means the tribe referred to probably became acquainted with him. When our zeal is brought in comparison with that of those ignorant Indians in obtaining a knowledge of the true God, with what force may we take to ourselves the charge of Paul to the brethren: "Some have not the knowledge of God. I speak this to your shame."

CHAPTER XXIX.

In Niles's Register, sixth volume, page 394, may be found the earliest suggestions of a canal from Lake Michigan to the navigable waters of the Illinois River that we have found in print. The date is August 6, 1814, in the time of the war, and it is a paragraph from a series of editorial articles on the great importance, in a National point of view, of the States and Territories of this now great central valley. We give the extract: "By the Illinois River it is probable that Buffalo may be united with New Orleans by inland navigation through Lakes Erie, Huron, and Michigan, and down that river to the Mississippi. What a route! How stupendous the idea! How dwindles the importance of the artificial canals of Europe compared with this water communication! If it should ever take place, the Territory of Illinois will become the seat of immense commerce, and a market for the commodities of all regions." Governor Bond, at the first session of the General Assembly, in 1818, brought this subject before that body in his inaugural message. He suggested an early application to Congress for a certain per centage from the sales of the public lands, to be appropriated to that object. In his valedictory message, in December, 1822, he again refers to it, and to his first address, and states: "It is believed that the public sentiment has been ascertained in relation to this subject, and that our fellow-citizens are prepared to sustain their representatives in the adoption of measures subservient to its commencement." His successor, Governor Cole, in his inaugural address, December 5, 1822, devoted four pages to this subject, and referred to an act of the preceding Congress, which gave permission to the State to cut a canal through the public lands connecting the Illinois River to Lake Michigan, and granting to it the breadth of the canal, and ninety feet on each side. With this was coupled the onerous condition "that the State should permit all articles belonging to the United States, or to any person in their employ, to pass free forever." The Governor, who was a zealous and liberal advocate for an economical and judicious system of internal improvements, proposed to create a fund from the revenues received, from taxes on the military bounty lands, from fines and forfeitures, and from such other sources as the Legislature in its wisdom might think proper to set apart for that purpose. He further proposed the examination and survey of the river and the canal route in Illinois, and to memorialize Congress for a liberal donation of land in opening the projected lines of communication. An act and memorial to Congress on the subject was passed by the Legislature during the session. This act, which was approved February 14, 1823, provided for a board of commissioners, whose duties were to devise and adopt measures to open a communication by canal, etc., also to invite the attention of the governors of the States of Indiana and Ohio, and, through them, the Legislatures of those States, to the importance of a canal between the Wabash and Maumee Rivers. Thomas Sloe, jr., Theophilus W. Smith, Emanuel J. West, and Erastus Brown were elected commissioners. At that time Sangamon River and Fulton counties were the boundaries of settlements. Only a military and trading post existed at Chicago. A dozen families, chiefly French, were at Peoria. The northern half of Illinois was a continuous wilderness, or, as the impression was, an interminable prairie, and not likely to be inhabited for an age to come. Morgan county, which then included Scott and Cass counties, contained about seventy-five families, and Springfield was a frontier village of a dozen log cabins. Some of the commissioners, with the late Colonel Justice Post, of Missouri, as their engineer, made an exploration in the Autumn of 1823–24. Colonel R. Paul, of St. Louis, was also employed as engineer, with the necessary men to assist in making the survey complete. The party was accompanied by one commissioner. Two companies were organized, and five different routes examined, and the expense estimated on each. The locks and excavations were calculated on the supposition that the construction was to be on the same scale of the Grand Canal, of New York, then in process of making. The probable cost of each route was reported by the engineers, the highest being $716,110, the lowest $639,940. At the next session of the Legislature an act was passed—January 17, 1825—to incorporate the Illinois and Michigan Company. The capital stock was one million of dollars, in ten thousand shares of one hundred dollars each. The stock not being taken, at a subsequent session the Legislature repealed the charter. During these movements within the State, the late Daniel P. Cook, as the Representative in Congress, and the Senator of Illinois, was unceasing in his efforts to obtain lands from the National Government to construct this work. As the result of these efforts, on the 2d of March, 1827, Congress granted to the State of Illinois each alternate section of land, five miles in width, each side of the projected canal. The finances of the State were so embarrassed as to prevent much being done till January, 1829, when the Legislature passed an act to organize a board of commissioners, with power to employ agents, engineers, surveyors, draughtsmen, and other persons to explore, examine, and determine the route of the canal. They were authorized to lay off town sites, sell lots, and apply the funds. They laid off Chicago near the lake, and Ottowa at the junction of Fox River. The Illinois survey and estimate were again made, but the improbability of obtaining a full supply of water on the surface level, and the increase of cost to near double the original estimate by reason of the rock approaching so near the surface on the summit level between Chicago and Desplaines, led a subsequent Legislature to authorize a reexamination, to ascertain the cost of a railway with a single track for ninety-six miles. It was estimated at one million and fifty thousand dollars. It was a great mistake that this railway was not constructed. At a special session of the Legislature, 1835-36, an act was passed authorizing a loan of half a million of dollars for the construction of the canal, and the board of commissioners was reorganized. On the 4th of July, 1830, the first ground was broken. At the session of 1836-37 the internal improvement system became the absorbing question, and the canal was brought under the same influence. Loans to a vast extent were obtained for both objects, and the most extravagant expectations were raised, never to be realized. As a financial measure, the canal loans were distinguished from internal improvements and other loans, but all failed, with the credit of the State, before 1842. Contracts were made, and the work, on the scale projected, was pushed till over five millions of dollars had been expended, and the work still unfinished. By this time the credit of the State had sunk so low that no further loans could be obtained. The contractors were obliged to abandon their work, with heavy claims against the State, and, in 1843, a law was passed to liquidate and settle the damages at a sum not exceeding two hundred and thirty thousand dollars. At the session of the Legislature of 1842-43 an act was passed to provide for the completion of the Illinois and Michigan Canal, and for the payment of the canal debt. Under this act the bondholders subscribed six hundred thousand dollars, the estimated amount necessary to complete the canal. In 1845 a board of trustees was organized, three in number, one appointed by the Governor, and two by the subscribers. The canal and its remaining lands and lots were transferred by the State to the board of trustees. Under this board the location of the canal between Chicago and Lockport was changed to a summit level eight or ten feet above the lake level. Work on the canal was resumed in the Summer of 1845, and it was completed and opened for navigation in the Spring or Summer of 1848. The first sale of lands and town lots under the board of trustees took place in the Fall of the same year.

I am indebted to Colonel Manning for the following correction to the above:.

"At the session of the Legislature of 1842–43 an act was passed of the following title:

"'*An Act to provide for the completion of the Illinois and Michigan Canal, and for the payment of the Canal Debt.*'

"Of which the following is the preamble, to-wit:

"'WHEREAS, it has been represented that certain holders of the bonds of this State are willing to advance the necessary funds for the completion of the Illinois and Michigan Canal on being secured the payment of their said advance and of their said bonds by a vested lien upon the said canal, lands, and revenues: For the purpose, therefore, of accomplishing an object so desirable and beneficial to the said bondholders and the State, Be it enacted,' etc.

"Under the provisions of this act $1,600,000, the estimated cost of completing the canal, was subscribed by the said bondholders, and, in 1845, a Board of Trustees of the Illinois and Michigan Canal was organized, three in number, one appointed by the Governor, and two by the subscribers—the canal and its revenues, lands, and lots transferred by the State to the said board in trust.

"Under the said board of trustees the place of the canal between Chicago and Lockport was changed to a summit level eight or ten feet above the lake level, on 'the rough cut.' Work on the canal was resumed in the Summer of 1845, and it was completed and opened for navigation in the Spring or Summer of 1848. The first sale of lands and town lots under the board of canal trustees took place in the Fall of the same year."

It was in the year 1816—the same year of the rebuilding of the fort after its destruction by the Indians—that the land on which Chicago now stands, and a strip twenty miles wide running to the southwest along a contemplated canal route, was ceded to the United States by the Pottawotamies. They remained the peaceful occupants of it for twenty years afterward. It was not till 1836 that they were removed by the Government to lands appropriated for their use west of the Mississippi. Black Hawk contended for the lands north-west of this contemplated canal route, and a line running through to the mouth of Rock River. It appears that a treaty had been made by General Harrison at St. Louis, in November, 1804, with the chiefs of the Sac and Fox nations—elsewhere referred to—in which they had ceded to the United States all their lands on Rock River, and considerable more elsewhere. Mr. Peck says in the Western Annals, page 546, that the tract of lands ceded by them in 1804 embraced all the country lying between the Mississippi, Illinois, and Fox River of Illinois, and Wisconsin River, comprehending fifty millions of acres. It was in the same year—1804—in which General Harrison made the above treaty that the first fort was built in Chicago.

CHAPTER XXX.

A SHORT sketch of Rev. John Hill and his arrival at Peoria Conference is among the matters of interest in the settlement of the State and the progress of Methodism. Hill was born in the State of Massachusetts, on the 15th of September, 1768, town of Berry, county of Worcester. His father moved to Hampshire county, in the same State, when John was about four years old, and remained there to the day of his death. His mother belonged to Mr. G. Whitefield's Church, and the boy often heard her in earnest prayer in his behalf. He emigrated to Canada in his early manhood, where, at times, he felt a most earnest concern for his soul, sometimes praying, and sometimes almost in despair. In the year 1800 he went to hear Rev. Joseph Jewell preach, near Queenstown, on the Niagara. He says: "His whole sermon seemed directed toward myself, and I seemed such a great sinner that I cried for mercy, for it seemed to me that I was in the depths of despair. Happily for me, however, I resolved that, if I went to hell, I would go praying. With this resolution, I continued praying, till, by faith, I claimed the promise, 'He will have mercy, and our God, he will abundantly pardon.' The change was so great, and the evidence was so clear that I shouted at the top of my voice. I was in the depths of a forest, and the thought came to me, It is well you are in the woods, or you would frighten all around you. This did not deter me from continually saying, 'Glory to God,' and in this happy frame of mind I continued, both on meeting in class and attending preaching, till Joseph Jewell gave me the privilege of uniting with the Methodist Episcopal Church. In the year 1805 Robert Perry was sent to our circuit, and came in the fullness of the blessing of the Gospel of Christ. He seemed to live in the full enjoyment of perfect love, and preached it to saint and sinner. He gave me to see such a beauty, and such a satisfying portion in this great blessing, that I never rested till I entered into its full enjoyment; and since that time I have had such a love for souls that I have prayed, exhorted, and preached for nearly fifty years, pointing sinners to the Lamb of God, and I trust that my feeble labors have not been in vain in the Lord. To God be all the glory."

Hill emigrated to the State of New York in 1812, and labored with great acceptability and usefulness in the counties of Genesee and Livingston. In the Spring of 1838, April 2d, he came west, and arrived at Princeville, Peoria county, Ill. The population was scarce, and but one Methodist sister in the neighborhood. He found in the "far West" a great opening for ministerial labor, and he commenced to work in good earnest for God and the good of souls. In a short time he had formed a class of nine members, and soon commenced preaching in the neighborhood. In the Fall of 1840 there was a camp meeting about fourteen miles west, at Cutler's Grove. E. Thompson and W. Pitner were preachers, and N. Berryman presiding elder. The little class at Princeville concluded to have a tent on the ground, and several of the neighbors, both professors and non-professors, joined with them. A certain Mr. B. had several daughters at the meeting, and he gave orders to the teamster, if his daughters got religion, to hitch up the team and bring them home before the Methodists opened the doors of the Church for the reception of members. He had anticipated rightly. His daughters were among the converts. His teamster, according to orders, had up his team, and no entreaties would prevail on him to stay. The daughters were obliged to go home. Soon after this a Christian preacher was sent for, and the daughters were baptized by him, and they joined that body. They did not remain long as members, however, but came back and joined the Methodists, among whom they first found peace. In 1841 W. Pitner was appointed to Peoria circuit, and held a camp meeting at Princeville. I had the privilege of attending this camp meeting. It was increasingly prosperous till Sabbath evening, when W. Pitner was to preach, and I to exhort and call up the mourners. We expected that evening to result in reversing the history of the past few days. The preacher began in his odd way of portraying the downward path of the sinner. His apt and unvarnished illustration of a sinner on the way to hell excited laughter all over the house. Every one seemed too merry and trifling to have any good result from such a sermon, and most of us gave up all expectations of inviting in the mourners at its close.

I felt that I could not exhort after that sermon, and told the elder so, when, all of a sudden, he changed to one of the most terrific descriptions of the finally impenitent, and the wailings of the damned, till it seemed as if the sound of those wailings reached our ears, and we could almost feel the darkness of despair brooding over the sinner, and see his tearless eyeballs rolling in their burning sockets, and his poor unsheltered soul cry out, "Lost, lost, lost!" All eyes seemed as if turned toward the yawning pit, and the deep sighs heaved from a thousand breasts—Lord, save; Lord, save the sinner! And then he pointed to the Savior as the sinner's only refuge, telling how, through him, there was yet hope, that all might come and receive pardon, and that the joys of heaven were freely offered, without money and without price. I have never witnessed another such a scene. It was as if they realized that the judgment was near at hand. Some fell, and lay all night and cried for mercy; others screamed as if hell was moving from beneath to meet them at their coming. And then how beautifully he cleared up the way and invited the sinners to the altar! Such as had strength came rushing and fairly tumbling along, some, with uplifted voices, crying, "Thou Son of David, have mercy on us!" In the midst of all this the preacher's mellowing tones, and his invitation to come to Jesus, beggar all description. The cries for mercy, the bursting forth of praise, and the preacher's voice sounding out over all with its melting tones of pardon produced a scene, I imagine, like that of God's ancient people when laying the foundation of the second temple, "when the old men wept with a loud shout, so that they could not discern the noise of the shouts of joy from the voice of the weeping people." This camp meeting ended with glorious results, which may be seen to this day. That class suffered a great loss when Rev. John Hill left and settled near Plainfield. His labors were greatly blessed during his short stay of eighteen months with us, from which place he returned again to Princeville, and labored on faithfully till he entered upon his great reward. His son Benjamin, who was, in his father's lifetime, a faithful co-laborer with him, is yet among us, and a firm Methodist, battling for the Lord. Many of Rev. J. Hill's grandchildren are living in and around Princeville, pillars of the Methodist Episcopal Church. May God's blessing rest upon them till they all meet in heaven!

John Hill received his license to preach from Nathan Bangs. A short time before his death he seemed to have a presentiment that his life was near its close, and one Sabbath, at the close of a sermon, he told his congregation that on the next Sabbath he should preach his farewell sermon. On the next Sabbath a large concourse of people met, filling the house. It may be easily imagined with what zeal and pathos he delivered his last words—a dying man to a dying congregation. His last sermon will not soon be forgotten, and eternity alone will reveal its results. In a few days after this, when a brother had called to see him, he requested that he would once more unite with him in prayer, and while he was commending his soul to God his happy spirit took its flight, and entered that rest which remains for his people. He died in the eighty-second year of his age, and fiftieth year of his ministry.

CHAPTER XXXI.

THE following circumstance, relating to Bishops Roberts and Soule, was given me by Dr. P. Akers. They were on their way to Conference, and journeyed on pleasantly till they came to Columbus, on the Tombigbee River, Alabama. They left this place early in the morning, in the hope of being able to reach a house among the Choctaw people in time to avoid lying out among wild beasts and hostile Indians. About noon they stopped to let their horses graze, turning them loose with their saddles off and their bridles tied up. Before long a company of Indians approached, and Bishop Soule's horse, a high-spirited animal, took fright and started off at full pace through the woods, followed by the rest. The Indians, seeing what they had done, made signs that they would pursue the horses and bring them back, and started off rapidly.

The Bishops remained there till the next day, entirely without provisions, and at last concluded that they would walk around and see if they could see their horses, or some human being to relieve their hunger. They soon saw a smoke in the distance. Hastening to the spot, they found an old squaw cooking some kind of meat. Making signs of hunger, and of a wish to enjoy her hospitality, she soon placed the food before them. Bishop Roberts sat upon the ground, taking the platter in his lap, and seemed to relish his food. The other two, however, after taking a mouthful or two, seeing the filthy manner in which it was dressed and cooked, were not only compelled to refrain from eating more, but lost what they had already eaten. But the Bishop kept on eating, and laughing as heartily as he ate at the daintiness of his companions. Before they left they found that they had been served to skunk's meat.

They soon returned to the place where they had camped, and after waiting long and anxiously, at last saw the Indians returning with all their horses. They had gone back, had swum the Tombigbee, and had been caught and retained till the Indians claimed them. Some years after this, Dr. Akers was accompanying Bishop Soule to a Conference through the same wild region, and when they arrived at the spot where they had camped, the Bishop related the circumstance, and they had a hearty laugh over it.

The following reminiscences are kindly furnished me by Rev. Hooper Crews:

"In 1832, in the town of Russellville, Kentucky, God graciously converted some sinners, among whom was a merchant, who for several years had sold dry goods in the place. He was remarkable for his morality—a quiet, diffident, retiring disposition. On one Sabbath morning, at the opening of public service, he, with a number of others, was to be baptized. He spent the day before his baptism in fasting and prayer to God, that he might be baptized with the Holy Ghost at the same time. Nothing occurred during the time of administering the ordinance more than what is common. After all were composed, and the more public service was about to commence, he was seen trembling as a man shaking with an ague. Almost at the same instant he arose from his seat and rushed into the pulpit, and commenced a most powerful appeal to the congregation. His eloquence was astonishing, and a most extraordinary influence came down upon the people. The unconverted were confounded; God's people shouted for joy. In a few minutes he left the pulpit and ran out into the congregation, and began to lead the penitent to the altar. None of the unconverted resisted him, and he continued till all the space around the altar was occupied with scores, crying for mercy. All thought of preaching was given up, but the exercises of singing and prayer went on till long after dark. Many found peace in believing, who made very worthy and efficient members of the Church.

"An instance will serve to show the powerful influence of the occasion. An old gentleman, well known for his hostility to an earnest Christianity, for some cause had that day attended the church. He had taken his seat in the gallery, as nearly concealed as possible. Mr. H., looking up, saw him, and ran up the steps. No sooner had he reached the floor above than the old gentleman, seeing his eye fixed on him, rose from his seat, saying, 'I will go!' and without resistance he came.

"After that remarkable day and its occurrences, there was nothing in the life of Mr. H. more than in the life of any other good, humble Christian. He lived many years an honor to the Church of his choice."

I introduce a few characteristic sketches as appropriate in this connection, from Rev. James B. Finley's "Sketches of Western Methodism:"

"I never heard brother Axley preach, but, according to popular fame, his pulpit performances were practical, forcible, and left a deep and abiding impression on the multitudes that thronged together to hear him. To this day we occasioanlly hear allusion made to a sermon he preached in the city of Baltimore, during the General Conference of 1820, of which he was a member. It must have been a potent sermon to be remembered so distinctly for the third of a century. I have heard also very frequent allusions to his pulpit performances in different parts of the Western country, where he had operated to good purpose as a traveling preacher, more particularly in Kentucky and Tennessee. But perhaps the effort which occasioned the most talk and obtained the greatest notoriety was the one said to have been made in his own section of country, and was commonly known as Axley's Temperance Sermon, though not so designated by any preannouncement. It should be known that East Tennessee in those days was regarded as a great country for producing peach brandy, and for a free use of it; also, that the New Lights abounded there, familiarly called Schismatics, and that Church members who rendered themselves liable to a disciplinary process would occasionally go over to them, as a city of refuge, where they felt safe from its restraints. With this preliminary, I proceed to recite a passage from the sermon, reminding the reader that my authority is not personal knowledge, but the verbal statement of a highly respectable Methodist minister, Rev. Dr. G., of Tennessee. I write it substantially as I heard it:

"TEXT: 'Alexander the coppersmith did me much evil: the Lord rewarded him according to his works.' 2 Timothy iv, 14.

"Paul was a traveling preacher, and a bishop, I presume, or a presiding elder at least; for he traveled extensively, and had much to do, not only in regulating the societies, but also in sending the preachers here, there, and yonder. He was zealous, laborious, would not build on another man's foundation, but formed new circuits, where Christ was not named, 'so that from Jerusalem, and round about unto Illyricum, he had fully preached the Gospel of Christ.' One new place that he visited was very wicked—Sabbath-breaking, dancing, drinking, quarreling, fighting, swearing, etc., abounded; but the Word of the Lord took effect; there was a powerful stir among the people, and many precious souls were converted. Among the subjects of that work there was a certain noted character, Alexander by name, and a still-maker by trade; also, one Hymeneus, who was his partner in the business. Paul formed a new society, and appointed brother Alexander class-leader. There was a great change in the place; the people left off their drinking, swearing, fighting, horse-racing, dancing, and all their wicked practices. The stills were worked up into bells and stew-kettles, and thus applied to useful purposes. The settlement was orderly, the meetings were prosperous, and things went well among them for some time. But one year they had a pleasant Spring; there was no late frost, and the peach crop hit exactly. I do suppose, my brethren, that such a crop of peaches was never known before. The old folks ate all they could eat, the children ate all they could eat, the pigs ate all they could eat, and the sisters preserved all they could preserve, and still the limbs of the trees were bending and breaking. One Sunday, when the brethren met for worship, they gathered round outside of the meeting-house, and got to talking about their worldly business—as you know people sometimes do, and it is a mighty bad practice—and one said to another, 'Brother, how is the peach crop with you this year?' 'O,' said he, 'you never saw the like; they are rotting on the ground under the trees; I do n't know what to do with them.' 'How would it do,' said one, 'to still them? The peaches will go to waste, but the brandy will keep;

and it is very good in certain cases, if not used to excess.' 'I should like to know,' said a cute brother, 'how you could make brandy without stills?' 'That's nothing,' replied one, 'for our class-leader—brother Alexander—is as good a still-maker as need be, and brother Hymeneus is another, and, rather than see the fruit wasted, no doubt they would make us a few.' The next thing heard on the subject was a hammering in the class-leader's shop; and soon the stills in every brother's orchard were smoking, and the liquid poison streaming. When one called on another the bottle was brought out, with the remark, 'I want you to taste my new brandy; I think it is pretty good.' The guest, after tasting once, was urged to repeat, when, smacking his lips, he would reply, 'Well, it's tolerable; but I wish you would come over and taste mine; I think mine is a little better.' So they tasted and tasted till many of them got about half drunk, and I do n't know but three-quarters. Then the very devil was raised among them; the society was all in an uproar, and Paul was sent for to come and settle the difficulty. At first it was difficult to find sober, disinterested ones enough to try the guilty; but finally he got his committee formed; and the first one he brought to account was Alexander, who pleaded not guilty. He declared that he had not tasted, bought, sold, or distilled a drop of brandy. 'But,' said Paul, 'you made the stills, otherwise there could have been no liquor made; and if no liquor, no one could have been intoxicated.' So they expelled him first, then Hymeneus next, and went on for complement, till the society was relieved of all still-makers, distillers, dram-sellers, and dram-drinkers, and peace was once more restored. Paul says, 'Holding faith and a good conscience; which some having put away, concerning faith have made shipwreck; of whom is Hymeneus and Alexander; whom I have delivered unto Satan, that they may learn not to blaspheme.'

"Of course they flew off the handle, and joined the Schismatics. . . . . .

"Although the following anecdote of Mr. Axley may be familiar to many of our readers, we hope they will pardon us for inserting it, as it is worthy of a more durable record than the columns of a newspaper, from which we clip it. The late Judge Hugh L. White, who relates it, was a learned and able jurist and distinguished statesman, and for many years a conspicuous member of the United States Senate from the State of Tennessee.

"On a certain day a number of lawyers and literary men were together in the town of Knoxville, Tennessee, and the conversation turned on preachers and preaching. One and another had expressed his opinion of the performances of this and that pulpit orator, when at length Judge White spoke up:

"'Well, gentlemen, on this subject each man is, of course, entitled to his own opinion; but I must confess that father Axley brought me to a sense of my evil deeds, at least a portion of them, more effectually than any preacher I ever heard.'

"At this, every eye and ear was turned, for Judge White was never known to speak lightly on religious subjects, and, moreover, was habitually cautious and respectful in his remarks about religious men. The company now expressed the most urgent desire that the Judge should give the particulars, and expectation stood on tiptoe.

"'I went up,' said the Judge, 'one evening to the Methodist church. A sermon was preached by a clergyman with whom I was not acquainted, but father Axley was in the pulpit. At the close of the sermon he arose and said to the congregation, "I am not going to detain you by delivering an exhortation; I have risen merely to administer a rebuke for improper conduct, which I have observed here to-night." This, of course, waked up the entire assembly, and the stillness was profound, while Axley stood and looked for several seconds over the congregation. Then stretching out his large, long arm, and pointing with his finger steadily in one direction, he said, "Now, I calculate that those two young men, who were talking in that corner of the house while the brother was preaching, think that I am going to talk about them. Well, it is true, it looks very bad, when well-dressed young men, who you would suppose, from their appearance, belonged to some respectable family, come to the house of God, and instead of reverencing the majesty of Him that dwelleth therein, or attending to the message of his everlasting love, get together in one corner of the house"—his finger all the time pointing as steady and straight as the aim of a rifleman—" and there, during the whole solemn service, keep talking, tittering, laughing, and giggling, thus annoying the minister, disturbing the congregation, and sinning against God. I 'm sorry for the young men. I 'm sorry for their parents. I 'm sorry they have done so to-night. I hope they will never do so again. But, however, that 's not the thing I was going to talk about. It is another matter, so important that I thought it would be wrong to suffer the congregation to depart without administering a suitable rebuke. Now," said he, pointing in another direction, "perhaps that man who was asleep on the bench out there, while the brother was preaching, thinks I am going to talk about him. Well, I must confess it looks very bad for a man to come into a worshiping assembly, and, instead of taking a seat like others, and listening to the blessed Gospel, carelessly stretching himself out on a bench, and going to sleep. It is not only a proof of great insensibility with regard to the obligations which we owe to our Creator and Redeemer, but it shows a want of genteel breeding. It shows that the poor man has been so unfortunate in his bringing up as not to have been taught good manners. He do n't know what is polite and respectful in a worshiping assembly among whom he comes to mingle. I 'm sorry for the poor man. I'm sorry for the family to which he belongs. I'm sorry he did not know better. I hope he will never do so again. But, however, this was not what I was going to talk about." Thus father Axley went on, for some time, "boxing the compass," hitting a number of persons and things that he was not going to talk about, and hitting *hard*, till the attention and curiosity of the audience were raised to their highest pitch, when finally he remarked:

"'"The thing of which I was going to talk was *chewing tobacco*. Now, I do hope, when any gentleman comes to church who can't keep from using tobacco during the hours of worship, that he will just take his hat and use it for a spit-box. You all know we are Methodists. You all know that our custom is to kneel when we pray. Now, any gentleman may see, in a moment, how exceedingly inconvenient it must be for a well-dressed Methodist lady to be compelled to kneel down in a puddle of tobacco spit."

"'Now,' said Judge White, 'at this time I had in my mouth an uncommonly large quid of tobacco. Axley's singular manner and train of remark strongly arrested my attention. While he was stirring to the right and left, hitting those "things" that he was not going to talk about, my curiosity was busy to find out what he could be aiming at. I was chewing and spitting my large quid with uncommon rapidity, and looking up at the preacher to catch every word and every gesture—when at last he pounced upon the tobacco, behold, there I had a *great puddle* of tobacco spit! I quietly slipped the quid out of my mouth, and dashed it as far as I could under the seats, resolved never again to be found chewing tobacco in the Methodist church.'

. . . .

"Samuel Hamilton belonged to a class distinctly marked. His position among the itinerant ranks the reader will be able to fix after he shall have read our sketch. He was the youngest son of William Hamilton, who emigrated from Western Virginia, in 1806, and settled in the wilds of Muskingum. Having purchased his land, and made every preparation for settling upon it, he called all the members of his household together, and, like Abram in Mamre, erected an altar, and consecrated his family and possessions all to God. This patriarch, with his devoted and pious wife, having given themselves and children to God in an everlasting covenant, were encouraged, by God's promise, to expect that the children of their faith, and prayer, and godly example, would soon give evidence of the work of grace upon their hearts. At the removal of his father to Ohio, Samuel was in the fifteenth year of his age. His mind was early impressed with the importance of religion, and his tears and prayers gave evidence that the world and its pleasures could not fill the aching void in his aspiring soul. In the year 1812, when he was in the twenty-first year of his age, he attended a camp meeting, held on the lands of Joseph Thrap, in the bounds of Knox circuit, where he was powerfully awakened under the ministration of God's Word. It was impossible for him to suppress the deep and overwhelming convictions of his soul, and in agony he cried aloud for mercy. For days and nights, in a distress bordering upon despair, he sought for pardon. We had witnessed his anguish, and the unavailing cries of his heart for mercy, and all the sympathies of our nature were deeply aroused in his behalf. We took him to the woods, and there, in the solitude and deep silence of the night, with the curtains of darkness around us, we fell prostrate before God in prayer. We arose upon our knees, and embraced him in our arms, while, with streaming eyes and faltering voice, he exclaimed, 'O Lord, I do believe! Help thou mine unbelief!' Then, in a moment, quick as thought conveyed by lightning, the blessing of pardon came down, and heaven filled his soul. Instantly he sprang to his feet, and, like the man in the 'beautiful porch,' he 'leaped, and shouted, and praised God' for the delivering grace he had obtained in that distressful hour. At this time we were traveling the circuit on which his father lived, and we had the pleasure of aiding the young convert in taking up his cross. He was zealous, determined, and active, and the Church and world alike saw that God had a work for him to do. He exercised his gifts in exhortation, and sinners were awakened and converted through his instrumentality. In the year 1814, at the Conference held in Cincinnati, he was admitted on trial as a traveling preacher. His first field of labor was the Kanawha circuit. The circuits in Western Virginia at that time were called the Colleges of the Methodist Church, where the young preachers were sent to get their theological education, or, in other words, take their theological course. Sometimes they were called 'Brush Colleges;' at other times, the fields where the Conference broke its young preachers. Some of the most prominent of our Western preachers took their first lessons in the itinerancy upon this field. Here, amid the dense forests and flowing streams, the logical and metaphysical Shinn pored over his books, on horseback, as he traveled to distant appointments; and here, among the craggy mountains and deep glens, the eloquent Bascom caught his sublimest inspirations. In this wild region the preachers had to encounter much toil and hardship; and while they lived on the simple fare of the country, consisting of hominy, potatoes, and 'mountain groceries,' they were not afflicted with those fashionable complaints denominated dyspepsia and bronchitis. As a specimen of the trials of Methodist preachers, we will relate an incident that occurred in the year 1836. One of the preachers of the Ohio Conference, having reached his circuit, and finding no house for his family, built for himself a shanty out of slabs, on the bank of the

Gaulley River. Having furnished his wife with provisions for a month—that being the time required to perform his round—consisting of some corn-meal and potatoes, he started out upon his circuit. To reach his appointments, which were sometimes thirty miles distant, it was necessary for him to take an early start. One morning, after he had progressed about half round his circuit, he started for an appointment which lay on the other side of one of the Gaulley Mountains. It had rained through the night, and having frozen, the earth was covered with a sheet of ice. The travel was difficult even on level ground, so slippery was the surface; and unless it should thaw, the itinerant felt an apprehension that it would be difficult to ascend the steep sides of the mountain. Instead of thawing, however, the weather grew colder; but there was no retreat. His appointment was before him, and the mountain must be crossed. At length, after passing for some distance through a narrow valley, he came to the point where his narrow path led up the ascent. It was steep and difficult, and his horse would frequently slip as he urged him on. On the right the mountain towered far above, and on the left, far down, were deep and frightful precipices; a single misstep, and horse and rider would be dashed to pieces on the rocks below. After ascending about two-thirds of the elevation, he came to a place in his mountain path steeper than any he had passed over. Urging his tired but spirited steed, he sought to ascend; but the horse slipped. Seeing his danger, the preacher threw himself off on the upper side, and the noble animal went over the precipice, bounding from rock to rock, deep down into the chasm below. The preacher retraced his steps, and on coming round to the point where his horse had fallen, he found him dead. Taking off the saddle, bridle, and saddle-bags, he lashed them to his back, and resumed his journey, reaching his appointment in time to preach. The balance of the round was performed on foot, and at the expiration of four weeks from the time of starting, he joined his companion in her cabin, on the bank of the river, thankful for the providence which had returned him safely home.

"Here young Hamilton studied theology and human nature, in both of which he became well versed. His preaching talents were peculiar, and often did he make his discourses sparkle with wit and eloquence. Sometimes he would indulge in a rich vein of humor, which, without letting down the dignity of the pulpit, would send a thrill of delight among his audience. No one enjoyed a little pleasantry more than himself; and having a peculiar horror for any thing like a sour godliness, he may, at times, have gone a little too far over to the other extreme. He had a quick perception of the ridiculous, and was not very well able to command himself even in the pulpit when any thing occurred to excite that sense in his mind. We recollect of his telling us of an occasion of this kind, which occurred at a meeting on the waters of the Little Kanawha. At a certain appointment there lived a Colonel ———, whose family were members of the Church, and who had a respect for religion, though he was too fond of the world to make a profession thereof. He was regular in his attendance, and on the occasion to which we have alluded, he was in his seat, attended by a neighbor of his, who was respectable enough, with the exception that at times he would lose his balance under the influence of intoxicating liquor. He had taken on this occasion just enough to make him loquacious without being boisterous. Hamilton, after singing and prayer, arose and gave out for his text the first Psalm, which reads as follows: 'Blessed is the man that walketh not in the counsel of the ungodly, nor standeth in the way of sinners, nor sitteth in the seat of the scorner,' etc. He entered upon the discussion of his subject by showing what was to be understood by walking in the counsel of the ungodly; and as he entered upon the description of the ungodly, and their various wicked ways and bad examples, he saw the friend of the Colonel punch him in the ribs with his elbow, and overheard him say, 'Colonel, he means you.' 'Be still,' said the Colonel, 'you will disturb the congregation.' It was as much as the preacher could do to control his risibles; but he progressed with his subject; and as he described another characteristic of the ungodly in standing in the way of sinners, the force of the application was too strong to be resisted, and the Colonel's friend, drawing up closely, elbowed him again, saying, 'He certainly means you, Colonel.' 'Be quiet, the preacher will see you,' whispered the annoyed man, while he removed as far from him as he could to the other end of the seat. The preacher had arrived at the third characteristic of the ungodly; and as he, in earnest strains, described the scorner's seat, the Colonel's friend turned and nodded his head at him most significantly, adding, in an under tone, 'It's you, it's you, Colonel; you know it's you.' By this time the most of the congregation were aware of what was going on, and cast significant smiles and glances at one another. Those who understood the features of the speaker could easily discover that he was moving along under a heavy press of feeling, and unless something should occur to break the excitement, he must yield to the impulses of his nature. Just at this crisis a little black dog ran up the aisle, and, stopping directly in front of the pulpit, looked up in the preacher's face, and commenced barking. The scene was ludicrous enough; but how was it hightened when the Colonel's friend rose from his seat, and deliberately marching up the aisle, he seized the dog by his neck and back, and began to shake him, exclaiming, 'Tree the preacher, will you? tree the preacher, will you?' Thus he kept shaking and repeating what we have written, till he arrived at the door, when, amid the yells of the dog and the general tittering of the audience, he threw him as far as he could into the yard. This was too much for Hamilton, and he sat down in the pulpit, overcome with laughter. It would have been impossible for him to have resumed his subject, or even to have dismissed the congregation. Suffice it to say that preaching was done for that day; and ever after, when the Colonel went to Church, he was careful that his friend was not by his side.

"Samuel Hamilton was well instructed in the doctrines, and Discipline, and peculiarities of Methodism, and wherever he went his labors were appreciated, and souls were blessed."

CHAPTER XXXII.

"An important Western character appeared in this field in 1816. Young failed to reach the district after the General Conference of that year. James B. Finley came to supply his place, and continued to superintend it till 1819, with extraordinary zeal and success. Few men have attained more distinction as evangelical pioneers of the West. He was, in all respects, a genuine child of the wilderness—one of its best 'typical' men—of stalwart frame, 'features rather coarse,' but large, benevolent eyes, 'sandy hair, standing erect,' a good, expressive mouth, a 'voice like thunder,' and a courage that made riotous opposers, whom he often encountered, quail before him. He did not hesitate to seize disturbers of his meetings, shake them in his athletic grasp, and pitch them out of the windows or doors. Withal, his heart was most genial, his discourses full of pathos, and his friendships the most tender and lasting. All over the North-West he worked mightily, through a long life, to found and extend his Church, traveling circuits and districts, laboring as missionary to the Indians, and chaplain to prisoners, and, in his old age, making valuable historical contributions to its literature.

"Though born in North Carolina—in 1781—his

childhood was spent in Kentucky, where he grew up with all the hardy habits of the pioneer settlers. In early manhood he and all his father's family were borne along by the current of emigration into the North-Western Territory, where he lived to see his State—Ohio—become a dominant part of the American Union. He had been a rough, reckless, and entirely irreligious youth, associating with Indians, a 'mighty hunter' among the 'backwoodsmen,' fond of nearly every excess, and of the most hazardous adventures with savage men and beasts. The camp meetings of the Presbyterians and Methodists in Kentucky had spread, about the beginning of the century, a vivid religious interest all over the West. Finley's sensitive, though rough nature, could not escape it. He went with some of his associates to Cane Ridge, Kentucky, his former home, to witness one of these great occasions. His own story gives us a striking view of them in their primitive, their rude Western grandeur and excesses. 'A scene presented itself,' he says, 'to my mind, not only novel and unaccountable, but awful beyond description. A vast crowd, supposed by some to have amounted to twenty-five thousand, was collected together. The noise was like the roar of Niagara. The sea of human beings seemed to be agitated as if by storm. I counted seven ministers, all preaching at the same time, some on stumps, others on wagons, and one, William Burke, standing on a tree which, in falling, had lodged against another. Some of the people were singing, others praying, some crying for mercy in the most piteous accents. While witnessing these scenes a peculiarly strange sensation, such as I had never felt before, came over me. My heart beat tremendously, my knees trembled, my lip quivered, and I felt as though I must fall to the ground. A strange, supernatural power seemed to pervade the mass of mind there collected. I became so weak that I found it necessary to sit down. Soon after, I left and went into the woods, and there strove to rally and man up my courage. After some time I returned to the scene of excitement, the waves of which had, if possible, risen still higher. The same awfulness of feeling came over me. I stepped up on a log, where I could have a better view of the surging sea of humanity. The scene that then presented itself to my eye was indescribable. At one time I saw at least five hundred swept down in a moment, as if a battery of a thousand guns had been opened upon them. My hair rose up on my head, my whole frame trembled, the blood ran cold in my veins, and I fled to the woods a second time, and wished that I had staid at home.' He went to a neighboring tavern, where, amid a throng of drinking and fighting backwoodsmen, he swallowed a dram of brandy, but afterward felt worse than before; 'as near hell,' he says, 'as I could wish to be, in either this world or that to come.' Drawn irresistibly back to the meeting, he gazed again, appalled, upon its scenes. That night he slept in a barn, a most wretched man.

The next day he hastily left for his home, with one of his companions. They were both too absorbed in their reflections to converse as they journeyed; but, says Finley, 'When we arrived at the Blue Lick Knobs I broke the silence which reigned between us, and said, "Captain, if you and I do n't stop our wickedness the devil will get us both."' Tears gushed freely from the eyes of both. The next night was spent without slumber, at a place called May's Lick. 'As soon as day broke,' adds Finley, 'I went to the woods to pray, and no sooner had my knees touched the ground than I cried aloud for mercy and salvation, and fell prostrate. My cries were so loud that they attracted the attention of the neighbors, many of whom gathered around me. Among the number was a German, from Switzerland, who had experienced religion. He, understanding fully my condition, had me carried to his house and laid on a bed. The old Dutch saint directed me to look right away to the Savior. He then kneeled by my bedside, and prayed for me most fervently in Dutch and broken English. He rose and sang in the same manner, and continued singing and praying alternately till nine o'clock, when suddenly my load was gone, my guilt removed, and presently the direct witness from heaven shone fully upon my heart. Then there flowed such copious streams of love into the hitherto waste and desolate places of my soul that I thought I should die with excess of joy. So strangely did I appear to all but the Dutch brother that they thought me deranged. After a time I returned to my companion, and we started on our journey. O what a day it was to my soul!' . . . . .

"Astonishing—superhuman, almost—as seem the travels and labors of many of the earlier itinerants, none of them could have surpassed the adventurous energy of Nolley, on his Tombigbee circuit, among the rudest settlements and Indian perils. For two years he ranged over a vast extent of country, preaching continually, stopping for no obstructions of flood or weather. When his horse could not go on he shouldered his saddle-bags and pressed forward on foot. He took special care of the children, growing up in a half-savage condition over all the country, and catechised and instructed them with the utmost diligence as the best means of averting barbarism from the settlements. To his successor on the circuit he gave a list of them by name, solemnly charging him, 'Be sure to look after these children.' He labored night and day, also, for the evangelization of the blacks. When Indian hostilities prevailed the settlers crowded into isolated forts and stockades. Nolley sought no shelter, but hastened from post to post, instructing and comforting the alarmed refugees. He kept 'the Gospel sounding abroad through all the country,' says our authority. The people could not but love him, admiring and wondering at his courage, and the very savages seemed to hear a voice saying unto them, 'Touch not mine anointed, and do my prophets no harm. It was in this wild country that happened the fact often cited as an illustration of the energy of the primitive Methodist ministry. 'The informant, Thomas Clinton,' says a Southern bishop, 'subsequently labored in that region, and, though a generation has passed, he is not forgotten there. In making the rounds of his work Nolley came to a fresh wagon track. On the search for any thing that had a soul, he followed it, and came upon the emigrant family just as it had pitched on the ground of its future home. The man was unlimbering his team, and the wife was busy around the fire. "What!" exclaimed the settler upon hearing the salutation of the visitor, and taking a glance at his unmistakable appearance, "have you found me already? Another Methodist preacher! I left Virginia to get out of reach of them, went to a new settlement in Georgia, and thought to have a long whet, but they got my wife and daughter into the Church; then, in this late purchase—Choctaw Corner—I found a piece of good land, and was sure I would have some peace of the preachers, and here is one before my wagon is unloaded." Nolley gave him small comfort. "My friend, if you go to heaven you'll find Methodist preachers there, and if to hell I am afraid you will find some there; and you see how it is in this world, so you had better make terms with us, and be at peace."' . . . .

"Nathan Bangs was at this Conference as a

spectator. He had been laboring on Canada circuits, and had hardly heard of M'Kendree, whose fame, nevertheless, now filled all the West. Bangs went, on Sunday, to Light-Street Church, the center of interest, the cathedral of the occasion and of the denomination. He says: 'It was filled to overflowing. The second gallery, at one end of the chapel, was crowded with colored people. I saw the preacher of the morning enter the pulpit, sun-burned, and dressed in very ordinary clothes, with a red flannel shirt which showed a large space between his vest and small-clothes. He appeared more like a poor backwoodsman than a minister of the Gospel. I felt mortified that such a looking man should have been appointed to preach on such an imposing occasion. In his prayer he seemed to lack words, and even stammered. I became uneasy for the honor of the Conference and the Church. He gave out his text: "For the hurt of the daughter of my people am I hurt; I am black; astonishment hath taken hold on me. Is there no balm in Gilead? is there no physician there? why, then, is not the health of the daughter of my people recovered?" As he advanced in his discourse a mysterious magnetism seemed to emanate from him to all parts of the house. He was absorbed in the interest of his subject; his voice rose gradually till it sounded like a trumpet. At a climactic passage the effect was overwhelming. It thrilled through the assembly like an electric shock; the house rang with irrepressible responses; many hearers fell prostrate to the floor. An athletic man sitting by my side fell as if shot by a cannon-ball. I felt my own heart melting, and feared that I should also fall from my seat. Such an astonishing effect, so sudden and overpowering, I seldom or never saw before.'

"Bangs refers again, in his History of the Church, to this sermon, and says he saw 'a halo of glory around the preacher's head.' M'Kendree's general recognition as leader of Western Methodism, together with his evident fitness for the Episcopal office, doubtless led to his nomination, but this remarkable discourse placed his election beyond doubt. 'That sermon,' said Asbury, 'will decide his election.' Asbury had formerly favored Lee's appointment to the Episcopate. M'Kendree had become endeared to him in the conflicts of the West, and he now saw reason to prefer him even to Lee. The Church had become rich in great and eligible men."

CHAPTER XXXIII.

I HAD a mode of administering Discipline which, though not in the usual way, was in order, and effective. Several years since, in the first quarterly meeting of Clark county, it was my lot to have a presiding elder who filled that important office for the first time. After he had asked me the regular questions, and I had answered them, he asked me what was my method of admitting probationers into full membership at the expiration of six months; also, if I admitted seekers of religion after they had given satisfactory evidence that they desired to flee from the wrath to come and be saved from their sins, upon the recommendation of their class-leader, after having met with the class six months. I said that I admitted all such into full membership. Said he, "You are not Methodistical in that particular; for none ought to be admitted before they profess religion." "Well," said I, "before I can change my practice I must have higher authority." He replied, "I shall have an Episcopal decision next Conference." It seems that some reporter had understood Bishop Hamline to say that professors of religion alone were to be admitted into full membership, and it was published in the Christian Advocate.

The Bishop discovered and corrected it as follows:

"CORRECTION.

"NEW YORK, *June* 4, 1847.

"REV. MESSRS. BOND & COLES—*Dear Brethren*,—One thought in the address reported in the Advocate was so inaptly set forth by me that it was misunderstood; and as it bears on the Discipline, it were better to notice it. The fifth paragraph, instead of reading, 'Our rules *require* members,' etc., should have expressed the following sentiment:

"'Our rules do *not* require that persons received into our Church profess conversion, and in more than half our bounds they are often received without conversion. Possibly there may be fifty thousand such, marked "S." on our class-books, as "seekers;" and in harmony, too, with our Discipline, which makes "a desire to flee from the wrath to come, and be saved from sin," duly "manifested" the only condition. But is there nothing in the Discipline to be set off against these terms of membership? The class is one thing. Here the catechumens mingle with the more mature in grace, enjoy their prayers, and from them, with God's blessing, learn the way. But we can not safely receive and retain members who refuse to visit the class-room. If they become incurably neglectful, let their names, by due forms, be taken from the class and Church records. I solemnly believe that if this plan,' etc., as reported.

"I do not know that I used these words, but such is the sentiment I aimed to express. The error is not at all surprising, as the remarks were strictly *extempore*, and no doubt wanting in precision, as hastily uttered thoughts often are.

"Respectfully yours,   L. L. HAMLINE."

At the next quarterly meeting I asked the elder if he was still of the same opinion respecting the reception of seekers into the Church. "Yes," said he; and then very confidently quoted Bishop Hamline's views, as published in the Christian Advocate. I then handed him the correction. He read it over twice; and I then requested him to read it to the members of the quarterly conference, which he refused to do. This was the last I heard, however, of an Episcopal decision, on receiving seekers into full membership.

In 1844, when I traveled Milford circuit, John Hunter was my colleague. It was his first year. He was a young man of great promise, and, although his attainments were limited, had more than ordinary ability. Luke Hitchcock was my presiding elder. This year was the first and only time that any thing like a charge ever came up against me at Conference. This charge was for maladministration.

Brother M. had been on trial for several years, and he wished to be admitted into full membership, and if not found worthy, that he might be dropped out of probation. As there were some members who were bitterly opposed to his admission, on account of some reports not favorable to him having been circulated, in order to decide the matter satisfactorily to all parties, I gave M. the privilege, which he wished, of answering to all the charges or complaints which were afloat concerning him, before a number of male members of the Church. This was more than the Discipline required, yet I wished to give all a fair chance. I thought it the most satisfactory course to pursue, and when he was permitted to answer for himself, the committee decided that nothing worthy of "death or of bonds" could be found against him. He came up the next day for admission. The class-leader and nearly all of the class were present, and I then said: "If any one has any objections to this brother, let him speak now, or let him hereafter hold his peace." There being no objections raised, I then received him into full membership. One of our preachers, hearing of the matter, objected to the manner in which I put the question. He said that I should have asked the class-leader if he could recommend him, and made out a charge against me. When the Bishop asked Hitchcock, my presiding elder, if there was any charge against me, he said: "There is nothing against brother Beggs." "Yes," said the preacher, "there is a charge of maladministration." The Bishop asked the elder again: "Is there anything against brother Beggs?" and he again replied: "There is nothing." Said the Bishop: "Pass his character." And here ended the charge of maladministration.

I give a sketch of the life of the Rev. John Sinclair, to whom reference has been frequently made in this volume. He was born in Virginia. At the age of five years he came with his father into East Tennessee, and there, in the midst of privations and many hinderances to intellectual training, he remained during his boyhood. The opportunity for attending school was limited; the qualifications of teachers were very inferior. Brother Sinclair used to relate that his first teacher in East Tennessee was a Mr. Rowe, who could read and write *a little*. He taught us to pronounce the vowels as follows: A was *ablesome*, fa; E was eblesome, fe; I was iblesome, fi; O, oblesome, fo; U, ublesome, fu; Y, yblesome, fy; & was called *ampersand;* and Z was called izzard, or zed. Rowe knew nothing about figures. In spelling Aaron, it was, Great A, wee a, r-o-n. The few advantages, however, that he possessed in relation to acquisition of letters in the schools, he labored to improve under very trying and peculiar circumstances. He states in relation to himself, that by reading by fire-light, he was enabled to retain what little learning he had, and made some advancement. He remarked that he had heard it said that "A little learning is a dangerous thing," but he had never had enough to expose him to that danger.

At the age of twenty, with his father and family, he removed to Kentucky, and on the 19th of February, in 1819, he was married to Lydia Short, who is now his bereaved widow. It was about one year after this when God forgave his sins, and renewed his heart in so gracious and powerful a manner, that he could never doubt the change that was wrought. Shortly after his conversion he was made a class-leader, and soon the impression was made upon his mind that he ought to preach the Gospel. This impression seems to have at first found no response in his companion. Many now dread the trials of an itinerant life; many still look upon it as connected with privations that they could not endure, but, compared with what then must have been presented to any one that would dare look into the future before engaging in such a work, it must now be an easy task. How she felt as to any particular trial I do not know. We learn, however, from a little scrap that he has left, probably written in 1855, that one night, when he supposed that all were asleep, and that no one on earth knew any thing of his anxiety, when struggling in relation to his duty, he heard a voice, of which he says, "It was not the voice of God—it was not the voice of an angel, but it was the voice of my wife, saying, 'Go, and do all the good you can.'" This was in September, 1825, and some time between the 15th and 20th of that month he was admitted on trial in the Kentucky Conference. In 1831, however, having for some time felt that the existence of slavery in the State of Kentucky was a serious thing, and dreading its consequences upon after generations—and this was the feeling generally of Methodist ministers at that time—he resolved to take a transfer to the Illinois Conference. He came, and was appointed to the Jacksonville circuit. Here his labors in this State commenced. They continued till, perhaps, 1836, when they were slightly interrupted, and he sustained a supernumerary relation, and took work in Peoria. It was probably in 1846 that for one year he was returned upon the Minutes as superannuated. With the exception of these brief interruptions, till here he took the superannuated relation, each year, from the time he came—1831—he continued to perform "effective labor," and I will add that it was also *efficient labor*—labor that told favorably upon the Church in building it up in holiness, extending its borders, and multiplying its numbers. I discover from the Minutes, that when, in 1833, he was placed upon the Chicago district, that while it embraced what now is the city of Chicago, it also took in Galena on the west, and Peoria on the south! Think of such a district as that!—traveling around it!—what is now two Annual Conferences! To this field of labor he went, leaving an afflicted wife in the wilds of Fox River. But privations could not deter him. It was frontier work, a sparse population, neighborhoods remote from each other, roads without bridges, and vast plains without a stake or mark to direct his course, except the points of timber, miles apart; but he undertook and did accomplish the work of superintending such a district.

The next year he was returned to the same district, with a little change. Galena was taken off on the west, but it still extended from Chicago to the Sangamon River on the south, including all the region of country intervening, or Peoria, Bloomington, and all the settlements in that extent. This will give you some idea of his toils and conflicts. I am sorry that I can not give the details of his labors on this extended district. In 1835 he was removed from the Chicago district. It was a painful occurrence to him, of which he thought and spoke to his own personal friends; and though he felt there was some mistake, still he harbored no resentment, and spoke of it as a man of God. He was placed upon the Sangamon district. I was then in charge of the church at Springfield. Owing to his financial condition, his poor health and that of Mrs. Sinclair, it was quite inconvenient, if not almost impossible for him to remove his family. They had been some years on Fox River, five or six miles above the city of Ottawa. He came to one quarterly meeting; he became sick, and nearly five weeks elapsed before he was able to leave. During this time, when I sat by his bedside, laid my hand upon his forehead scorching with fever, I have heard him talk of his invalid wife at home, and tears would wet his pillow. Yet amidst all the trials of such occurrences I never heard him complain. I never heard him wish he had not entered the work; I never heard him mention a word of retreat; no—it was "Onward!"

and as soon as he was able to sit alone he was desirous of reaching his home, and by the aid of friends soon set out to accomplish that object.

For several years before his death he was a resident of Evanston—for two years as pastor—and after that till his death as a superannuate. Up to the time that he entered upon this pastoral charge, I had never found a man who cared for consistent practical piety that did not love John Sinclair. Men were so universally impressed with the honesty of this minister and his Christian fidelity, that when, through the common infirmities and weaknesses of our nature, he erred, for I do not pretend to say he did not err—that he was not fallible—none charged him with evil motives. "It was a mistake—it was not intended." He was emphatically, in the judgment of men, as the apostle warned the Church to be, "without offense, blameless, harmless—a son of God without rebuke."

When he was tried, God took him to receive his crown. Long was it his wish that he might not linger when called to pass away, and if he did, he earnestly hoped that it might be under circumstances where he could care for himself without troubling—as he was wont to express it—his friends. God favored him in this matter! After all his wanderings to and fro amidst the pelting storms and the dreary wastes; after his going out and his coming in from an afflicted family for so many years; after all his privations, what a pleasing thought to have him die at home! Doubtless he desired to die without lingering; but, sudden as was his death, he was not unprepared. But a short time since he said to his family and friends, and especially his wife, "Do n't weep for me when I go away." What an idea was that of death! "Do n't weep for me when I GO AWAY!" *We* think about it as *death*. *He* did not see it. *He* looked on the shore of immortality. To him it was *going away;* it was *falling asleep.* Jesus said, "He that keepeth my saying shall not see death." "Do n't," said he, "put on mourning; it seems to me that it is very improper to mourn for a minister who has gone to so good a place as heaven!" This was his dying request. Death found him ready, no doubt. All the time he was ready.

CHAPTER XXXIV.

The first session of the Rock River Conference was held on the camp-ground near the Seminary. There were sixty-four large regular tents, besides many small temporary ones. We had heavy rains at the beginning of the meeting, but no one seemed inclined to leave the ground on account of it, and so graciously were they preserved that no case of sickness originated on the ground, and those who were sick recovered in the course of the meeting. The congregations were large, and very attentive, and many were brought from darkness to light, and from the power of Satan unto God. It was estimated that about four thousand persons were present on the Sabbath, who listened with eagerness to the sermon preached by the bishop. It is worthy of note that no guard was necessary, and that no disturbance took place during the meeting. The closing exercises of the Conference, which were delivered in the presence of the congregation, were short, but deeply impressive. An address was delivered by the superintendent, and the appointments read off. Our Conference room was an inclosure of twenty feet square, which consisted of logs hastily thrown up. The large cracks between the logs were badly chinked, and the earth was strewn with straw as a floor or carpeting. A large canvas tent was erected and filled with beds for the accommodation of the preachers who boarded with the tent-holders. Bishop Waugh, who was President of the Conference, took up his lodging with a private family. There had already been held three Conferences in this State where the preachers were accommodated in the same manner—the two first at Shiloh, and the last at Padfield's—and another, also, in Missouri. The minutes of this Conference are very imperfect, in consequence of the reports which have been mislaid, such as the report of the stewards, and, also, those of the missionary, centenary, and temperance questions.

Among those who were admitted on trial were P. Richardson, C. N. Wagar, H. Hubbard, N. Swift, W. B. Cooley, S. Wood, A. White, M. F. Shinn, D. Worthington, H. Whitehead, James Ash, R. A. Blanchard, A. M. Early, E. P. Wood, C. Campbell, P. Judson, H. P. Chase, H. Hadley. Those who remained on trial were S. Spater, A. Haddleston, George Copway—an Indian—William Vallette, John Johnson, J. W. Whipple, O. H. Walker, J. G. Whiteford. Those who were admitted into full connection were J. L. Bennett, N. Jewett, J. Hodges, J. M. Snow, R. Brown, H. J. Brace, M. M'Murtry, D. King, S. Bolles—all of whom were ordained this year, besides others—Jesse Halstead and Joseph L. Kirkpatrick—who were not ordained. The deacons were H. W. Frink, William Simpson, T. M.

Kirkpatrick, M. Bourne, William Gaddis, B. H. Cartwright. Those elected and ordained elders were J. Crummer, J. Pillsberry, J. J. Stewart, E. Springer, J. Halstead, J. L. Kirkpatrick. Located—F. O. Chenoweth. Supernumerary preachers—none. Superannuated, or worn-out preachers—A. Brunson, Robert Delap, T. Pope. None were expelled from the connection. None had withdrawn.

The eleventh question, "Were all the preachers' characters examined?" was strictly attended to by calling over their names before the Conference. None had died this year. Total number of members, 6,154.

The fourteenth question, "What amounts are necessary for the superannuated preachers, the widows and orphans of preachers, and to make up the deficiencies of those who have not obtained the regular allowance on the circuits?" was not answered.

Question 15th—"What has been collected on the foregoing accounts, and how has it been applied?" Stewards' report, not found among Conference papers.

Question 16th—"What has been contributed for the support of missions, what for the publication of Bibles, tracts, and Sunday school books?" Not answered.

Question 17th—"Where are the preachers stationed this year?"

CHICAGO DISTRICT, *J. T. Mitchell, P. E.*—Chicago, to be supplied, H. Crews, William Gaddis. Wheeling, J. Nason, one to be supplied. Elgin, Sims Bolles.*

Crystalville, O. H. Walker. Roscoe and Belvidere, M. Bourne. Rockford, S. H. Stocking.* Sycamore, L. S. Walker,* N. Swift. Dupage, William Kimball.* Napierville, C. Lamb.*

OTTOWA DISTRICT, *J. Sinclair, P. E.*—Ottowa, Jesse L. Bennett. Milford, E. Springer. Wilmington, R. Lunnery. Joliet, W. Weigley.* Lockport, W. Bachelor.* Indian Creek, A. White. Princeton, J. M. Snow. Bristol, H. Hadley.

MT. MORRIS DISTRICT, *John Clark, P. E., and A. M'Murtry, Superintendent.*—Buffalo Grove, R. H. Blanchard.* Dixon, L. Hitchcock.* Portland, William Vallette.* Stephenson, C. N. Wager. Savannah, P. Judson.* Galena, J. W. Whipple. Apple River, E. P. Wood.* Freeport, S. Pillsberry.*

T. T. Hitt, agent for Rock River Seminary. Dr. Hitchcock, a member of the Oneida Conference, located and came among us this year. He was a supply at Dixon till February, 1841, and then he was elected agent of the Mt. Morris Seminary, and R. A. Blanchard supplied Dixon the remainder of the year.

BURLINGTON DISTRICT, *A. Sommers,* P. E.*—Burlington, J. J. Stewart.* Mt. Pleasant, T. M. Kirkpatrick.* Richland mission, M. F. Shinn. Fox River mission, to be supplied. Philadelphia, Joel Arrington. Fort Madison, Moses H. M'Murtry, William B. Cooley. Bloomington, Nathan Jewett.* Crawfordsville, Joseph L. Kirkpatrick.*

IOWA DISTRICT, *Bartholomew Weed, P. E.*—Iowa

mission, Garrett G. Worthington.* Rockingham, Chester Campbell.* Camanche, Barton H. Cartwright.* Marion, John Hodges.* Bellview, Philander S. Richardson. Clarksville, Henry Hubbard. Dubuque, Washington Wilcox.

INDIAN MISSION, *Benjamin T. Kavanaugh, Superintendent.*—St. Peter's and Sioux mission, one to be supplied, David King. Chippewa mission, Henry J. Brace, George Copway, Henry P. Chase, Allen Huddleston, John Johnson. Sandy Lake, Samuel Spates.

PLATTEVILLE DISTRICT, *William H. Reed,* P. E.*— Platteville, to be supplied. Lancaster and Prairie du Chien, William Simpson, Alfred M. Early.* Mineral Point and Wiota, James G. Whitford, one to be supplied. Monroe, James Ash. Madison, to be supplied. Fort Winnebago, Stephen P. Keys.* Fon du Lac, Jesse Halstead. Green Bay, to be supplied. Oneida, Henry R. Coleman.

MILWAUKEE DISTRICT, *Julius Field,* P. E.*— Milwaukee, John Crummer.* Racine, Leonard F. Malthrop.* Root River, Henry Whitehead.* Southport mission, Solomon Stebbins.* Burlington and Rochester, D. Worthington. Troy, James M'Kean. Watertown, Sidney Wood. Summit, Hiram W. Frink.*

Austin F. Rogers, transferred to the Illinois Conference.

The next Conference was held at Platteville, August 25, 1841

Those whose names are marked with a star are yet living. There were three Indians laboring as preachers among us—George Copway, H. P. Chase, and John Johnson.

Our Conference district then embraced Iowa, Wisconsin, and Minnesota, besides our own, the Rock River Conference. At that time there were 71 ministers stationed, and now we have 781. Its membership then was 6,154, now 79,405. What was then embraced in one Conference now is ground enough for eight. In the place of six churches, we now, in seventeen years, have increased to 801.

INCREASE UP TO 1867.

Conferences.	Members.	Preachers.	Dist.	Churches.	Value.
Iowa	17,234	96	7	150	$251,975
Upper Iowa	14,540	97	7	106	322,700
Minnesota	7,193	75	7	59	174,800
Wisconsin	10,712	130	5	132	427,050
Rock River	18,859	171	6	180	1,447,100
Des Moines	11,159	85	6	63	154,905
West Wisconsin	6,932	79	5	86	161,650
North-West Wisconsin	2,796	48	3	25	54,700
Total	89,425	781	46	801	$2,994,880

CHAPTER XXXV.

The most remarkable and striking feature distinguishing Illinois from the other States consists in her extensive prairies, covered with a luxuriant growth of grass, and forming excellent natural meadows, from which circumstance they received their present name, from the early French settlers. They extend from the western part of Indiana more or less to the foot of the Rocky Mountains. Illinois is properly called the Prairie State; as it is, generally speaking, one vast prairie, intersected by strips of woods, chiefly confined to the banks and the valleys of the rivers. Their soil is from one to three feet deep; while nearly all of them possess an inexhaustible fertility, and but few are sterile. The eye sometimes surveys the green prairie without discovering, on the illimitable plain, a tree, bush, or other object save a wilderness of grass and flowers. The charms of a prairie consist in its extension, its green, flowery carpet, its undulating surface, and the skirts of forests whereby it is surrounded. The congenial rays of the sun soon ripen the plentiful harvest; and in Autumn the yellow harvest is gathered into the well-filled garner. Soon the green-carpeted prairie is changed to deep yellow, as Indian Summer dries up the grass, and then comes on the preparation against the flood of fire that sweeps over the broad surface. Of this I wish to give an idea, as I have seen it, run from it, and fought it till I could hardly stand, covered with sweat and dirt, and my eyes almost sightless amid the black clouds of smoke, to save the scanty crop of the settler's first year's toil, and the little cabin that I had preached in, in the morning of the same day. I will relate an incident that took place in the Missouri Bottom, above Boonville. A few families had settled on a very rich, broad bottom of prairie. The grass was as high as my head when on my horse, and so thick that it was with the utmost difficulty that I could ride through it. There was a heavy body of timber west of the settlers, and the fire had not passed through it for several years; and, of course, a great body of combustible vegetable matter had accumulated upon the ground, to which the last Summer's growth had added greatly. One family had moved into a small house about midway in the prairie. One warm, dry, windy day, one of the girls had started to a neighbor's house, about two miles, on the bluff, and having proceeded about half way, she heard a roaring as of a mighty tempest; and looking west toward the timber, she saw the flickering blaze kindled into a fierce torrent of flames, which curled up and leaped along with resistless force. The air was filled with clouds of crimson smoke, while the crashing sounds, like roaring cataracts, were almost deafening; danger and death filled the air, and seemed to scream for victims. At such a fearful crisis, one becomes irresolute, and almost unable to withdraw or seek refuge. As there was not a moment to lose, the girl fled back to the old domicile. The family had thrown all the household goods into one pile, and covered them as best they could, closing the door and window. The fire hastened in its devouring march, till its far-reaching flames enveloped the house, the inmates being almost stifled with heat and smoke. It lasted, however, but for a few moments. The green, brown carpet had been consumed, and black destruction sickened the heart. The inmates threw open the door, by which time the fire had began to blaze up through the cracks of the floor. They gathered up all the articles that they could, and threw them out into the yard, where the flames had consumed every thing, and having a well of water, saved most of their household goods; but the old house was soon in ashes, and the inmates left to do as best they might. Some perished in these terrific fires in an early day. It is said that two betrothed lovers perished on the banks of the Kankakee, their crisped forms being found near that of their horse the next day, by a hunter. The river flowed along to leeward of them, but the flames had outstripped their fleet charger, upon which both were riding, before they could reach the stream. Why did they not have the presence of mind to set a "back fire" or take refuge on the burned space?

Illinois seems destined, in a short time, to play a great part in the United States, being entitled to this not only by the vastness of its area—three hundred and seventy-eight miles from Cairo to Wisconsin, from south to north, and its greatest breadth, two hundred and twelve miles—but, also, by the fertility of its easily cultivated soil, the multitude of its rivers, railroads, canals, coal-beds, and its beautiful and abundant stone quarries, its water powers, and the rapid increase of its population, at once enterprising and intelligent. May our moral zeal increase, and our victories multiply in behalf of all that is good, till God shall "make us an hundred times so many more as we be!"

CHAPTER XXXVI.

THE first newspaper printed in Missouri was at St. Louis, in 1808, by Joseph Charles. It was first called the *Louisiana Gazette*, then the *Missouri Gazette;* and in 1832, going into the possession of other parties, it took the name of *Missouri Republican*. The census taken in 1810 gives 20,845 inhabitants in Missouri. In 1818 St. Louis commenced a greater progress in its building and commercial enterprises. During that year more than three millions of bricks were made, and one hundred buildings erected. The first *brick* dwelling-house was built in 1813 or '14, by Wm. C. Carr. The first steamboat that ascended the Mississippi, above the mouth of the Ohio, was the "General Pike," which reached St. Louis the 2d of August, 1817. It was commanded by Capt. R. P. Guyard. The country above Cedar Creek, a small stream on the western border of Galloway county, Missouri, which was then regarded as the boundary of the district—afterward the county of St. Charles—was called Boone's Lick, from the time of its first settlement, in 1797, till the organization of the State Government. In 1808 there was a small village, called Cote Sans Dessein, from a singular oblong hill in its vicinity. In 1810 a few enterprising families struck out into the wilderness, and formed a settlement in what is now known as Howard county. Here were several large salt springs and "Licks," at one of which Daniel Boone had his hunting camp, and where his son, Major Nathan Boone, made salt as early as 1807. This gave name to the "Lick," and, also, to a large district of counties. Boone's Lick settlement, at the commencement of the war with Great Britain, numbered about one hundred and fifty families. In 1815, throughout the county and town of St. Louis, the inhabitants numbered 9,395, the town population alone numbering 2,000.

I add a few more reminiscences of Chicago. Early in the Spring of 1834, brother Henry Whitehead and Mr. Stewart contracted with Jesse Walker to build a small but commodious house of worship, on the north side of the river, on the corner of Water and Clark streets. Father Walker and the local preachers occupied it every Sabbath alternately. In looking over the annals of Methodism found here and there in books, in my own experience, and in the relation of the experience of others to me, it seems as if God had sifted the whole inhabited region of North America, and selected the choice spirits therefrom, with their iron constitutions, to plant and cultivate the tree of Methodism in the West. Stevens says: "We have often been reminded of the adaptation of Methodism, by some of its providential peculiarities, for its self-propagation. Its class and prayer meetings train most if not all its laity to constant practical missionary labors; so that three or four of these, meeting in any distant part of the earth, by emigration, are prepared immediately to become the nucleus of a Church. The lay or local ministry, borne on by the tide of emigration, was almost every-where found prior to the arrival of the regular preacher, ready to sustain religious services."

The year 1790 was not the real epoch of Methodism in the United States. The sainted Barbara Heck, foundress of Methodism in the United States, went with her children, it is probable, into the province of Canada as early as 1774. Mrs. Heck and her three sons were members of a class at Augusta, under the leadership of Samuel, son of Philip Embury. Brother William Smith has truly said that there were many pious women among the early settlers who were Christian heroines in the true sense of the word. Having left their native State to accompany their husbands to territories where was naught but a howling wilderness, they have proved themselves to be helpmeets for the men who braved the dangers of a frontier life. They were equally brave in every moral conflict in battling for the Lord. In singing, what have they not done in congregations? I have often sat and listened till my own eyes, as well as those around me, were suffused with tears, and especially in prayer circles, when the heart of some mother in Israel went out in irresistible pleadings with her Lord and Savior for an only child or an erring husband, as if every word were an inspiration, every utterance an immediate communication from above, the language of the heavenly host. Indeed, it has often seemed to me as if woman, as if the *mother of the Son of God* was nearer the throne in earnest supplications than man can be. And then, like the women of the Bible, she will take no denial. She will not cease her importunities till the unclean spirit has gone out, and the soul is made a fit temple for the indwelling of the Holy Spirit. Sometimes, after an earnest prayer, I have known them to arise and exhort till it seemed like a visible influence all over the house, as if the powers of darkness had yielded, saints were rejoicing, and heaven had come down to earth, and the whole congregation would be shouting "Glory to God!" The Presbyterian definition of true eloquence—namely, shouting and tears, shouting and tears—may be justly applied to the women of early Methodism. But, alas! how few of them remain among us! I have followed one and another of them to their last resting-place, and, standing by their dying beds, have heard them testify "all is well," till their voices were lost in death. A few years more, and none of them will remain; they all will have passed over the swelling tide, and become inmates of the mansion on high. Though it may hardly seem in place here to mention these things, yet it has often seemed to me such a cruel, unjust thing that we have to cast so many unjust slurs upon our women. I have often thought of these things—the use of so many foul sayings which are looked upon as so many witticisms—such, for instance, as the rib out of which mother Eve was formed, denoting her crooked disposition; that woman is "all tongue," because she is gifted in conversation; that Mary Magdalene had seven devils cast out of her, while they seem to forget that one of the male sex possessed a legion. We have good authority for that, and we can not estimate how many more possessed the same number, for Paul gives one of the most fearful epitomes of man's unparalleled wickedness; and, from his summing up, one would think that man possessed not only a legion, but legions. If our State prisons contain more men, will not heaven contain more women? In either case it is a fearful thing to believe in the loss of a soul.

THE END.

www.ingramcontent.com/pod-product-compliance
Lightning Source LLC
Chambersburg PA
CBHW030012240426
43672CB00007B/923